The Myth of the Explorer

Polar Research Series

edited by Bernard Stonehouse

other titles are in preparation

The Myth of the Explorer

The Press, Sensationalism, and Geographical Discovery

Beau Riffenburgh

Belhaven Press
London and New York
Scott Polar Research Institute
University of Cambridge
*Distributed exclusively in the United States
and Canada by St. Martin's Press*

Belhaven Press
(a division of Pinter Publishers Ltd.)
25 Floral Street, Covent Garden, London, WC2E 9DS, United Kingdom

First published in 1993

Distributed exclusively in the USA and Canada by St. Martin's Press, Inc., 175 Fifth Avenue, New York, NY 10010, USA

British Library Cataloging in Publication Data
A CIP catalogue record for this book is available from the British Library

ISBN 1 85293 260 0

Library of Congress Cataloging in Publication Data

Riffenburgh, Beau, 1955-
  The myth of the explorer / Beau Riffenburgh.
    p. cm. -- (Polar research series)
  Thesis (Ph. D.) -- University of Cambridge.
  Includes bibliographical references and index.
  ISBN 1-85293-260-0
  1. Explorers in the press--United States. 2. Geographical discoveries in the press--United States. 3. American newspapers--History. I. Title. II. Series.
PN488.E97R54 1993
070.4'4991092--dc20   92-44358
                                              CIP

Typeset by Florencetype Ltd., Kewstoke, Avon
Printed and bound in Great Britain by Biddles Ltd., Guildford and King's Lynn

Contents

v

List of plates

List of figures

List of maps

Acknowledgements

This book is a revised version of my PhD thesis, which was undertaken at the Scott Polar Research Institute, University of Cambridge. Most theses require significant contributions by many people, and this was no exception: I received input and assistance from individuals in England, the United States, and Canada.

My initial thanks go to my parents, Ralph and Angelyn Riffenburgh, who gave me not only encouragement but financial support, counseling, and even occasional editorial input.

Clive Holland (my PhD supervisor) and Roland Huntford, two of the world's most respected polar historians, served as inspirational examples of how to conduct thorough research, led me to new and valuable directions with penetrating comments about my techniques and results, and regularly shared with me the findings of their own current work. Jonathan Kotler gave me similar input on the aspects of the book dealing with the history of the press.

I am also grateful for the editorial and historical suggestions of Terence Armstrong, William Barr, James Savelle, and Bernard Stonehouse; for the inspiration received from the late Kenneth Owler Smith; and for the translation assistance of Rosemary Graham.

During the course of my research and writing, the facilities of a number of institutions were made available to me. I would particularly like to thank the staff of the University Library, Cambridge, and most notably Stephen Lees. I am also grateful to the staffs of the British Newspaper Library at Colindale, the British Library, and the library at the Scott Polar Research Institute, including Janice Meadows, William Mills, and Shirley Sawtell.

Lastly, I would like to give special mention to the intellectual feedback, practical assistance, and enthusiasm given by Elizabeth Cruwys of Wolfson College, Cambridge.

As was my thesis, this book is dedicated to Maxie.

1

Introduction

More than three-quarters of a century has passed since the first week of September in 1909 when two men thrilled both the international scientific community and the public of the Western world by virtually simultaneously claiming to have attained what was considered the earth's most alluring geographical goal, the North Pole. For months the furor surrounding Dr Frederick A. Cook, Robert E. Peary, and which, if either, first reached the Pole received unprecedented coverage in the world press. The issue remains a topic of debate even today.

Ultimately, the attainment of the North Pole resulted in no imperial gain, it achieved no great scientific aim, it realized no commercial coup, and it lacked any essential benefit to mankind. Yet it was widely considered one of the most significant triumphs of its time. Why was there such commotion over an achievement lacking every attribute except personal priority? Part of the reason was that the claiming of the Pole was the culmination of centuries of exertion in exploration. By the time the North Pole was reached, geographical exploration, and particularly that of Africa and the polar regions, had become – like medical and scientific discovery – an integral part of the Western mentality. Equally important was that the claims of Cook and Peary, and their rivalry, were turned into the media event of the year, particularly by two of the most important newspapers in the United States, *The New York Herald* and *The New York Times*. In fact, the North Pole controversy was as much a competition between these newspapers as it was a feud between the rival explorers.

From a media-studies perspective, these reasons represent a chicken-and-egg argument about whether the press simply reported what was of interest to the public or whether it actually created that interest. But from a social-historical perspective, they relate the Cook–Peary controversy to the apogee of a Euro–American intellectual and social current that had been gaining strength throughout the second half of the nineteenth century. In

1

an era of imperialism and extreme nationalism, when the state was extolled as supreme and the individual was subordinated to, yet made to personify, the nation, men who achieved remarkable feats were more than just popular heroes; they were symbols of real and imagined nationalist or imperialist cultural greatness. Explorers, confirming as they did the heroism, romance, and adventure of empire, were a particularly celebrated genre. They were pictured as journeying into the blank spaces on the globe, where they were confronted by constant challenges and danger, both natural and human. With Social Darwinism and the Western demand for the conquest of the physical world serving as ideological justification for their actions, they forcibly opened the way for imperial or national expansion by overcoming the challenges of the natural world, defeating "barbarism," exporting Christianity, mapping and defining the unknown, and establishing trade. Since continued expansion represented a means to achieve or maintain moral, racial, spiritual, and physical supremacy, exploration thus became an instrument not only to justify imperial or nationalist political doctrine, but to embody the supposed collective cultural superiority of a nation.

By the late nineteenth century, explorers were being promoted through a number of powerful iconographies. They were widely desired and highly paid as public speakers. They, and the images of the new lands they discovered, were the subjects of painters, sculptors, and early photographers, as well as of artists for popular newspapers or journals, such as *The Illustrated London News* or *Frank Leslie's Illustrated Newspaper*. Some, such as Peary, Ernest Shackleton, and Henry Morton Stanley were unashamed personal promoters and their portraits were reproduced in countless advertisements. Explorers and their adventures were featured in both theatres and music halls, venues that maintained such popularity that by 1892 an estimated 14 million seats were sold annually in 35 London music halls alone (Bailey 1986). There was perhaps no better example of the public promotion of the myth of the explorer than one of the grand imperial exhibitions of the era, held at the Victoria Gallery in Regent Street, London, and entitled the "Stanley and African Exhibition." Visitors were asked to move through the stations in the main hall to "the heart of savage Africa," which included a "native hut, an African primeval forest and village scene" complete with two slave boys (Driver 1991: 140). Such exhibitions were one of the prime propaganda tools of the era, and they represented explorers, as they did all their subjects, in supremely heroic terms (MacKenzie 1984: 96–120).

Most importantly, however, explorers were also assiduously promoted in print. They and their heroic deeds were featured in expedition accounts, popular biographies, juvenile literature, and the popular press, the last the medium that reached the largest and most diverse audience throughout the late nineteenth and early twentieth centuries.

The interest of the press in Cook and Peary was not unique. Throughout the second half of the nineteenth and the early part of the twentieth centuries, explorers and newspapermen cultivated close ties with each other. During that period, newspapers were far more influential in establishing images of and interest in unexplored areas than has traditionally been acknowledged. Not only did members of the press sponsor numerous expeditions, they also encouraged exploration by paying large sums for exclusive accounts from the explorers. In addition, the volume and sensational style of press coverage helped make the exploration of the Arctic, Antarctic, and Africa (as well as the explorers of those areas), significant cultural factors in the developing mass markets of journalism.

Those involved in the business of exploration knew that it often bore little resemblance to the accounts that were presented to the public, but the depiction of exploration was rarely changed once formats were discovered that were not only mutually beneficial to the explorers and the newspapers, but popular with the hero-seeking public. Historians and geographers have agreed that what is perceived to exist or happen is equally as important as what actually exists or happens (Watson 1969; Belich 1986). This was particularly true of the images created of exploration and the explorers themselves, because they could be specifically designed for the consumption of select audiences – geographical societies, financial supporters, scientists, or the general public – bearing in mind little other than the benefit to the press and the explorers.

Regardless of the obvious importance of the journalist–explorer relationship, no previous study has focused on it or has attempted to place it in a wider context, despite the fact that the interplay between newspapermen and explorers not only reflects on the history of the press and the history of exploration, but relates to models of imperialism, modern nationalism, the growth of science, and the diffusion and incorporation of knowledge into society.

Both the history of the press and the history of exploration have traditionally been dominated by a rather Whiggish historiography, which has tended to focus on the role of individual newspapermen or explorers and to celebrate the triumphs of the press over the challenges of time and space and those of explorers over the mysteries of nature. In recent years, historians have begun to pay more attention to the role of exploration in nineteenth-century institutional, intellectual, and political contexts, particularly its relationship with the expansion of empire (Cairns 1965; Curtin 1965; Rotberg 1970; Bridges 1982; Stafford 1989).

This book, which is an examination of the encounter of the popular press with the exploring fraternity, approaches these current concerns about the wider contemporary significance of the practices of exploration in a new manner. By investigating the bargain struck between the press and explorers, it helps explain the public's growth of interest in exploration. By using newspapers as a primary source, a technique uncommon among historians, it indicates what the "common man" actually knew about explorers and newly discovered lands more clearly than would a study of expedition accounts, society publications, or private journals or letters. It also addresses the roles of science and the scientific community, commercial expansion, and nationalism in nineteenth-century exploration. Concurrently, it re-examines some common theories about newspaper sensationalism, giving a new interpretation of the development of sensation-

3

alism in English and American newspapers, and thereby illuminating the broader, and still active, issues of the control of the press over the knowledge and images held by the reading public.

"Sensationalism" is frequently perceived as a necessarily pejorative term. In the context of this book, however, it has no derogatory connotations. It refers to a full range of journalistic techniques used to interest, excite, or emotionally grip a vast readership that, for one reason or another is more concerned with being entertained than being educated with potentially dry, lifeless topics – such as events in government or business. The basic methods of attracting an audience by appealing to its interests are widely accepted normative goals adopted by journalists concerned with intellectual idealism as well as those who emphasize sinful pandering.

Many previous definitions of sensationalism attempted to confine it to specific categories of news (such as war or crime) or emphasized intent and effect, such as those stating it is "intended to arouse strong curiosity, interest, or reaction, especially by exaggerated or lurid details" (*American heritage dictionary* 1980) or is used to produce "startling effects, strong reaction, intense interest . . . by exaggerated, superficial, or lurid elements" (*Random House dictionary* 1978). However, the most important defining aspect of sensationalism is the treatment of news, which includes both literary content and style of display – for example, the use of artwork or photography, the selection of headlines and typefaces, and the techniques of layout and make-up. Juergens (1966: ix) indicated that sensational newspapers have both a specific prose style – "slangy, colloquial, and personal" – and a different way of determining the relative importance of stories, giving dominant placement, large headlines, and abundant photographs to articles that "quality" newspapers might relegate to modest back-page status.

What could be called the "conventional view of sensationalism" is expressed in those books – both American and British – that a recent study indicated are the most frequently used in university courses on the history of the press or are considered the outstanding references on newspaper history (Payne 1920; Bleyer 1927; Herd 1952; Mott 1962; Lee 1973; Hughes 1981; Brendon 1982; Williams 1984; Emery and Emery 1988; and Folkerts and Teeter 1989).

This conventional view indicates that modern sensationalism was born in the 1830s with the birth of the penny press in the US, but that it died out in the 1860s not only because the success of the sensational dailies tempered the technique, but because the American Civil War was so horrible it did not need sensationalizing. Sensationalism did not reappear, so it indicates, until the mid-1880s, when Joseph Pulitzer moved to New York to run *The World*. At about the same time, under the guise of the New Journalism, sensationalism entered mainsteam British journalism when W.T. Stead of *The Pall Mall Gazette* adopted techniques of layout, writing, and investigative reporting from the American papers. The conventional view also clearly differentiates between the sensational press, such as *The New York Herald* and the *Daily Mail*, which in theory attempted simply to gain circulation and therefore to entertain rather than to educate or lift the reader to new moral heights, and the quality press, such as the *The New-York Times* and *The Times* of London, which strove to sell news dispassionately, reliably, and without devious inspiration.

If British and American newspapers engaged in sensationalism, clearly they were not passive diffusers of scientific and geographical fact on the issue of exploration. On the contrary, they played active roles in translating the events of exploration into popular culture, even to the extent of embarking on heroic myth creation.

Heroic myths

Heroic myths are not, of course, unique to the era of the popular press, but have been found throughout history, from classical and ancient pagan mythology to the great world religions. When taken in conjunction, three studies give an indication why nineteenth-century explorers were so easily classified as heroic figures.

In his classic analysis of the hero, Joseph Campbell (1949) examined myths and folk tales from throughout the world, drawing together the parallels in order to determine generalities about the life cycle of the mythic hero. He divided the adventure of the hero into three stages: the departure, the initiation, and the return. In the first, the hero receives a call to adventure. Accepting it, he crosses a threshold to a zone of magnified power, a place of darkness, danger, and the unknown, frequently represented by those very things that nineteenth-century explorers challenged: deserts, jungles, or lands of perpetual ice. In the initiation stage, the hero encounters a multitude of trials, through which he is cleansed or purified before a discovery is made or an apotheosis reached. He then receives a boon or gift, such as the key to enlightenment or a major revelation. In the phase of the return, the hero makes a magical journey home, in which he is often confronted by every conceivable obstacle and difficulty, before giving his boon to his community, nation, or world. This is often accomplished only with aid from members of the natural world, who must rescue the hero.

In his noted discourses on war (1866), the British polymath John Ruskin not only indicated what he viewed as the morality and justification of chivalrous or heroic warfare, but included three criteria that helped make it so. First, Ruskin stated, although national in import, war was a matter of individual effort, not of massed troops hurling themselves at an enemy. This was particularly true of leaders, who had to do their own fighting and not expect others to do it for them. Second, war had a spiritual dimension, in that it required repeated acts of dedication and trust. And third, war served to differentiate between the genders, because while men fought in far-away places, women waited at home, encouraging these efforts with sympathy and understanding. Exploration also perfectly fit these criteria. It involved individual action, in which each member of an expedition (especially those on land) had not only figuratively, but all too often literally, to pull his own weight. In theory it required a close-knit brother-

5

hood that could constantly depend upon each other. Also, despite examples such as Florence Baker, it generally differentiated between the male explorers in distant lands and their wives at home.

Like Ruskin, in a recent analysis of "the hero," John MacKenzie (1992) focused on the military but used arguments equally acute in the context of heroic exploration. MacKenzie indicated that in the nineteenth century there were a number of keys to the creation of heroic myths. The first of these was the exotic setting. Explorers vanished not into the past as they frequently did in traditional myths, but into the remoteness of primeval regions, such as the Arctic or Africa, that co-existed with the progressive European and American world.

The second key was the supposed personal qualities and heroic characteristics of the individual, which allowed him the capacity to single-handedly change the world for the good. The hero had to be a man of extraordinary energy and action. He was single-minded in his drive and possessed an indomitable will, as much because of his unbounded intelligence and moral clarity as because of his almost miraculous courage. Physically, he combined incredible stamina with remarkable strength and a willingness to assist others. Thus the hero represented the attributes that would be used to personify his society and educate its youth in the traditions it wished to emphasize.

The third key to the heroic myth was the martyrdom of the hero. According to MacKenzie, the greatest influence of mythic figures is indirect, through the efforts of others. The mythic hero is an archetype, not only representing the qualities supremely valued by his society, but having instrumental power. This power comes through the hero being both a moral paradigm and an advocate of policy, a policy, however, that can be regularly reinterpreted in a fashion suitable to those using the hero as their exemplar. Thus the most powerful hero is the dead hero, particularly the martyred hero, since it is through his death for the cause that his heroic status can be most easily created, interpreted, and manipulated. It is important to note, however, that this was an important point of difference between the American and British heroes in the nineteenth century. The Americans preferred their heroes living; the British most honored (and most used) those who were dead.

The fourth key to the heroic myth was the creation of the icons of that myth. As MacKenzie states:

> The Roman Catholic Church sees the canonisation of new saints in each generation as a vital way of maintaining the energy of the Church, solidifying the loyalty of old adherents and inspiring the faith of the new. Imperial heroic myths operated in much the same way. (1992: 15).

Thus, heroic myths of the late nineteenth century developed their instrumental power because they justified and promoted the expansion of the state in geographical and economic terms, embodied the collective will and hopes of the governing elite, and offered guidelines for personal and national ascendancy to a new generation. At the same time, hero myths could be used for a variety of purposes: to influence the formation of policy; to justify decisions that had already been taken; and to intensify or eliminate the distinctions between groups, including social classes, political parties, church and state, and industry and military.

The cult that surrounded each hero required mediators who could develop, interpret, and manipulate the myths. This was most commonly done by the promulgation of carefully edited journals, diaries, and letters of the hero; the publication of numerous biographies; and the presentation of other forms of iconography, each in a manner that carefully and clearly indicated the message that the mediator (through the hero) wished to distribute. Thus, as Helly (1987) has shown, the selection of that mediator could be a factor as large in the creation of a mythic hero as any of the hero's actions.

The visual references that were frequently repeated during the myth creation of one of the most honored British explorers clearly demonstrate the iconography of the explorer–hero, as constructed by these theoretical perspectives. Many of the keys or stages mentioned are easily identified in the case of Robert Falcon Scott: the young naval officer plucked from obscurity by Sir Clements R. Markham (the call to adventure); the farthest south of the *Discovery* expedition (the threshold); the years of planning a new expedition, the trek to the South Pole, and the discovery of Amundsen's priority (the trials); his relationship with Edward Wilson (the close-knit brotherhood); the desperate march to One Ton Depot (the magic journey); the death of the entire polar party (martyrdom); the return of his letters and notebooks to Britain and its public (the return, conveying the boon of national inspiration: "Had we lived, I should have had a tale to tell of the hardihood, endurance, and courage of my companions which would have stirred the heart of every Englishman" [Scott 1913: I, 607]); and the role played by his widow in the creation of the icons of his myth.

That few heroes of exploration actually fully reached MacKenzie's final stage of mythic – almost messianic – status, as Scott did, is unimportant. Virtual deities, men such as Charles Gordon or David Livingstone, who become instrumental in determining, for example, political policy, are hard to create. However, lesser heroes can still personify the perceived greatness of their nation or culture, and can therefore still be used as symbols for those interested in justifying national, imperial, or scientific "progress." These other heroes could also serve equally well to perform the desired function of their most important mediator – the press – this being to sell newspapers.

Notes on the text

Although the title of this book refers to myths and explorers, its chapters do not give equal emphasis to all of the areas of the globe, just as the press of the nineteenth century did not. In both Britain and the United States, newspapers gave relatively little coverage to exploration in Asia, South America, or Australia, concentrating instead on that in Africa and the polar regions. Even the western part of North America did not appeal to

7

the major newspapers like these more remote areas. By the 1850s most of North America south of the Arctic, and certainly below the sub-Arctic, had been explored, and although there was a great deal of excitement in the American press about the settlement of the West, and particularly about relations with the Indians, this was not presented in the same manner as was the exploration of previously undiscovered lands.

The era of this book is 1855 to 1910. The former date corresponds with the beginning of new patterns of Arctic and African exploration, the birth of the popular press in Britain, and the first expedition accounts written specifically to enthrall the public. The latter date is that of the most significant, and most obvious, intervention of the press in the world of exploration.

Due to national, regional, and dialectal differences (occurring despite the languages all being agglutinative), there are many distinct self-appellations for the peoples who inhabit the far north. It is commonly accepted to call these peoples Eskimos in Alaska, Inuvialuit in western Canada, Inuit in eastern Canada, and Greenlanders on that island. However, Eskimo (or Esquimaux) has not only long been an English word – first used by Richard Hakluyt in 1584 (Taylor 1935: 269) – it was virtually the only term used for these peoples by the press of the nineteenth century. Therefore, it has been employed here. Similarly, the place names in this book comply with the common usage of the British and American press in the nineteenth century. The names used by the British Permanent Committee on Geographical Names and the American Board of Geographical Names, which recognize the version of the name officially used within the country as correct, are indicated in parentheses after first use.

Throughout this book, technical newspaper terms that might not be familiar to those outside of journalism have been used. These have been briefly defined in the glossary that forms Appendix 1. This study required a comprehensive examination of 30 daily and weekly papers, as well as of many more newspapers and journals for more limited periods of time. A number of these newspapers changed names during the 55-year period. When cited for a specific date, a paper is referred to by its name of that moment. However, when mention of a paper does not include a specific reference to a date, it is called by the name most commonly used during the period of the book, which is also the name it is listed under in Appendix 2.

The newspapers selected were limited to the United States and England. Although it might have been desirable to have included the other parts of the United Kingdom, there were a number of cogent reasons for not doing so, reasons also related to what might initially seem to be a disproportion-ately high number of newspapers from New York and London. The newspapers selected not only boasted of the largest circulations or greatest prestige, they were often the direct source of national and international news for papers from other parts of the country, had the largest number of reporters actively involved in overseas coverage of news stories, estab-lished the patterns for writing about exploration, and were the leaders in the sensationalization of the press.

2

Stereotyped images of the unknown

The most powerful image-makers of unknown lands prior to the nineteenth century were not the press, but authors of books, both non-fiction (such as expedition accounts and geographical treatises) and fiction (including novels, plays, and epic poems). Books were rarely read by vast numbers of people – the quantity available was even more limited than the relatively small literate population – but what they reported gained acceptance far beyond the reading public.

References to the exploration of Africa and the Arctic reach as far back in Western literature as classical Greece. About 457 BC Herodotus followed the Nile south to the first cataract at Aswan before turning back in defeat. In the next century, Pytheas of Masillia was probably the first southern European to pass the Arctic Circle or to give a description of the midnight sun, during a voyage in which he circumnavigated Britain before searching for a northern land he called Ultima Thule (Whitaker 1982). Later Greek geographers, particularly Strabo, doubted Pytheas' account, but his claims have more recently been accepted, although accompanied by debate over the location of Thule: Iceland, Norway, or the Shetlands. The importance of Pytheas' story was not so much his descriptions as the skepticism about them. His voyage was questioned because the Arctic was imagined to be such an inhospitable place that no one could visit, much less live, there. This belief influenced European perceptions of the Arctic until the nineteenth century as, indeed, did the Greek theories about Africa, the most popular of which was based on the map by Ptolemy, the second century AD geographer, who laid down the rough location of the source of the Nile in central Africa: the Mountains of the Moon.

In the next two millennia, India, China, and the Middle East became known to Europeans; North and South America were discovered, explored, and colonized; and Australia and the islands of the Atlantic and Pacific oceans were claimed and mapped by European sea powers. But the

Arctic remained a genuinely unknown region, as did the interior of sub-Saharan Africa. Despite establishing a trade route to India around the tip of Africa, the Portuguese did little to open up the continent. In 1482 Diogo Cão discovered the mouth of the Congo (Zaire) River and sailed some 100 miles upstream to where he was stopped by the falls below Stanley Pool (Malebo). But his efforts, like those of other Portuguese landing on the west, south, and east coasts of Africa, initially resulted in little more than the placing of stone pillars engraved with the royal arms of Portugal. Similarly, despite the Norse discovery and colonization of Greenland, their exploration north to Melville Bay, west to Newfoundland, and east into the White Sea, for all the impact they had on the English-speaking world, they might have never existed (Nansen 1911: II, 380–81).

It was the French humanist François Rabelais (1494–1553) who helped bring the Arctic into the consciousness of non-northern Europeans in his widely translated novel *Gargantua and Pantagruel*. The fourth book, which is a record of Pantagruel's maritime voyages, begins with his completion of the Northwest Passage and includes descriptions of his sojourn among the people of the far north and his stay on the edge of the frozen sea (Rabelais 1900: III, 55–8, 77–80, 202–4).

An analysis of the geographical background of the time (Lefranc 1905) suggested Jacques Cartier was Rabelais' main inspiration, but that he also was influenced by John Cabot. Cabot's first voyage created a sensation in England with tales of Newfoundland cold, fog, mosquitoes, and fish (Morison 1971: 189–90), but neither he nor Cartier ever reached high Arctic latitudes. Barbeau (1984) suggested Rabelais knew Cartier and used his accounts to create incidents on Pantagruel's voyages, but that the vision of the New World's north accepted at the court of François I (and, therefore, by the public) came from Rabelais' tales of danger and wonder in an area like the high Arctic rather than from Cartier's descriptions of the sub-Arctic.

Throughout the sixteenth, seventeenth, and much of the eighteenth centuries, travel accounts presented new pictures of unknown lands to the literate English public. The *Description of Africa* by Leo Africanus was translated into English in 1600, and in the next 150 years many accounts of North and West Africa appeared, including some 20 that became classics of the genre (Curtin 1965: 11). Many gave detailed ethnographic or geographical descriptions, but more were simply tales of adventure, often spiced with facts of dubious accuracy. Few of the descriptions of the Arctic were more fanciful, or more popular, than that of Pierre Martin Bruzen de la Martiniere, a French surgeon who served on the Danish exploring expedition of 1653, which sailed to the Barents Sea and Novaya Zemlya. Martiniere's book owed as much to fantasy as fact, both in the narrative of strange fauna and native peoples, and the accompanying map, which was remarkably unrepresentative of the known geography of the time and of today. Nevertheless, his account was circulated in six languages and at least 16 editions, and had much influence on European perceptions of the Arctic for many years (Holland in press).

The English public, like others, was most interested in the achievements of its own explorers, so there was a passion in the first two-thirds of the eighteenth century for Northwest Passage expeditions, which were encouraged by Parliament's offer in 1745 of a £20,000 reward for anyone discovering a Passage through Hudson Strait (Cyriax 1939: 3). But the very failure of voyages such as those led by Christopher Middleton (1741–42) and William Moor (1746–47), and the secrecy of the Hudson's Bay Company (which hoped to protect its trading monopoly) made the Arctic more fascinating. Like the hunt for El Dorado in the mountains and jungles of South America or the search for the kingdom of Prester John in the interior of Africa, the fact that so little was known about the Northwest Passage after centuries of exploration added to its power in the imaginations of the public (Ruggles 1971). It seemed that nature was manifested not only at its harshest but its most inscrutable in the Arctic and Africa.

References to Africa and the Arctic in seventeenth- and eighteenth-century literature encouraged these images, using unknown areas as sources of mystery, vastness, and danger. Most writers were ignorant of Africa and the Arctic; in their works, descriptions of these regions were mere trope, a convenient source of stock phrases about "tropical luxuriance" or "icy grandeur." Mountains played a greater part in the English mentality, and the intense public interest in Africa and the Arctic that later developed was over-shadowed until late in the eighteenth century by images of alpine scenery (Nicholson 1959: 30–47). Yet this fascination with alpine areas included the same stereotypes as Africa and the Arctic. What they shared was "an asymmetry that violated all classical canons of regularity" (Nicholson 1959: 32), a feature known as the "sublime."

The sublime and the picturesque

Although Africa and the high Arctic had been scantily explored by the beginning of the nineteenth century, the English-speaking public had specific ideas about them (Curtin 1965). "The geography of any place," Watson (1969: 10) has argued, "results from how we see it as much as what may be seen." Exploration entailed just such a process of identification, combining healthy doses of expectation and illusion with empirical reality. Thus the Anglo-American perceptions of the world developed out of these combinations at the start of the nineteenth century were not just distorted imaginings, they were truths of their time (McManis 1975; Ruggles 1988).

It has been suggested that the visual world can be represented only by widely held schemata (Gombrich 1960). For British explorers of the late eighteenth and early nineteenth centuries, the two most important schemata for representing nature in words and pictures were the sublime and the picturesque.

The sublime had been a concept popular in rhetoric and poetry since Nicolas Boileau-Despréaux's French translation in 1674 of a treatise by Longinus, a first-century AD Greek author. However, with the publication of *A philosophical enquiry into the origin of our ideas of the sublime and beautiful* (1758), Edmund Burke made the sublime a coherent and unified

11

theory that became the chief aesthetic of the age, was a major influence on the philosophy of Kant and Diderot, and was particularly indispensable to all who viewed nature.

The sublime referred to the marvellous, the surprising, the awe-inspiring, those phenomena the effect of which was "to lift up the soul; to exalt it into ecstasy; so that, participating, as it were, of the splendors of the divinity, it becomes filled with joy and exultation" (Knight 1805: 329). Sublimity was said to be present in the natural world when a landscape reflected nature at its extreme, beyond human control and inspiring fear and wonder: enormous open spaces whose dimensions defied definition or even imagination, open stretches of ocean or prairie, perilous mountain peaks or abysses, thunderstorms or tornadoes.

The keystone to Burke's sublime was the emotion of terror, most notably displayed in the confrontation with the unknown (Monk 1960: 84–100). Burke classified the concepts he considered sublime and justified each, the most important of which were: obscurity, where darkness, uncertainty, and confusion aroused dread and terror; power, where the mind was impelled to fear because of superior force; privations, such as darkness, solitude, and silence, because they were terrible; vastness in dimension; infinity, which had the tendency "to fill the mind with that sort of delightful horror, which is the most genuine effect, and truest test of the sublime"; uniformity, which produced the illusion of infinity; magnificence, a great profusion of something splendid or valuable in itself; and difficulty, where an object owed its existence to an immense expenditure of force and effort (Burke 1758). According to Burke, these attributes had the power to overwhelm the senses with sheer terror.

Although Burke's treatise was a general philosophical discussion, the clear-cut categories into which he divided the sublime were much more easily appreciated as aspects of nature than as abstract concepts. Thus to the general British public they soon came to define nature, both in its actual state and as portrayed in art, architecture, and literature. Based upon Burke's classifications, no part of nature was more terrible or sublime than the Arctic.

The picturesque was the response of aesthetic theorists who felt unable to categorize all landscapes in Burke's sublime and beautiful. Popularized by William Gilpin (1792) and Uvedale Price, the picturesque was keyed to a lower emotional threshold and had as a basic premise that when individuals looked at nature they found combinations of elements that corresponded to what they had already experienced in art. Thus, the picturesque became the "habit of viewing and criticizing nature as if it were an infinite series of more or less well composed subjects for painting" (Hussey 1927: 1).

Variation was at the core of Gilpin's picturesque, requiring landscapes that were irregular in detail, coarse in surface texture, variable in color and shading, and intricate in pattern. Despite this emphasis, the picturesque became conventional, formulaic, and oversimplified, at least in part because Gilpin so completely defined its aspects, such as the correct disposition of hills in a view and even the number of cows permissible in a painting. The typical picturesque painting became "a prospect . . . usually set on a moderate rise, [looking] out over a foreground, a lower middle ground through which a river meandered, and an enclosing background of bluish hills or mountains . . . at the side of the view, trees in clumps or rows would . . . 'frame' the scene and encourage the single perspective" (MacLaren 1985: 90).

However, finding the picturesque where it did not exist opened a dangerous gulf between imagination and actual nature and imperiled those who could not understand what adaptations were demanded (MacLaren 1985: 101). An example of this occurred on John Franklin's first overland expedition (1819–22). In the autumn of 1820, Fort Enterprise was erected on a hill chosen partly for aesthetic reasons (MacLaren 1984). John Richardson commented on this in a letter to his mother: "We could not have selected a more convenient or beautiful spot. The surrounding country is finely varied by hill and dale and interspersed with numerous lakes connected by small streams" (McIlraith 1868: 63). Yet that prized site, so picturesque by English aesthetic standards, lacked the food, water, fuel, and wind shelter that were to be found down the hill by the lake. After their grueling journey the next year, when Franklin, Richardson, and company arrived back at Fort Enterprise, they did not have the strength to walk down the hill to the lake to catch the fish that would have forestalled their starvation (Franklin 1823). Without the assistance of the Indians, their aesthetics would have precluded them from saving themselves.

Thus the sublime and the picturesque were ingrained as the qualities of scenery for which British and American travellers looked in the late eighteenth and early nineteenth centuries, a time when books on travel and exploration were outsold in Britain only by those on theology. Through the use of the sublime and picturesque in travel accounts, novels, and art, the Anglo-American public developed stereotyped views of the far north, the interior of Africa, and much of the rest of the world.

In North America, James Fenimore Cooper effectively used both aesthetics in his novels, while Francis Parkman wrote about the "sublimity of desolation" and travel writers such as Timothy Dwight discovered the picturesque (Dwight 1822; Parkman 1872; Nevius 1976). British writers and travellers also viewed and presented the world through both aesthetics, from Samuel Taylor Coleridge's sublime images of the Antarctic in *The rime of the ancient mariner*, the eighteenth century's most influential vision of the polar world, to picturesque accounts of India and both East and West Africa (Allen 1840; Parkyns 1853; Archer 1980).

Developments in exploration also encouraged these ways of viewing unknown lands. When Parliament stipulated in 1776 that as a condition of the reward for discovering the Northwest Passage it should be found north of the fifty-second parallel, the search moved from the relatively cramped confines of Hudson Bay to the vast, uncharted (and therefore sublime) waters of the Pacific (Williams 1962). The most noted northern Pacific voyage of the time (1776–80) was led by James Cook. The publication of the account of Cook's previous voyage, during which his ships had become the first to cross the Antarctic Circle, brought polar works to new heights of popularity in England (Beaglehole 1961). Cook was killed on Hawaii before he could write an account of the far north, but his journals delighted an eager public (Beaglehole 1974: 691).

Other travels added to the notion of the sublime because of their failure to illuminate the mysteries of the unknown. Samuel Hearne's expedition to the mouth of the Coppermine River in 1771 and Alexander Mackenzie's trip down the Mackenzie River to its mouth in 1789 added only small points in a vast, unexplored map (Hearne 1795; Mackenzie 1801). Mungo Park's first expedition to the Niger in 1795–96 did not ascertain its course, source, or termination (Park 1799), and Park and virtually his entire company were killed on a second expedition in 1805–06, although it was years more before any confirmation came of their deaths. The mystery of such areas also increased because there was a considerable time-lag in the publication of many expedition accounts, and in the interim fantastic rumors circulated about the journeys. It was not until 1795, more than two decades after Hearne's expedition, that the Hudson's Bay Company allowed the publication of his narrative (Williams 1970: 169), and Mackenzie's account also took more than a decade from when he began his travels to reach the readers. Similarly, James "Abyssinian" Bruce reached the source of the Blue Nile in 1772, but, after a skeptical reception in London of his strange tales, he did not publish his account until 1790.

By the early nineteenth century, Africa and the Arctic were regarded as exotic backgrounds for adventure stories, closer to fiction than to reality. During this time, explorers continued to wander over the unmapped spaces of the globe, but the great mysteries remained unsolved. When Europe became engaged in the Napoleonic wars, to a great extent exploration lost its place of importance, and the blank spaces on the map were again unchallenged. But the wars in Europe did not last. It was only a short time before both Britain and the young United States were drawn irresistibly toward opening the Arctic and Africa to the world.

The search for new water routes

It is one of the coincidences of Arctic exploration that 1818 marked not only the revival of the British search for the Northwest Passage and the North Pole but the appearance of a novel that used the Arctic as effectively as any ever written. Mary Shelley's *Frankenstein* was prophetic: the changes it traced in the character Walton anticipated those that the Victorian audience underwent during the next half century. Initially Walton's dream was of a tropical paradise surrounding the Pole, and his belief in the Arctic's sublime power was highlighted by his meeting Frankenstein, of whom he wrote: "The starry sky, the sea, and every sight afforded by these wonderful regions, seems still to have the power of elevating his soul from earth" (Shelley 1818: I, 34). It was only by exposure to Frankenstein's tale that Walton learned of the more ominous aspects of the sublime. Thus, by the end of the novel he was able to recognize the terror of his own expedition: "I am surrounded by mountains of ice, which admit of no escape, and threaten every moment to crush my vessel. . . . There is something terribly appalling in our situation" (Shelley 1818: III, 163–4).

Despite the success of *Frankenstein*, it was the only significant work of fiction about the Arctic in the first half of the nineteenth century. This is partly because there was no need for creating stories – in an era that focused on exploration, there were plenty of expedition accounts available.

The moving spirit behind the new British expeditions was the Second Secretary of the Admiralty, John Barrow. Called the "Father of Arctic Exploration," Barrow viewed exploration as a means of occupying the Royal Navy, which was beginning to stagnate after Napoleon's defeat. There was also a possibility of commercial profit in exploration, but more compelling reasons were national pride and the quest for scientific knowledge (Barrow 1847).

Perhaps influenced by the work of James Rennell, Britain's foremost geographer, whose reputation was initially earned on a land and river survey of Bengal, Barrow emphasized water routes – rivers and the Northwest Passage – in the expeditions he encouraged the Admiralty to sponsor or finance.

The first major expedition for which Barrow was responsible was sent in 1816 to explore the Niger and Congo rivers, and, hopefully, to find out if they were part of the same waterway. One of the two prongs of the richly financed expedition, under the command of John Peddie, was to follow Park's route down the Niger. The other, under the command of James Kingston Tuckey in *Congo*, the first steamship ever built for the Royal Navy, was to follow the course of the Congo. A memorandum of 7 February 1816 from Barrow to Tuckey stated that even if the Congo, which had never previously been mapped far inland from the coast, did not follow a northeast course that would take it to the Niger, it was still worth investigating: "That a river of such magnitude as the Zaire . . . should not be known with any degree of certainty . . . is incompatible with the present advanced state of geographical science, and little creditable to those Europeans, who, for three centuries nearly, have occupied various parts of the coast, near to which it empties itself into the sea . . . ." (Tuckey 1818: xxxi).

This memorandum captured the essence of Barrow's interest in exploration, but it was not the fetid jungles of Africa that most caught his fancy; it was the Arctic. Barrow pressured the Royal Society to persuade Parliament to amend the Act of 1776, offering prize money for the completion of parts or all of the Northwest Passage or the journey to the North Pole (Cyriax 1939: 3–4). He convinced the Admiralty that national honor was at stake in the Arctic, writing that it would be mortifying if Russia, having only recently built a modern navy, should complete the Northwest Passage before Britain.

Despite the African expedition being a catastrophe – 21 of 54 men in the Congo party (including Tuckey) died within several months and both halves of the expedition failed miserably at their goals – Barrow's further

15

machinations led to two expeditions being sent to the north in 1818. One, under the command of David Buchan, was to attempt to reach the Pole in *Dorothea* and *Trent*, the former just back from having served as Tuckey's transport ship. The other, under John Ross, was to renew the search for the Northwest Passage in *Isabella* and *Alexander*. Both expeditions failed in their objectives – Buchan was stopped west of Spitsbergen, and Ross barely penetrated Lancaster Sound before turning back – but they initiated one of the most determined periods in the history of exploration.

During the next 25 years, the British mounted a series of overland and maritime expeditions that added many pieces to the jigsaw puzzle of the Canadian Arctic. Throughout this time, the emphasis was on the completion of the Northwest Passage. Everything else – the mapping of the continental coastline, the collection of botanical and geological specimens, the taking of magnetic and hydrographic measurements – was secondary. It was the Passage itself that fired the imagination of the Admiralty, the explorers, the press, and the public. And it was the explorers who attempted to complete the Passage, endured dreadful ordeals but persisted in the face of adversity, and demonstrated British hardihood and courage even in failure, who became national heroes: William Edward Parry, John Franklin, James Clark Ross, and George Back.

The story was the same in Africa. From 1822 to 1826, Owen and Vidal carried out a 7,000-mile coastal survey of sub-Saharan Africa, which was one of the glories of the hydrographical service. But the public was interested in exploration, not in surveying. In the next several decades, the route of the Niger was solved, it was proven that it did not meet with either the Congo or Lake Chad, the fabled city of Timbuktu on its banks was reached, and the principal investigators – Hugh Clapperton, Dixon Denham, Alexander Gordon Laing, and Richard and John Lander – became household names.

These men, from both African and Arctic efforts, stood at the head of a long line of British exploring heroes; they became folk figures, larger than life, and their failings, flaws, and human frailties were ignored by the press and public, which saw in them everything grand and honorable. One of the first was Parry, whose exploits so impressed young Emily Brontë that she adopted his name as a pseudonym (Gerin 1971: 12–14). Her sister Anne had a similar devotion for John Ross (Gerin 1971: 15).

The new explorers also wrote books about their travels and the strange world of the far north. One of the earliest and most popular of these accounts was Parry's *Journal of a voyage for the discovery of a North-West Passage* (1821). Viewed from a later perspective, the text seems subdued, devoting many pages to the mundane details of daily life aboard ship. But such details were not mundane at the time. Wintering in the Arctic was new in 1820, and it was something that thrilled the British public. Thus, as unromantic as the book seems today, it created a very romantic image. Even Parry's understatement and logic in describing the unusual – his unwillingness to indulge in raptures – emphasized the strangeness and vastness of the Arctic. When, for example, he commented on the dreariness of the long winter, he evoked sublimity:

16

Not an object was to be seen on which the eye could long rest with pleasure, unless when directed to the spot where the ships lay, and where our little colony was planted. The sound of voices . . . served now and then to break the silence that reigned round us, a silence far different from that peaceable composure which characterizes the landscape of a cultivated country; it was the deathlike stillness of the most dreary desolation, and the total absence of animated existence. (Parry 1821: 125)

The winter was only one aspect of this extraordinary world; at times, the Arctic was the home of weird visual effects: parhelia (or "mock suns"), the aurora borealis, and "loomings" created by refraction. Above all, it was a world made constantly unstable by the pack ice that could trap or crush the strongest ship, and against which even the new steam engines of the industrial age were helpless. The knowledge the public thus gained of the Arctic was a compound of fact and fantasy, and was dominated by the power of the sublime.

Few explorers made more of an impression on the public than John Franklin, a Royal Navy officer who, after serving under Buchan in 1818, led two overland expeditions to explore the north coast of British North America (1819–22 and 1825–27). On the first, 11 men died from starvation, exhaustion, and murder. But Franklin survived, became known as "the man who had eaten his shoes," and emerged a hero. On his return from his second expedition, he was knighted and Oxford University awarded him an honorary degree.

It was certainly not Franklin's ability as a writer that gained him prominence. His books were plodding, tedious, and formal. Even when he attempted to describe the Canadian scenery in terms of the picturesque, the result was not evocative:

Steel River presents much beautiful scenery; it winds through a narrow, but well-wooded, valley, which at every turn disclosed to us an agreeable variety of prospect, rendered more picturesque by the effect of the season on the foliage, now ready to drop from the trees. The light yellow of the fading poplars formed a fine contrast to the dark evergreen of the spruce, whilst the willows, of an intermediate hue, served to shade the two principal masses of colour into each other. (Franklin 1823: 29–30)

Instead, the public delighted in Franklin's account of suffering, murder, and cannibalism, all of which fitted the prevailing taste for gothic tales. Simultaneously, his books included an unintentional use of the sublime: the very lands that reduced his company to such desperate conditions must have been powerful, vast, brooding, obscure, and terrible.

But why Franklin's personal popularity? There had been earlier accounts of hardship and death, yet the attention that he received had not been previously forthcoming (Wallace 1980: 13). An answer is hard to provide – perhaps it was because the public could sense his noble character; perhaps because he, unlike his predecessors on land expeditions, was a Royal Navy officer; perhaps the public approved of the scientific investigations by John Richardson, who accompanied Franklin; or perhaps Franklin's expedition was such an overwhelming disaster that the very idea that he could come back alive from such a terrible place captured the public's imagination. For whatever reason, Franklin had laid the groundwork for both his and later explorers' roles as tragic heroes, the kind the English preferred.

It was a situation that led Dr John Rae, a Hudson's Bay Company surveyor, to write, "The way to get into credit . . . is to plan some . . . scheme . . . and after having signally failed, return with a lot of . . . reasons – sufficiently good to gull John Bull – for your failure" (Rae to George Simpson, 19 November 1852, in Rae 1953: 233).

Thus the stage was set for the greatest concentration ever on Arctic exploration. It was also the period for the beginning of the serious involvement of newspapers in exploration.

The roots of the popular press

The English-language popular press was born in the United States several decades before it reached England. One important reason was that the three great prerequisites of a mass reading public – literacy, leisure time, and spending money – were generally available in America before they were in England (Cole 1948; Webb 1955; Altick 1957; Brown and Browne 1968; US Bureau of Census 1975).

Another prerequisite of the mass press was the technology enabling the production and distribution of large quantities of periodicals. These developments continued into the twentieth century, but dramatic strides were made in the early and middle decades of the nineteenth. Before that, the printing press had changed little in 350 years. To the simple platen press had been added a metal screw (1550), a sliding bed and an anti-twist device (1620), and a cast-iron frame (1800). Worked by strong men, these hand presses could produce 200 to 300 impressions an hour (Isaacs 1931: 10–13).

Major breakthroughs were initiated by Friedrich Koenig. Between 1811 and 1816, he patented the world's first steam-driven press, built a two-cylinder press, and invented a perfecting press capable of printing on both sides of the paper in one operation. In 1814 *The Times* became the first newspaper to use one of Koenig's perfectors, which could print approximately 1,100 impressions per hour (Howe 1943: 2–3). Design improvements, first by William Cowper and Augustus Applegarth and then by David Napier, made it possible to print 3,000 sheets per hour, but that was still not fast enough to keep up with rapidly increasing circulation. The problem was that a bed weighing more than a half ton had to be moved 76 inches, brought to a dead stop, and started again in the other direction; this meant a tremendous waste of power and an impression of inconsistent quality (Lee 1976: 55).

The solution to this dilemma came in 1846 when the American Richard Hoe combined the concept of rotary motion with locking movable type onto a horizontal cylinder. Hoe sold his first type-revolver to *La Patrie* in Paris, and another to the *Public Ledger* of Philadelphia (Musson 1958: 416). In 1849 *The New York Herald* installed a Hoe six-cylinder press capable of printing 12,000 impressions an hour. Five years later, *The Herald* became the first newspaper to change from turtles (the segmental chases in which movable type was locked in columns) to stereotypes – curved, solid plates of type. Stereotypes, which allowed the duplication of pages so that several presses could print simultaneously, were introduced to the English press in 1858 by *The Times* (Berry 1958: 694–701).

The effect of technological developments on the speed and scale of newspaper production was not confined to printing. Distribution and news-gathering were accomplished at a pace previously unimaginable. Railways so expedited the delivery of newspapers that by the 1840s areas outside the home counties were able to obtain same-day London papers, and by the 1870s Bristol, Norwich, and Birmingham received the London morning dailies before business hours (Hitchman 1880: 506; Redivivus 1899). In the early 1840s *The New York Herald* established a regular system of carriers so that subscribers in Newark, Albany, and Philadelphia could read their papers at the breakfast table (Hudson 1873: 438).

The most important step in the rapid transmission of news was the invention of the telegraph. On 21 May 1844, the same day that Samuel Morse sent the first telegraphic message, he also wired the results of a vote in the House of Representatives to the *Baltimore Patriot & Commercial Gazette*, unfortunately sending inaccurate figures in the process (Cray *et al.* 1990: 38). A year later, the first message transmitted by telegraph to an English newspaper was sent from Portsmouth to *The Morning Chronicle* of London (Lee 1976: 60). Newspapers all over America and Britain were quick to exploit the wire.

The birth of the American penny press

If one date were to be selected for the birth of the modern American press, it undoubtedly would be 3 September 1833, when Benjamin H. Day first published his four-page New York newspaper, *The Sun*.

Before Day's entry into journalism, American metropolitan dailies served primarily as mouthpieces for political parties, while also attracting a small audience interested in business news. The price of the papers – 6¢ per copy or $10 per year – was prohibitive for most people, who had little interest in partisan editorials or detailed mercantile listings. The bulk of the remaining space was filled with mundane features clipped from other newspapers, few of which would meet modern standards of quality or interest. The mercantile papers were almost without exception dull and heavy in appearance and tone, and their very names – such as *The New-York Mercantile Advertiser* – bespoke of products that would gain small circulations; in fact, the largest was about 4,000 (Crouthamel 1964).

Day's *Sun* cost only a penny, and it revolutionized circulation methods in the United States by ignoring the usual subscription requirements and introducing the "London plan" of distribution, in which newsboys hawked papers in the streets. Day realized that the key to popular journalism lay in appealing to the emotions of the masses rather than to their intellects. Thus he filled his paper with interesting but trivial local news, features, for example, about animals and children, and humorous "human-interest" stories, which were interesting not on account of the significance of the people or events reported, but because they were amusing or pathetic, or meaningful in terms of the texture of universal human life. *The Sun* also began a trend toward sensationalism, covering murder, suicide, and duels, while deliberately ignoring economic and political news (O'Brien 1918: 31–63). Perhaps Day's most sensational effort came in September 1835, when the *The Sun* ran a series of articles purporting to describe discoveries made by the English astronomer John Herschel, including strange amphibious creatures and "man-bats" that inhabited the moon. *The Sun*'s circulation rocketed, and even after the series was exposed as deception, the paper retained much of its new readership. The result of these innovations was that within two years *The Sun* had the highest daily circulation in the nation, more than 15,000 (O'Brien 1918: 78).

Within four years of the start of *The Sun*, four imitators had come and gone from the New York scene (Coggeshall 1856: 148), but one proved even more successful than Day's paper. This was *The New York Herald* of James Gordon Bennett, founded in 1835. The subject matter and style of *The Herald* were initially similar to those of *The Sun*, but Bennett, who had a seemingly unerring news sense, soon expanded his coverage to include hitherto neglected areas as well as economic and political news. In this way, he challenged both the penny and mercantile papers by not only doing what they were, but by doing it better and by doing more. Bennett appealed to the business class by developing the best financial section in the country. He devoted space to society news, religion, and sport, none of which had yet been prominently featured in the press. And he showed that a paper could flourish without the backing of politicians (Fermer 1986: 13–30).

In a short time *The Herald* began to outdo *The Sun* in its sensational reports of crime and scandal, delighting in describing itself as "saucy" and "spicy." "I have seen human depravity to the core," trumpeted Bennett, "I proclaim each morning . . . the deep guilt that is encrusting over society" (*The Herald* 19 August 1836).

The Herald's readers were fed a steady diet of murder, suicide, seduction, and rape. Bennett calculated that his audience was "more ready to seek six columns of the details of a brutal murder, or of testimony in a divorce case, or the trial of a divine for improprieties of conduct, than the same amount of words poured forth by the genius of the noblest author of the times" (Pray 1855: 225).

The story that above all others assured *The Herald*'s success was the Jewett-Robinson murder case of 1836. Bennett's energetic reporting of this brothel killing included an interview with Rosina Townsend, who ran the house the murder was committed in. Recently, the consensus has been to credit this as the beginning of using the interview as a journalistic technique (Eberhard 1970; Nilsson 1971; Francke 1974: 44). Bennett's imaginative exploitation of the investigation not only boosted *Herald* sales enormously but made Bennett himself an item of news, something that, over the next three decades, he never allowed to change. When he was not announcing his plans – such as publicizing his upcoming wedding on page one – he was touting his success: "I know and I feel I shall succeed. Nothing can prevent . . . success but God Almighty, and he happens to be entirely on my side" (*The Herald* 20 July 1836).

Bennett's sensational coverage was not limited to local violence or crime. Anything new or different could be sensationalized in a series of stories: the death of Aaron Burr, the capture of a giraffe, the discovery of the ruins of Mayan civilization, or Millerite meetings predicting the impending end of the world and Christ's second coming. Bennett also realized that unusual places had appeal. This was one reason *The Herald* was so comprehensive in its coverage of the Mexican War (1846–48), to which it was the only New York paper to send a full-time correspondent (Hudson 1873: 476–7).

Bennett was also a great believer in the effect of sensational illustrations. Perhaps having been encouraged by the success of the two-column wood-cut captioned "Herschel's Forty-Feet Telescope" that accompanied the bogus astronomical series in *The Sun* in September 1835, he began by using a woodcut to supplement an account of a fire in New York's business district (21 December 1835). A decade later, *The Herald* ran the first full-page illustration on page one – "The Grand Funeral Procession in Memory of Andrew Jackson" (28 June 1845). Although such illustrations were rare in American journalism until the founding of *Frank Leslie's Illustrated Newspaper* in 1855, *The Herald* printed about 20 a year by the 1840s (Crouthamel 1973: 313).

Bennett's innovations had their desired effects. Despite a price increase to 2¢ in 1836 – whereas *The Sun* remained a penny until 1864 – *The Herald* outsold all its rivals, and in 1860 boasted a circulation of 77,000, the largest of any daily in the United States (Seitz 1928; Fermer 1986: 323–4).

The next two decades saw the beginning of countless penny papers, the two most important of which were the *New-York Tribune* of Horace Greeley (1841) and the *New-York Daily Times* of Henry J. Raymond, George Jones, and E.B. Wesley (which was founded in 1851, but dropped the "Daily" from its name in 1857, becoming *The New-York Times*). Greeley was one of the greatest editorial writers in American newspaper history and a champion of the press as a democratic forum. He had more credibility with the people of the United States than perhaps any other journalist in history. In general, Greeley eschewed sensationalism, and although the *Tribune* had brief flashes of it, neither Greeley nor his successors ever truly adopted the sensational practices of their chief rivals (Van Deusen 1953).

Similarly, Raymond, the editor of the *Daily Times*, was determined that it should be decent, reliable, fair, and complete, even at the risk of some dullness. Under Raymond's leadership, the *Daily Times* soon established a reputation for supreme objectivity (Brown 1951). Although Raymond did not believe in the eccentric idealism of Greeley, he loathed the sensationa-lism of *The Sun* and *The Herald*, which he called "cheap, filthy, false and extravagant" (*The New-York Times* 26 August 1859). At the same time, he

21

acknowledged Bennett's ability to understand what his readership demanded, commenting that he would pay the Devil one million dollars to whisper to him each evening "as he does Bennett, what the people of New York would like to read about the next morning" (quoted in Carlson 1942: xi).

Despite the presence of three nationally important rivals in New York City, from the early 1850s (when it surpassed *The Sun*) to the mid-1880s *The Herald* remained not only the nation's leader in circulation, but also in the creation of images from around the world. There were three reasons for this success other than those already mentioned. First, *The Herald* gained an enormous following because of the publicity it received during the "moral war" waged against both Bennett and his newspaper by the New York competition in the early 1840s – a war supposedly launched because of the outrageous language and defiance of convention by *The Herald*, but in reality a circulation war aimed at *The Herald* because of its very success (Three Lookers-on 1840; Mott 1952: 51). Second, *The Herald* issued successful editions for the midwest and California. And third, Bennett was the undisputed master of the crucial point of journalistic competition – news-gathering. As one critic who was appalled by the sensationalism of *The Herald*, admitted, "it is impossible any longer to deny that the chief newspaper of that busy city is *The New York Herald*. No matter how much we may regret this fact, or be ashamed of it, no journalist can deny it" (Parton 1866: 379).

Bennett's innate understanding of what news to obtain was equalled by his ability to procure it. He led the way in gathering news from distant places, quickly adopting the steamship, railroad, and telegraph when they superseded sailing ships, ponies, and pigeons (Giddings 1958; Fermer 1986: 33–9). *The Herald* was the most frequent user of the telegraph in the 1840s (Rosewater 1930: 41–2), and Bennett was the first American publisher to set up a regular team of European correspondents (Wikoff 1880: I, 464–96).

Bennett was also at the front in the collection of national and local news. He was one of the first Washington correspondents and his inquiring methods helped *The Herald* establish a reputation for political coverage that made it the most widely read American paper in Britain (*Foreign Quarterly Review* 1843; McCullagh 1929). He asserted the right of his reporters to go into spheres of society and enter places previously regarded as private. Congressmen, businessmen, and socialites were affronted by this intrusion, but, knowing that to snub a *Herald* reporter could mean a cruel lampooning, they had to accept it (Nevins 1936: 289–90, 464–5; Fermer 1986: 21). Being the best at news-gathering necessarily put *The Herald* in first place in the collection of sensational material. Sensational stories were missed by the other papers, but nothing escaped the attention of *The Herald* unless it was dull and uninteresting (Crouthamel 1973: 315–16).

The beginning of English sensationalism

By the late 1840s, *Herald*-style sensationalism was widespread in American journalism, but across the Atlantic, such sensationalism had been flatly rejected by the English dailies, which by comparison were conventional, staid, and – until 1855 – still a luxury of the upper classes (Wadsworth 1955: 2).

An underlying difference between the English and American press was the existence in Britain of "taxes on knowledge" that did not allow newspapers to reach the general public. The Newspaper Stamp Act of 1819 defined as a newspaper (and thus subject to a 4*d*. tax) every periodical containing news or comments on the news that was published more frequently than every 26 days, was printed on two sheets or less, and was priced at less than 6*d*. exclusive of tax (Wickwar 1928). The result of the Stamp Act was that a mass press could not legally or viably exist, due to the prohibitive prices charged for a newspaper (Collet 1899).

The first major steps towards the creation of cheap newspapers were taken the same year the penny press was born in America. In 1833 the advertisement tax was cut from 3*s*.6*d*. to 1*s*.6*d*. per ad. Three years later, the newspaper stamp tax was lowered to a penny per issue and the paper duty was cut in half (Aspinall 1949). But more than two decades were to pass before the struggle for a popular press was won. In 1853 the advertising duty was repealed; two years later, the newspaper tax was abolished; and in 1861 the duty on paper was removed. For the first time since the reign of Queen Anne (1702–14), the English press was completely free of fiscal restrictions.

In the meantime, daily newspapers were remarkably uniform. In 1833 *The Times* adopted a six-column, eight-page format that most English newspapers imitated for the next half century (Hutt 1973: 44). This new look included small type, run-on text, and single-column, titling headlines of minimal size. With the exception of *The Times*, the circulation of these dailies was very small throughout the 1830s and 1840s. By 1846 *The Times* had achieved a circulation of 28,600, while its three largest competitors – *The Morning Herald*, *The Morning Advertiser*, and *The Morning Chronicle* – combined for sales of less than 15,000.

The largest circulations belonged rather to the representatives of that peculiarly British institution, the separate Sunday paper. By the early 1850s three weeklies, *The Illustrated London News*, *Lloyd's Weekly Newspaper*, and *The News of the World*, had circulations of more than 100,000, while two, *The Weekly Times* and *Reynolds's Newspaper*, outsold even *The Times* (Wadsworth 1955).

The Sunday papers traditionally were considered to have been the stronghold of the radical press, but it has been indicated more recently (Lee 1974: 51–2; Berridge 1978: 254–64) that the keynote of those that were the most successful by the mid-nineteenth century was rather their emphasis on commercialism. The fact that the papers were under the control of middle-class businessmen instead of artisans or radical politicians, and the very way in which they were run – with an emphasis on sales,

23

marketing, and business techniques – suggest that their origin lay not in a natural outgrowth of working-class concerns but in an assessment of the possibilities of an expanding working-class market.

This drive toward commercialization led to the same result as when the American newspapers began to attract a new, wider audience: the relationship between the newspapers and their readers became based not so much on a mutuality of political interest as on sensational and salacious stories. The Sunday papers presented a basic political analysis to their relatively unsophisticated readership, but the formula that gave them such great success was that of Bennett and Day. As a street-vendor commented: "I read *Lloyd's Weekly Newspaper* on a Sunday, and what murders and robberies there is now! What will there be when the Great Exhibition opens!" (Mayhew 1861–62: I, 269).

By the late 1850s, more than a third of the material in *Lloyd's* could be classified as sensational, only slightly more than in *The Weekly Times* or *Reynolds's Newspaper* (Berridge 1976: 184–89). Approximately three-quarters of this sensational writing covered murder, other crimes, and scandal (Berridge 1978: 255), but special coverage also was extended to unusual events, such as the completion of the Northwest Passage or McClintock's discovery of the remains of the Franklin expedition. The diminishing interest in politics and the corresponding emphasis on sensationalism made the Sunday papers a direct progenitor of the English popular press of the second half of the nineteenth century.

Despite the beginning of sensationalism in the newspapers of both England and the United States, the press had not yet discovered exploration as a topic suitable for sensationalization. The dominant views of unknown lands were those of the sublime and picturesque, not the sensational. The ascendancy of the last had to await the death of the first two.

The Franklin search

The year 1845 was a busy one in the business of exploration. In central Asia, two French missionaries, Regis-Evariste Huc and Joseph Gabet, started their return journey after being the first Europeans to reach Lhasa from Peking. In Australia, three separate expeditions, under Charles Sturt, Thomas Mitchell, and Ludwig Leichhardt, opened up enormous sections of the interior. But these all paled in comparison to an expedition that left London under the command of Sir John Franklin on 19 May 1845. The largest and most well-equipped expedition ever to seek the Northwest Passage, Franklin's party consisted of two ships, *Erebus* and *Terror*, and 129 men. The Franklin expedition was intended to be the final step in the completion of the Passage, and the Royal Navy felt so assured of success that it made no contingency plans for search and rescue. Arctic experts, the public, and the press were equally optimistic about the outcome of the expedition, and one journal lectured skeptics: "The evident design of Providence in placing difficulties before man is, to sharpen his faculties for their mastery . . . [and] an expedition is at present on foot which will probably complete the outline of the American continent towards the Pole" (*Blackwood's Edinburgh Magazine* 1847: 516).

England had a considerable material investment in the Franklin expedition. The ships were fitted with screws powered by high-pressure steam engines; their keels were extended in order to obtain a more advantageous vertical alignment and to protect their interiors; and their sterns were redesigned to allow the raising and lowering of the new propellers (Smith 1938: 124; Wallace 1980: 55–7). The expedition supposedly had every other possible benefit as well: the latest technology in food preservation and canning (Morris 1958), the most recent advances in Arctic land travel (*The Observer* 15 May 1845), crews that were the cream of the Royal Navy (*The Times* 20 May 1845), and a leader described by Joseph Conrad (1926: 15) as "the dominating figure among the seamen explorers of the first half of the nineteenth century."

Britain also had a huge emotional investment in the expedition. It not only involved national pride, but represented man's capacity to conquer nature at its most mysterious and intimidating. Its members were seen as idealists "whose aims were certainly as pure as the air of those high latitudes where not a few of them laid down their lives for the advancement of geography" (Conrad 1926: 16).

However, Franklin's expedition took place during one of the least favorable climatic periods within the last thousand years (Alt *et al.* 1985: 91), and this, together with other problems for which the expedition was unprepared, resulted in a disaster of unequalled proportion in the history of exploration (Neatby 1970).

The shock came gradually to a nation that for several years was not seriously alarmed that no news had been received. Only in 1848 did it begin to occur to the English public that Franklin, his two ships, and all of his men had utterly disappeared into that strange, cold world of the north. That year searches for Franklin were initiated on three fronts: from the east through Lancaster Sound (under Sir James Clark Ross), the west through Bering Strait (under Thomas Moore), and the south down Mackenzie River and along the Arctic coastline (under Sir John Richardson and John Rae). Despite the potential horrors of the findings, the public attitude about the expedition still was supremely relaxed. When Richardson left England, *The Times* commented: "We do not ourselves feel any unnecessary anxiety as to the fate of the ships. . . . We place great hope in the *matériel* as well as the *personnel* of the expedition, for ships better adapted for the service, better equipped in all respects, or better officered and manned, never left the shores of England" (16 March 1848; emphasis *The Times*).

The searchers as well could not yet break free from their complacency. Richardson wrote in the same terms he had almost three decades before: "Here only, of all the countries I have seen, can I understand the deep blue shades of the ancient Italian masters. . . . The depth of shade which marks out low snowy waves of the lake when the sun is low would surprise a painter" (quoted in McIlraith 1868: 236–7).

Although Richardson's aesthetic was the picturesque, most English

25

newspapers contained little in the way of such description, their cliché-filled writing concentrating on the toughness or nobility of the explorers in terrible and sublime places:

> The return of Sir James Ross from his voyage in search of Sir John Franklin recalls our attention from the ordinary topics of discussion to those distant and desolate regions of eternal ice from which man and his interests seem for ever banished. That where there is danger men should be found to brave it, is not a matter of surprise. There will always be forthcoming adventurous spirits . . . ready to grapple with peril for peril's sake. . . . To men of such stern, unyielding stuff, the human race has been greatly indebted. (*The Weekly Times* 25 November 1849)

It was not only description that English newspapers generally avoided, but lively portrayals in general. They maintained an understated, phlegmatic tone throughout stories that were much longer than they would be later. For example, on 1 October 1850 *The Times* ran 78 column inches quoting the dispatches of John Ross, William Penny, and Erasmus Ommanney, and on 11 May 1853 *The Morning Herald* printed 94 column inches from a testimonial for Joseph-René Bellot, the French volunteer for the Franklin searches, who had been tragically killed in the ice. As in these cases, much of the time the accounts were not even written by journalists. The majority of articles about the Arctic fell into one of six categories, none of which made for scintillating reading. These included first, official dispatches from the expedition commanders to the Admiralty, frequently printed word for word; second, pre-expedition sailing orders from the Admiralty to the ship captains; third, letters received from expedition members; fourth, reports of lectures, also generally recorded verbatim; fifth, and most frequent, letters to the editor, most unsigned and many from obvious novices in Arctic affairs; and last, editorials.

In these forms, the English newspapers – particularly *The Times*, *The Weekly Times*, and *The Morning Herald* – gave far more coverage to the Franklin search than they had earlier Northwest Passage expeditions. Similarly, newspapers in the United States gave greater coverage to the Arctic after the first American Franklin search (1850–51), sponsored by Henry Grinnell and led by Edwin Jesse De Haven.

Stories in American newspapers were written in a more personal way than those in England. For example, after the return of *Advance*, one of the two ships Grinnell had sent out, *The New York Herald* printed an article that discussed the crew's interactions with the Eskimos, the curiosities they had brought home, and the methods of measuring distance and height when frozen in the ice (2 October 1851). While not truly sensational, the American stories printed personal details that would never have been allowed in the stuffy English press:

> The majority of the crews, as if relieved from a heavy responsibility, and it seemed by common consent, a sympathetic, upheaving, sicking consent – rushed almost to a man for the bulwarks of the vessel, and then and there gave full flow to their 'pent-up' feelings without a murmur or reproach from anyone. (*New-York Daily Times* 3 October 1851)

For seven years, expedition after expedition sailed into the Canadian archipelago and returned with only scraps of information about what had happened to Franklin. These fruitless efforts influenced not only the press, but popular writers. Herman Melville's greatest novel, *Moby Dick*, had a polar setting. And Henry David Thoreau's *Walden* was replete with references to the Franklin search, arguing that all exploration other than that of one's self was futile:

> Are these the problems which most concern mankind? Is Franklin the only man who is lost, that his wife should be so earnest to find him? Does Mr. Grinnell know where he himself is? Be rather the Mungo Park, the Lewis and Clark and Frobisher of your own streams and oceans; explore your own higher latitudes . . . .(Thoreau 1854)

The author who made the period's most significant contribution to the images of the Arctic was Charles Dickens, who helped keep the English public in a frenzy over Franklin throughout the search, and even after. Dickens did not feature the Arctic in his novels, but he did in his magazine *Household Words*:

> Think of Christmas in the tremendous wastes of ice and snow, that lie in the remotest regions of the earth! Yet it has been kept in those awful solitudes, cheerfully, by Englishmen. Where crashing mountains of ice, heaped up together, have made a chaos round their ships, which in a moment might have ground them to dust; where hair has frozen on the face; where blankets have stiffened upon the bodies of men lying asleep, closely housed by huge fires, and plasters have turned to ice upon the wounds of others accidentally hurt; where the ships have been undistinguishable from the environing ice, and have resembled themselves far less than the surrounding masses have resembled monstrous piles of architecture which could not possibly be there, or anywhere. . . . (McCormick and Dickens 1850: 306–7)

Dickens' image of the Arctic sublime endured as long as the Admiralty was interested in the Franklin search and as the lucrative rewards for the settling of the fate of Franklin and the completion of the Northwest Passage remained unclaimed. However, in October 1853 word arrived that Robert McClure, who had sailed from England in 1850 in *Investigator*, had completed the Passage (Osborn 1856). In their dull, stolid manner, the English dailies gave the story unrivalled attention: on 21 October *The Morning Herald* ran 94 column inches about it, followed in its next two issues by 91 inches and 104 inches.

McClure's completion of the Northwest Passage also occasioned one of the last classic representations of the sublime in *The Illustrated London News*, which recalled age-old images of the ice:

> The ice was floating in broken detached masses, with frosted summits, beautifully brilliant beneath a bright sun and azure sky, assuming the most extraordinary and grotesque appearances – from ships under full sail to whole squadrons of gun-boats, spires of churches . . . towers, domes, and pinnacles, which lent a strange charm to these lonely regions. (22 October 1853)

Three months later, on 20 January 1854, the Admiralty announced that if nothing concrete were heard by 31 March the officers and crews of *Erebus* and *Terror* would "be considered as having died in Her Majesty's service" (*London Gazette* 12 January 1854). Despite Jane Franklin's fervent request for a continuation of the search because "where Esquimaux can live, there also Englishmen can live" (Great Britain 1854: 10), the Admiralty had lost interest in pursuing an interminable, unrewarding, and expensive task. Any hopes for further Franklin searches were crushed when, four days before the deadline, the Crimean War broke out. The navy needed its ships, officers, and men to battle with Russians instead of icebergs.

It is a coincidence of Arctic history that virtually as soon as the Royal Navy abandoned the Franklin search, the first definite evidence about the crews of *Erebus* and *Terror* was uncovered. In the autumn of 1854, John Rae, the consummate Arctic traveler of his time (Rich, in Rae 1953: xcviii–xcix), reported to the Admiralty the fate of the Franklin party, and in so doing, he ended the Arctic sublime and opened the way for the sensational reporting that was to follow.

3

A decade of change: 1855–65

The decade between 1855 and 1865 was remarkable from the standpoint of change. The Anglo-American public's long-established ways of perceiving the unknown – through traditional aesthetics related both to nature and art – disappeared because they were no longer consistent with the horrible realities exposed by the discovery of the fate of the Franklin expedition. In particular, the sublime view of the Arctic began to be replaced by a vision based on new concepts of man's continuing struggle against nature.

On a less philosophical level, political, technological, and scientific developments influenced both national and personal participation in exploration. Meanwhile, large numbers of scientists, explorers, and adventurers began to become interested in new lands for their own sake, particularly in the far north and the interior of sub-Saharan Africa. Travelers to these areas presented fresh, exciting images that, together with changes in the press in Britain and the United States, set the stage for the subsequent sensationalization of exploration.

The death of the sublime

Edmund Burke argued in his *Philosophical enquiry* that natural sublimity had to be kept at a distance for it to enthrall the spectator. Once the sublime approached too near (whether through familiarity or geographical proximity), the accompanying terror erased any appreciation of it. In the autumn of 1854, this is exactly what happened to the British nation.

For six years, the Anglo-American public's fascination with the Franklin search was undiminished by a growing concern that nothing would ever be discovered. On 23 October 1854, when *The Times* published a report that John Rae had sent to the Admiralty on 29 July, the English public finally received some clarification about what had happened, but it was not the type of information for which it had hoped. Rae stated that, while surveying on Boothia Peninsula, he had received from a group of Eskimos what he considered incontestable evidence that the bodies of many white men – almost certainly members of Franklin's expedition – had been found along the shores of King William Island. Rae's conclusion – that Franklin's men had died of starvation and scurvy while heading south toward Back's Great Fish River – was bad enough, but the report contained a further statement that shocked the Western world:

> Some of the bodies had been buried (probably those of the first victims of the famine); some were in a tent or tents; others under the boat, which had been turned over to form a shelter; and several lay scattered about in different directions. . . . From the mutilated state of many of the corpses and the contents of the kettles, it is evident that our wretched countrymen had been driven to the last resource – cannibalism – as a means of prolonging existence. . . . (*The Times* 23 October 1854)

There was an immediate outcry of horror and skepticism from the public, which assumed that the Eskimos had murdered Franklin's men (*The Times* 26 October 1854). Rae was excoriated in the press (*The Morning Herald* 27 October 1854; *The Times* 30 October 1854), particularly when he insisted that he believed the Eskimos (*The Times* 31 October, 3, 7 November 1854). Then, into the fray entered the formidable figure of Charles Dickens (Stone 1987), who, in *Household Words*, voiced the outrage and disbelief of many: "It is in the highest degree improbable that such men as the officers and crews of the two lost ships would, or could, in any extremity of hunger, alleviate the pains of starvation by this horrible means" (Dickens 1854a: 361). Although Rae maintained his position (Rae 1854a, 1854b), *Household Words* continued to protest that the pride of English manhood could not stoop to the level implied (Dickens 1854b; Morley 1857a, 1857b). Even when Rae's full account was printed in the magazine, it was accompanied by an editorial questioning his accuracy (Rae 1855). Ultimately, Dickens became so involved in the issue that he joined with Wilkie Collins to produce a play, *The frozen deep*, which dramatized the nobility of British explorers faced with a plight similar to that of Franklin's men (Brannan 1966).

Despite Dickens' reaction, the British seemed to consider the topic something better left unaddressed. After a burst of indignation, the press turned its attention to the grim struggle in the Crimea and ignored Rae's findings: "Our work amid the ice is now limited to certain investigations which may throw light upon the matter in which FRANKLIN and his friends came by their end" (*The Times* 8 November 1854). Rae himself was also ignored, an early example of an explorer shunned for presenting facts with which the establishment, the public, or the press were not pleased. Unlike almost every other major contemporary British explorer of the Arctic – Parry, both Rosses, Franklin, Back, Richardson, McClure, and McClintock – Rae was neither knighted nor accepted into the circle of national heroes (Richards 1985: 178).

But the damage had been done to the British psyche. The press and public alike tried to disregard Rae's findings, but the suspicion that they were accurate crept slowly into the public consciousness, beginning to change the image of the north. For centuries, the English had imagined the Arctic as a place of terror, but one that God had created for its wonder, beauty, and fascination. Knowing that the Franklin expedition had disappeared forever was terrible, yet sublime. But knowing that the men of the expedition had died slowly of scurvy and starvation was different. The reality and proximity of the horror had eliminated the sublimity:

No; there are no more sunny continents – no more islands of the blest – hidden under the far horizons, tempting the dreamer over the undiscovered seas; nothing but those weird and tragic shores, those cliffs of everlasting ice and mainlands of frozen snow, which have never produced anything to us but a late and sad discovery of the depths of human heroism, patience, and bravery, such as imagination could scarcely dream of. (*Blackwood's Edinburgh Magazine* 1855: 589)

Thus, it was almost anticlimactic when, four years after Rae's report was published, Francis Leopold McClintock and William Hobson, in an expedition sent by Jane Franklin, searched King William Island and found relics, bodies, and a note in a cairn, which combined to confirm what had happened to the expedition: after being beset in the ice of Franklin Strait, Franklin had died on *Erebus* in 1847; under the command of Francis Crozier, the men had left the ships in April 1848; and they had died as they walked to the Canadian mainland, the last of them reaching Starvation Cove on Adelaide Peninsula.

The English press reports gradually accepted the disaster and were able to salvage something positive by stressing the courage and self-sacrifice of the expedition members. *The Illustrated London News* was typical when it commented:

Who shall tell how they struggled, how they hoped against hope, how the fainting few who reached Cape Herschel threw themselves on their knees and thanked their God that, if it so pleased Him that England and home should never be reached! He had granted them the glory of securing to their dear country the honour they had sought for her – the discovery of the North-West Passage. (15 October 1859)

No more was the Arctic romantic or sublime. And, for a few, no more was the north desirable as the backdrop for heroic adventure:

. . . at last the mystery of FRANKLIN'S fate is solved. We know where he died, we know the very day of his death. . . . Alas! There can be no longer those sad wailings from an imaginary Tintagel to persuade the credulous that an ARTHUR still lives. . . . We must learn that there are yet powers in nature too strong for man to overcome. The dauntless soul dies out amid frost and snow; the spirit is never quenched though the body may perish. . . . We retire now from the contest with honour, if with grief, and we leave the name of FRANKLIN engraved on the furthest pillars which the energy of mankind had

31

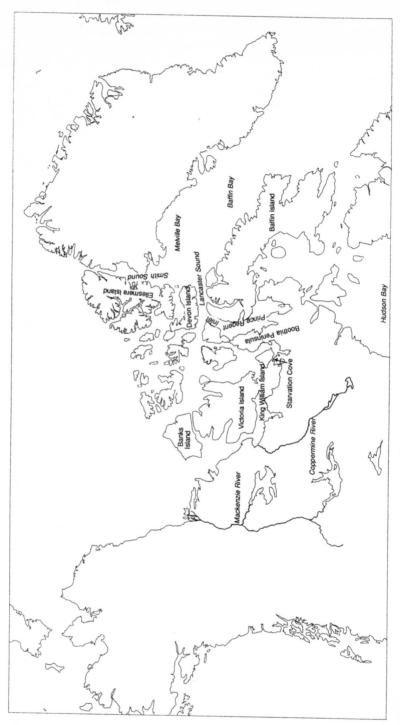

Map 1 The Canadian Arctic: scene of the Franklin searches

dared to erect as the landmark of its research in the dull and lifeless region that guards the axis of the world. (*The Times* 23 September 1859)

The conquest of the world

Even as *The Times* rejected future Arctic exploration, popular interest in unexplored areas began to increase. This was in part due to the spread throughout Western civilization of a new perception of man's relationship to the world, of his "mission of dominion over nature" (Powell 1977: 107). Around 1860 there was a resurgence in the Biblical notion of man as a force above nature, given powers to subdue the earth. When combined with popularized Darwinian theory, Social Darwinism, the prevalent racial beliefs of the time, and interpretations regarding man and nature by popular theoreticians such as George P. Marsh and John Ruskin, this led to the intellectual growth and triumph of the "desire for the conquest of the world" (Marsh 1864; Ruskin 1866; Ellegard 1958; Himmelfarb 1959; Curtin 1965).

Man's role as conqueror of the world was a persistent theme during the late nineteenth century: it was perceived that character was built by this challenge and from an early age boys were prepared for competition with nature (Mack 1941). No one more clearly espoused this belief than Henry Morton Stanley, who positively revelled in the name Bula Matari, the "breaker of rocks," which he was given by the natives of the Congo during his work there for King Leopold of Belgium. To Stanley, the name portrayed him as the man who could conquer all of nature (Stanley 1885: I, 237).

The Western attempts to make man the master of nature found expression in numerous facets of life. In technology, machines were developed to increase output and reduce manpower; in medicine, age-old diseases were identified and eradicated; and in science, secrets in geology, chemistry, and physics were uncovered. In geography, the desire for knowledge, combined with the attitude that not only could everything be known but that it should be, made it both a sufficient and honorable reason to go somewhere merely because no one had been there before.

Thus the new era of geographic inquiry was not marked simply by the fascination with the blank spaces on the map that had prevailed in the late eighteenth century under the influence of men like Sir Joseph Banks, the president of the Royal Society and one of the founders in 1788 of the African Association. Rather, in this last great age of terrestrial discovery, such areas were more than merely interesting; they were at first paradoxes, then unacceptable, and finally national insults (Barrow 1847). By the 1850s subjugating nature and filling in the blank spaces had become the aim of numerous organizations, including the Royal Geographical Society (RGS) and the American Geographical Society. In his 1852 Presidential address, Sir Roderick Murchison told the RGS:

there is no exploration . . . to which greater value would be attached than an

33

ascent of [Mount Kilimanjaro and Mount Kenya] from the east coast, possibly from near Mombasa. The adventurous travellers who shall first lay down the true position of these equatorial snowy mountains . . . and who shall satisfy us that they not only throw off the waters of the White Nile . . . will be justly considered among the greatest benefactors of this age . . . . (Murchison 1852: cxxiii–cxxiv)

But it was not just the learned societies that wanted to complete the map; the public was thrilled with the idea of a struggle against the wilderness. "Let any man," wrote the explorer Charles Sturt, "lay the map of Australia before him, and regard the blank upon its surface, and then let me ask him if it would not be an honourable achievement to be the first to place foot in its centre" (quoted in Cameron 1980: 51–52). Perhaps the American explorer Anthony Fiala best summed up the thinking of the time when he wrote:

Beyond the geographical and scientific value of the discovery of the North Pole, and the solving of questions of popular curiosity, another reason exists to explain the ceaseless effort to reach that mystic point: The Spirit of the Age will never be satisfied until the command given to Adam in the beginning – the command to subdue the earth – has been obeyed, and the ends of the earth have revealed their secrets. . . . (Fiala 1907: 4)

The conquest of the world was also an important element in nationalism – itself a driving force in exploration. That the public's preoccupation with exploration had nationalist overtones is apparent from the newspapers of the day, and some sponsors of polar expeditions – notably the Peary Arctic Club and the RGS – were blatantly nationalist. Nationalism was also a significant motivation for explorers such as Fridtjof Nansen, who saw success in exploration as an important tool in the struggle for Norwegian independence. Nansen understood that characteristics such as physical courage, stamina, scientific expertise, and ingenuity not only identified the individual as being of heroic stature, but became synonymous with national traits, thereby adding to the prestige of his country (Wechter 1941: 1–16).

A change of emphasis in exploration

In addition to the destruction of the sublime and a new way of viewing man's relationship to nature, several other factors helped set the stage for new images of the unknown. Among these were changes in both the participants in exploration and the techniques of travel and survival.

Before the end of the Franklin search, the Arctic explorers who made the most significant impact on the English and American publics were in the Royal Navy or were members of expeditions associated with those sent by the Admiralty. This was altered by Britain's decision in 1854 to withdraw from the Arctic, where the Royal Navy was not to reappear in strength for another two decades. Around the same time that the British decreased their participation in the exploration of the Arctic, they became much more active in the exploration of East Africa. British efforts had previously concentrated on the Niger, but the meticulous observations by Heinrich Barth on his overland journeys helped dissipate the mysteries that had surrounded that river for so long. Now the emphasis turned instead to the sources of the Nile and the lake regions in the central and eastern parts of the continent.

Meanwhile, countries without major previous involvement in international exploration began to appear in the Arctic. Alaska was purchased by the United States in 1867, the same year that the British North America Act provided for the Confederation of Canada. Within a decade, the US and Canada had initiated systematic exploration of their far northern areas, and the Danes had begun active research in Greenland. A number of countries in central and northern Europe also developed or expanded their Arctic interests.

This change in participation affected ideas about the travel, clothing, and food used in the north. Whereas the British continued the man-hauled sledging described as "about the hardest work to which free men have been put in modern times" (Mackinnon 1985: 133), the Scandinavians began to change polar travel. The first ski club was established in Norway in 1861 (the year of Nansen's birth), leading directly to the expansion of Scandinavian polar exploration in the 1880s. Similarly, whereas Royal Navy expeditions had neglected to adapt their clothing to the cold, in the 1860s American explorers began to learn from the Eskimos how to dress so as to be warm in the coldest climates and yet not to be too hot when doing heavy work (Hall 1865).

Many European and American explorers also effectively defeated scurvy by learning to live off the land, with a vitamin C-rich diet that included large amounts of fresh meat. Although several private British expeditions were scurvy-free, almost every major polar expedition led by Royal Navy officers in the six decades after the Franklin search was affected (Carpenter 1986).

These developments had different effects on the American and English press' presentation of the north. The newspapers in the US presented more exciting accounts as Americans moved to the fore. The English built images based on overcoming appalling conditions that were, to a great extent, of their own making.

The growth of Arctic science

The entry of new countries into the Arctic meant an influx of many individuals who also inspired fresh visions of the north. These were not commonly politicians, military heroes, or men of international power; they were people with concerns and interests specific to the Arctic.

Of the many developments in polar exploration during the mid-Victorian era, none was more significant than the growth of interest in the Arctic for its own sake. This was not a new phenomenon, but it was prevalent after 1855, whereas before it had been sporadic. Traditionally, the Arctic had been seen as an unfortunate reality: an inescapable obstruction on the way to the markets of the Orient and Siberia and to the efforts of the whaling or sealing industries; a maze of mysteries hiding knowledge about missing expeditions behind thousands of miles of uncharted ice and rock; a hostile region holding secret deposits of wealth within areas dominated by tundra, enormous lakes, and aimlessly wandering rivers.

Although British naval officers had eagerly volunteered for Arctic duty during the search for the Northwest Passage, this was generally not due to any strong personal interest in the area. Rather it was a path to promotion; it gave an individual a chance both for distinction and to avoid either stagnating on half-pay in an English seaport or being stationed in a colonial backwater. Once having served in the Arctic, officers frequently chose to return there, and many of the junior officers of one generation became the leaders of the next, such as McClintock, James Clark Ross, and George S. Nares. The same was true of the lower ranks. Seamen were not only keen to receive double pay for Arctic duty in the post-Napoleonic depression, they found the north more appealing when it became common knowledge that the death rate was lower than in the tropics.

Certainly there were notable British exceptions in the first half of the century, men who were versatile natural historians with absorbing curiosity about everything strange and new. John Richardson, for example, wrote the botanical appendices to Franklin's account of his first expedition; included observations about physical geography, currents, flora and fauna, ichthyology, magnetism, and meteorology in both of Franklin's books; and wrote the most comprehensive work of North American Arctic zoology of his time, *Fauna boreali-Americana* (Franklin 1823, 1828; Richardson 1831). John Rae made glaciological and anthropological studies as well as recording local flora and fauna. His publications considered subjects as diverse as the movements of boulders by ice, the native peoples of the American north, the birds of the Arctic coast, and the frozen remains of mammoths (Richards 1985). William Scoresby Jr made what remained for a century the definitive survey of the East Greenland coast, studied the "baffling lights" of the Arctic sky, and drew pictures of snow crystals that were not surpassed until the mid-twentieth century, with the development of the photographic microscope (Stamp and Stamp 1975; Martin 1988).

Scientists from other European nations also showed interest in the study of the Arctic. The German Karl Ludwig Giesecke pioneered the geological study of Greenland during his seven-year expedition under the Danish flag (1806–13). Zoologist Sven Lovén was the leader of the first Swedish Arctic scientific expedition, to Spitsbergen in 1837 (Nathorst *et al.* 1909: 4). And from 1848 to 1851, Hinrich Johannes Rink, a Danish administrator, made detailed studies of the geology, mineralogy, and social conditions of Greenland, as well as of the formation of the ice sheet and the calving of glaciers (Holland in press).

But there was still a basic difference between many of these individuals and those who were active after 1855. Most of the British engaged in scientific research in the Arctic in the first half of the century had other reasons for being there. Richardson was a surgeon in the Royal Navy, Rae worked for the Hudson's Bay Company, and Scoresby was a whaling captain. The same was true of many Europeans: Giesecke remained in Greenland so long only because he was stranded by the Napoleonic wars, and Rink was there primarily as an administrator.

Similarly, even though British naval officers added to the scientific knowledge of the Arctic, it was not their principal aim, nor did they necessarily have any specific training for it. On naval voyages, the Arctic was usually investigated in addition to prescribed duties, above and beyond the primary aims of the expedition. A memorandum from the Admiralty relative to the compilation of a manual of scientific enquiry stated:

> Their Lordships do not consider it necessary that this Manual should be one of very deep and abstruse research. Its directions should not require the use of nice apparatus and instruments: they should be generally plain, so that men merely of good intelligence and fair acquirement may be able to act upon them. . . . The several heads of inquiry are as follows: Astronomy, Botany, Geography and Hydrography, Geology, Mineralogy, Magnetism, Meteorology, Statistics, Tides, Zoology. (Herschel 1871: iii–iv)

The man who reversed this trend, who proposed scientific study of the Arctic as a goal and not just as an addendum to commercial or geographical investigations, was the Swedish glaciologist Otto Torell. In 1850, at the age of 22, Torell completed his first significant fieldwork, under the direction of Lovén. In 1857 Torell visited Iceland to study its glaciers and maritime fauna. The next year he led an expedition to the west coast of Spitsbergen for the collection of geological, zoological, and botanical information.

In 1861 Torell was the driving force behind the Swedish Arctic Expedition to Spitsbergen, which included nine scientists, among them Adolf Erik Nordenskiöld. The expedition embraced two objectives: a comprehensive scientific investigation of Spitsbergen and its coast, and a geographical excursion to the north. The plan, unique both in its emphasis on science and in the careful distinction of its scientific and geographical aims, was designed so that the first goal of the expedition (the scientific studies) could be accomplished even if the geographical survey proved impossible. Indeed, despite the failure of the survey, the scientific program exceeded all expectations and resulted in a wealth of geological, glaciological, zoological, botanical, magnetic, meteorological, and hydrographic data. As Nathorst wrote (1900: 458): "With Torell's expedition of 1861 scientific polar research had been founded. The radical influence which this research had on the various areas of research in the natural sciences can only be hinted at. . . ."

Although this was Torell's last expedition to the Arctic, his pattern of comprehensive investigation was taken up by Nordenskiöld and eventually became a model for other European and American scientific expeditions. In 1864 Nordenskiöld led a Swedish Arctic expedition to Svalbard, where he carried out zoological, botanical, and meteorological work. But Nordenskiöld also crossed over to areas of interest to the common man; he was a leader both in the exploration and commercialization of the Arctic. Thus, more than Torell, he began to generate public interest in the far north.

Science in the exploration of Africa

Science also played a major role in the exploration of the interior of sub-Saharan Africa. However, the most significant figure in the science-exploration equation in Africa was not a man whose influence came about because he was doing active fieldwork there, but rather because of his political, professional, and institutional connections in Britain. Sir Roderick Murchison was recognized as one of Britain's foremost geologists, was Director-General of the Geological Survey of the United Kingdom, and was on the council of both the Royal Society and the Geological Society for many years. But his most important, and most visible, position was that of President of the RGS.

There were a multitude of complex and overlapping reasons for Murchison's sponsorship of African exploration through the RGS (Stafford 1989). At one level, he wanted to solve the mystery of the continent's general geological structure, and to be able to apply it to the Silurian System that he had postulated. At a second level, his control of exploration marked his bid for personal and institutional dominance over the scientific community. At a third, he hoped that, through directing science and exploration, the RGS could achieve a position as an independent source of national overseas policy, while at the same time winning broad public recognition and support not only for the institution but for geology. And at a fourth, he believed that science and exploration could be useful tools in serving Britain's global interests – promoting the economic progress, expansionist goals, and public emotional aspirations of British imperialism.

Murchison was not only interested in Africa: the RGS sponsored expeditions throughout the world, and he was both a personal champion of Jane Franklin and a supporter of Sturt, Leichhardt, and Burke and Wills in Australia. But it was with Africa that Murchison was most visibly linked, and particularly with Richard Francis Burton, John Hanning Speke, and David Livingstone. For nearly two decades, from 1850 to 1870, Murchison played a role in organizing virtually every British expedition to Africa (Stafford 1989: 187). He influenced what goals were established, what routes were taken, and what scientific measurements were made. And at the same time, he manipulated the information that came from the explorers and that was released to the press or the public about them. In this way, he helped promote public interest in not only science and exploration, but in the images of new lands. At the same time, he served as a creator of the heroic stature of explorers, and as a mediator of their myths.

The lure of the unknown

It was not only scientists who became fascinated with unknown lands in the second half of the nineteenth century. A growing number of private, independent explorers initially went to Africa or the Arctic with specific missions – resolving geographical problems, finding Franklin relics, lifting the natives from savagery, or opening up commerce – but returned because they were captivated by the lure of these lands. Such men were so smitten with the beauty and perceived purity of these areas, with the challenges to their intellect and manhood, or with their capacity to become free and nomadic in such undeveloped environs, that they were prepared to face anything to return. This love of unexplored parts of the globe simply because of the freedom they gave was expressed by Joseph Thomson, the first European to cross Kenya to Lake Victoria through the territory of the Masai, when he wrote: "I am doomed to be a wanderer. I am not an empire-builder. I am not a missionary. I am not truly a scientist. I merely want to return to Africa to continue my wanderings" (quoted in Moorehead 1960: 121). Anthony Fiala, who participated in two North Polar expeditions, gave a strong indication of how powerful this lure could be, when he wrote:

> It was odd how quickly the Arctic lost its terrors after the return to civilisation. During the long, dark winter . . . we would huddle together for warmth around a tiny stove in the cabin of the *America* and talk of warmer countries. Two of the men avowed their intention of going on an expedition to the island of Borneo as soon as the *America* returned to Norway; two others stated that they were going to Mexico; another expressed a wish to explore Africa, and one of the doctors of the party said he meant to go to the equator and never travel farther than five degrees north or south of it the rest of his days. Yet on the eve of another expedition these men applied to go north once more. (Fiala 1907: 11–12)

Such men were not above using exploration for personal gain. Like their predecessors in the Royal Navy, many adventurers saw the investigation of new lands as a way to fame and fortune. Yet, there was a significant difference between these travellers and those in the Royal Navy: these men had several options in the way they pursued their fame but chose exploration. Their forerunners proceeded in a more-or-less straight course on their journeys, and when they were done their desire was to return home. Many of the new explorers lived for the wild and traveled in circles, with their true mission beginning and ending there.

There are few better examples of the lure of the unknown than two American explorers, Elisha Kent Kane and Charles Francis Hall. Kane, a restless naval surgeon and inveterate wanderer who had already traveled to Brazil, Ceylon, China, the Philippines, and Egypt, volunteered for the first American Franklin search expedition (1850–51) out of a romantic desire for heroic adventure (Corner 1972: 70). The expedition's year in the Arctic included experiences Kane considered exciting, such as meeting Sir John Ross, killing a polar bear, and discovering the Grinnell Peninsula on Devon Island. But it also included rampant scurvy, terribly cold conditions, and being locked in the ice for months (Kane 1854).

Nevertheless, Kane was caught by the Arctic as tightly as had been his ship, *Advance*. Immediately upon arriving back in the US, he started working toward returning north. When ultimately he led a second American Franklin search expedition (1853–55), his official purpose was to sail to the most northerly penetrable point in Baffin Bay, and from there to search for Franklin and to carry out scientific investigations relating to magnetism, meteorology, and the existence of an open polar sea (Kane 1856). Whether by this time Kane had any honest belief in the possibility of finding Franklin or reaching an open polar sea is debatable. It is more likely that he had discovered that honorable motives were needed to obtain the financing to return to the Arctic. And his real goal was simply that – to get back to the Arctic, where he could simultaneously achieve contentment and fame.

Like Kane, Hall – a printer and journalist from Cincinnati – began his Arctic involvement with noble goals: "It seemed to me as if I had been called, if I may so speak, to try and do the work" (Hall 1865: I, 3). Hall apparently believed that God had chosen him to solve the mystery of Franklin's fate. There was another motive seemingly just as important: Hall wanted to escape from life in Ohio to the wilderness because "in his ignorance he idealized the world that lay in the Canadian north" (Loomis 1972: 46). On his first expedition (1860–62), when he spent two winters living with the Eskimos of Baffin Island, Hall found that the Arctic was not a land of romance or storybook tales. It was a simpler life than the one he had led in the US, but vastly harsher. Yet it was also more alluring, and Hall started planning his return almost immediately.

Hall's next expedition to find Franklin relics, again virtually on his own, occupied him in northern Canada for five winters, 1864–69 (Nourse 1879). Before he returned home he was already planning an expedition to the North Pole, and his powers of persuasion were such that he received US government backing for his scheme. Whether Hall truly believed he could reach the Pole and whether he actually cared about scientific objectives are unanswerable questions. But the Arctic had become an essential part of his existence: he lived for the north, where he found both honor from the world and personal contentment. He explained this in a speech to the American Geographical and Statistical Society in 1871:

> Many who have written to me, or who have appeared to me personally, think that I am an adventurous spirit and of bold heart to attempt to go to the North Pole. Not so. It does not require that heart which they suppose I have got. The Arctic Region is my home. I love it dearly; its storms, its winds, its glaciers, its icebergs; and when I am there among them, it seems as if I were in an earthly heaven or a heavenly earth. (Hall 1873: 406)

Although Hall appeared eccentric, he was not alone in preferring wild and unexplored areas to day-to-day life in the cities of Europe or North America. Henry Morton Stanley contrasted life in England with his toils in Africa when he wrote: "One brings me an inordinate amount of secret pain, the other sapped my strength but left my mind expanded and was purifying" (Stanley 1872–74: Journal 12 August 1872).

Unlike many contemporary Arctic scientists, the explorers of Hall's breed usually were not from Scandinavia or central Europe, but from the US or Britain. This played no small part in the fact that it was these adventurers, and the men who funded them, who helped to change the old images of the Arctic that had been passed down from the British naval expeditions.

Few individuals were more important in encouraging independent Arctic explorers than Henry Grinnell, a wealthy New York merchant called by Hall the "father of American Arctic exploration" (Cruwys 1991). Grinnell became actively interested in the Arctic after Jane Franklin's appeal to US President Zachary Taylor for aid in the search for her husband's expedition. With Grinnell's financing, four US Franklin-search expeditions were sent out, and he also backed two North Polar expeditions, one (1860–61) led by Isaac Israel Hayes and the other (1871–73) beginning under Hall.

Perhaps Grinnell's most important contributions were his efforts to promote interest in and influence opinion about the Arctic among the American government and the public. Grinnell's efforts first brought the US Navy into the Franklin search (Cruwys 1990: 212–13). His constant campaigning helped maintain government involvement in later expeditions, while also encouraging other wealthy individuals to support them (Grinnell 1850–73: MS248/414/33).

One reason Grinnell wielded such influence was his ability to read the American public. When interest in the Arctic began to decline, or opinion became negative, Grinnell encouraged the press to whip up support for his projects. He wrote letters to newspapers calculated to stir up public interest in the Arctic (Grinnell 1850–73: MS248/414/29), expressed his belief that America had a humanitarian duty to join the Franklin search (Grinnell 1850–73: MS248/414/30), published the letters of Jane Franklin and the captains who commanded the expeditions she sponsored (Grinnell 1850–73: MS248/414/30, 55), and even sided with Lady Franklin in the controversy over whether her husband or McClure had discovered the Northwest Passage (Grinnell 1850–73: MS248/414/37, 40, 41).

The explorers whom Grinnell sponsored were among the first caught by the lure of the unknown. If their expeditions had goals similar to those of the earlier British voyages, they attempted to attain those goals in an original, North American manner. For example, the two Grinnell expeditions were fitted out with ships and crews much smaller than the large and extensively manned vessels used by the Royal Navy. On the second of these expeditions, Kane established a pattern of exploration that included co-operation with the Eskimos, the adoption of some of their ways of life, and the use of dogs to haul sledges (Kane 1856).

Hall adopted Eskimo life-style almost entirely (Hall 1865; Nourse 1879). He wrote in his journal: "The fact is, to effect the purpose I have at heart – to carry out successfully what I have undertaken to perform . . . I *must learn to live as Esquimaux do!*" (quoted in Loomis 1972: 88; emphasis Hall's). This method differed considerably from that of most British expeditions (although it greatly resembled the techniques of Rae), but it was subsequently followed, at least in part, by many of Hall's North American successors.

New expedition accounts

As explorers learned how to operate more successfully in new environments, they developed different concepts of the places to which they traveled and of the peoples living there. These perceptions were presented to the public of the 1850s and 1860s in books notable for their exciting images. Not even, however, when their fascination with these areas impelled the explorers to return again and again, was the presentation always pleasant. Invariably, they showed a love-hate relationship, railing against the regions and their inhabitants, seeing Africans and Eskimos as ugly, scheming, debauched, and hopeless, and the wilderness as seldom touched by beauty or grandeur, but rather as hostile and in need of the order imposed by civilization.

These books were something new for the Anglo-American public. Most previous travelers had gone to exotic destinations with preconceptions based on the reports of their predecessors. Thus they had, not surprisingly, assimilated the information that most closely confirmed their expectations, while ignoring that which seemed contradictory. This circular pattern was self-perpetuating, as most of the books published about distant lands reinforced the others. But now the new genre broke with the past and looked at the Arctic and Africa as if with newly opened eyes.

The presentation of these books was also different. As opposed to the earlier stolid accounts frequently transcribed directly from private journals or official logs, these new works were not only thrilling but often quite personal. They were based on tales of danger, bravery, and heroism, but the authors also frequently became propagandists, intertwining throughout the adventurous happenings passionate arguments for their causes and using scientific, religious, or humanitarian reasoning to intensify their appeal to the sympathy or indignation of the readers.

There was a powerful response to these new books, in part because of their style and in part because of their immediacy. With books based in such settings, there was always the chance that the author or some of his compatriots might be dead before the book was published, or that they might again be lost in a remote corner of the world. This made the books even more thrilling. But these gripping narratives of adventure were not written solely because the explorers had seen the world in a new light or because they had a special cause to promote. The writers were serving their own ends in two additional ways. First, the more thrilling and dangerous unknown regions were seen to be, the more explorers would captivate a public anxious for heroes. So the Arctic became a backdrop for the daring voyages and heroic exploits of bold explorers, imprisoned by snow and ice and struggling against overwhelming natural forces, and Africa became the setting for struggles not only with nature, but with natives, animals, and diseases.

Second, large amounts of money were needed to return to these regions, so private explorers, invariably impoverished, constantly had to solicit patronage, both from wealthy benefactors and from the public. So they not only had to show that they were doing important work, they had to thrill the public with stories that would ensure book sales. Fame and wealth were interrelated: fame enhanced the chances of achieving wealth, while obtaining the financing to return to the wild was the first step to gaining fame.

Thus, travelers were explorers first, but writers as well. They began to tour the lecture circuit, both before and after expeditions. In fact, they began to do anything to create images of lands that not only needed to be conquered, but needed them as conquerors. In time, fund-raising became what was frequently the most gruelling aspect of a hazardous occupation, about which Hall stated, "lecturing is the curse of my soul." Roald Amundsen later insisted that no one except an explorer could appreciate the agony fund-raising involved, and that, despite his justly deserved fame, the burden of constantly having to seek financial support almost broke his constitution (Hunt 1986: 16).

The entire process became such an integral part of exploration that Clements R. Markham, the president of the RGS from 1893 to 1905, once assured the Danish explorer Ejnar Mikkelsen that he would eventually become accustomed to pleading for funds. Mikkelsen should feel less like a beggar and more like a benefactor of mankind, Markham said, because "it isn't for ourselves we do it, but for the cause" (Mikkelsen 1955: 14).

One of the early self-promoters in the "cause" was Kane, whose lectures were frequently sold out and whose books were best-sellers. He presented a world of enormous icebergs, towering cliffs, and tiny brigs battered by gales and running a gauntlet between crushing rocks and ice. And he showed himself to be truly heroic, a bold explorer and brilliant leader able not only to overcome nature but to master men. Kane won enormous praise both in the US and England, where it was written about his second book: "We cannot but feel proud that the English language should be the mother tongue of the hero of such a tale. Looked at merely from a literary point of view, the book is a very remarkable one" (*Saturday Review* 1856: 661).

Kane's efforts were a remarkable example of the power of the pen. The praise that was lavished upon him by the public and the press was to a certain extent misguided, because nowhere were they able to gain insights into his weak leadership, his erratic temperament, or his overwhelming ego. Kane was a far better writer than he was an explorer, and that ability not only made his reputation, it fired the imagination of the American public to an extent to which prior exploration had never been able.

American explorers were not the only ones to cater to the public with new-style accounts. In 1859 McClintock's *The voyage of the 'Fox' in the Arctic seas* became one of the best-selling books of its time. Seven thousand copies of McClintock's tale of unraveling the Franklin mystery were ordered before publication (Hodgson 1985: 10), and the inventory of Mudie's Subscription Library, arguably the best index to the tastes of the English middle-class reading public at that time, included 3,000 copies of it, more than any other book of that year, including Darwin's *Origin of species*, Dickens' *A tale of two cities*, and Hughes' *Tom Brown at Oxford* (Griest 1970: 21).

Inevitably, McClintock's tale had different origins from its American counterparts. McClintock undertook the journey because of his friendship with Jane Franklin and his desire for a successful conclusion to the Franklin search, rather than a driving interest in fame or promotion (Markham 1909). But there was more to its popularity than the story. It was the first

English narrative of the Arctic to rival the adventure and excitement of Kane. McClintock gave the public what it wanted more than did his contemporaries.

At the same time that Kane and McClintock were entertaining the public, a new genre of expedition literature began to appear, written by a breed of explorer who was wealthy; had no connection with the government, the Church, or scientific/exploring societies; was under nobody's instructions; and was out simply to please himself by pursuing various forms of sport. Despite this lack of official sanction, these individuals could still make important contributions to exploration. The classic example was Sir Samuel White Baker, who became determined to engage in travel of a more ambitious nature than had previously been popular. Originally interested primarily in hunting, Baker had discovered in the jungles of Ceylon (Sri Lanka) that he was fascinated by unexplored and uncharted lands (Baker 1855). In 1861, accompanied by his wife Florence, Baker traveled down the Nile, hoping to reach its source. At Gondoroko, they met Speke and James Augustus Grant returning from Lake Victoria. Informed by Speke of the probable existence of another large lake to the west, the Bakers set off, on 4 March 1864 reaching the body of water that they named the Albert N'yanza. Baker's four-year journey earned him a knighthood, and his expedition account, published in 1866, not only made him a hero in Britain, it helped give him an international reputation that led to his appointment in 1872 as the governor-general of Equatoria in the Sudan.

The first account popularizing tourism of the Arctic was Lord Dufferin and Ava's *Letters from high latitudes*, which, written in 1856 in the form of 13 letters, told of his voyage in the yacht *Foam* to Iceland, Jan Mayen, and Spitsbergen in the same pleasant, intimate, privileged way as if he were simply on a jaunt to Brighton. Dufferin's writings stimulated other wealthy adventurers to go north: artists, hunters, casual tourists, and reporters. One of the best known was James Lamont, who, sensing that even on a private journey he needed to pay his respects to science, dedicated his first book to geologist Charles Lyell with the note, "I shall esteem myself fortunate if any of the observations contained in it shall be the means of rivetting or strengthening a link in the beautiful chain of evidence by which you have . . . demonstrated the perfect adequacy of present causes to remodel the surface of the earth" (Lamont 1861: v).

Lamont was, like Baker and Speke had initially been, foremost a hunter, and he wrote in great detail about his slaughter in the vicinity of Svalbard and Novaya Zemlya of virtually every animal he could kill with gun or harpoon. He concluded his first book with a list of more than 200 animals bagged, including walruses, seals, polar bears, reindeer, and a whale. Lamont's writings were enormously popular, even though they seem by today's standards to show a lack of concern with life, animal or human. At one point, Lamont bemoaned that the mate of *Ginevra* had fallen from the crow's-nest and broken the last telescope. That the fall had killed the mate was acknowledged virtually as an afterthought (Lamont 1861: 25–6).

Lamont's popularity is not surprising considering that the culture of Victorian times considered big-game hunting a manly sport. That huge animals might not be difficult to kill was of little importance to many Victorians because the image of the "great white hunter" was as important as the hunt itself. Similarly, the image presented of exploration was more important than what actually occurred, because, as Vilhjalmur Stefansson commented (1943: 278): "Doubtless the average man turns to polar narratives, when he turns to them at all, with the desire and expectation of reading about suffering, heroic perseverance against formidable odds, and tragedy either actual or narrowly averted. Perhaps then, it is partly the law of supply and demand that accounts for the general tenor of arctic books."

The birth of the English penny press

The birth of the popular press in Britain coincided with technological developments in news-gathering, printing, and distribution. In fact, one of the reasons for the repeal of the paper duty was the development of esparto, a North African grass, as a replacement for rags in the production of newsprint (Plant 1939: 334–40). By the 1860s newsprint could be made from wood pulp, which reduced the price so much that popular papers were able to make considerably higher profits (Ellis 1960: Appendix, 10–17).

In the mid-1850s, technological changes, combined with the elimination of the taxes on knowledge, caused a proliferation of English newspapers representing virtually every class and political orientation. The three most popular of these were penny dailies: *The Daily Telegraph*, founded (as *Daily Telegraph & Courier*) in 1855; *The Manchester Guardian*, changed from a bi-weekly the same year; and *The Standard*, changed from an evening to a morning paper in 1857. Within five years *The Daily Telegraph* had surpassed *The Times*, which still cost 4*d*., as the largest daily in Britain. By 1870 *The Daily Telegraph* and *The Standard* had attained the two largest circulations in the world, and *The Daily News*, which dropped to a penny in 1869, had also surpassed the circulation of *The Times*.

Although the penny dailies diverged from *The Times* in many areas, their initial similarities encouraged the historian H.R. Fox Bourne to indicate that the 1860s was the period of the "highest level of real value" of English newspapers. He noted that not only could well-printed reasonably priced newspapers supplying up-to-date information from all over the world be easily distributed, but that the competition was keen enough to encourage rival papers to "use all their wits in seeking and winning public favour, but not yet so keen as to drive them to often unworthy ways of attracting and amusing readers" (Fox Bourne 1887: II, 284).

The aspects of the press of which Fox Bourne approved did not remain long. It has been commonplace to accept that English newspaper proprietors before 1880 believed the duty of the press was to uphold the classic liberal vision. However, it has more recently been suggested that many proprietors were in the newspaper business simply to make profits (Lee 1976: 49).

It was the English daily press' following of the pattern of commercialism and sensationalism set by the Sunday and the American press that led the change from newspapers "being the organ of democracy . . . [to] the sounding-board for whatever ideas commend themselves to the great material interests" (Hobhouse 1910: 365). Or, as G.M. Trevelyan stated more vitriolically (1901: 1047): "The Philistines have captured the Ark of Covenant [the printing press] and have learnt to work their own miracles through its power. 'The pen,' as our grandfathers optimistically observed, 'is mightier than the sword.' Mightier indeed, but, as we now have learnt, no whit more likely to be in good hands."

The press and exploration in a decade of change

Although the basis had been established for its sensationalization, the English daily press did not immediately accede. There are few indications of sensational writing in the 1860s, and even fewer about exploration, which, in general, received considerably less attention than had the Franklin searches. This was principally a result of the Crimean War and the Indian Mutiny, events that dominated newspaper coverage for much of the decade. A lack of attention to individual heroic efforts was mentioned by Isabel Burton in the preface of the memorial edition to her husband's *First footsteps in East Africa*: "This was one of his most splendid and dangerous expeditions, and the least known, partly because his pilgrimage to Meccah was in every man's mouth, and partly because the excitement aroused by the Crimean War had to a large extent deadened the interest in all personal adventure" (Burton 1894: xii).

The great exceptions to this lack of press exposure were McClintock's search for Franklin, Burton and Speke's discoveries of Lake Tanganyika and Lake Victoria, and the journeys of the Scottish missionary David Livingstone. Livingstone first attracted the attention of the RGS in 1849 when, with William Cotton Oswell, he discovered Lake Ngami, after making the first crossing of the Kalahari Desert by Europeans. In rapid-fire succession, he made a series of breathtaking discoveries that, through the auspices of Murchison, both gained the RGS immense prestige and made Livingstone a living legend. In 1851 he reached the headwaters of the Zambezi River, in 1854 he discovered Victoria Falls, and between 1853 and 1856 he made an epic crossing of Africa from Luanda to Quelimane (Livingstone 1857). With the intriguing of Murchison and the support of a compliant press, Livingstone attained as great a mythical status as any nineteenth-century explorer; his book *Missionary travels and researches in South Africa* sold more than 70,000 copies in the first few months after it was published in 1857, making it one of the best-selling exploration accounts of all time (Brantlinger 1985). But Livingstone was even more. He seemed greater than the sum of his parts: more than a medical doctor, missionary, geographer, scientist, and heroic explorer. His elevated moral position allowed him (and his myth) to be used effectively as a spokesman for the abolition of slavery, the "civilizing" of Africa, and expansionist commercialism, including white emigration to Africa (MacKenzie 1992:

121–25). Even Livingstone's disastrous expedition of 1858–64 was generally viewed as a success by the British press, which focused not on the difficulties and deaths, but on the discovery of Lake Nyasa (Lake Malawi).

By contrast, the American newspapers were little interested in Livingstone. Even *The New York Herald* did not give extensive coverage to his exploits before the end of the American Civil War. The press of the United States was still, to a great extent, very inward looking, and the expedition that most excited it was that led by Kane.

When Kane's expedition returned in August 1855, every New York newspaper, even the *Tribune*, gave extensive coverage to what had been essentially a disaster. The *New-York Daily Times* gave over its entire first page to Kane's self-serving claims (12 August 1855), and *The Sun* printed stories about the expedition for five successive days (12–16 August 1855). Concurrently, the *Chicago Daily Tribune* proclaimed Kane one of the greatest explorers since Columbus (21 August 1855), and a new weekly, *Frank Leslie's Illustrated Newspaper*, made the expedition the cover subject of its first issue (15 December 1855).

After Kane's death, no explorer so fired the American press until Robert E. Peary, although Hall, among others, did receive extensive coverage. On 24 August 1862 the announcement in *The New York Herald* of Hall's imminent return from the Arctic was accompanied by a banner headline and a map larger than was given to the Civil War battles of Antietam or Shiloh, both fought that year. Bennett also showed his belief in the public's interest in distant places and demonstrated his intention to cultivate it by commenting in the same story about Hall: "Fondness for adventure will lead men, so long as the world lasts, to seek new sources of excitement, and Arctic explorers will never be found wanting; consequently we had better be familiar with the localities they have a fondness for, that we may be able to follow their movements without the necessity of constant reference to a cumbersome atlas."

Several weeks later, *The Herald* devoted almost four columns and 11 decks to Hall's return. The space was extraordinary considering that the main feature was the battle of Antietam; in fact, Hall's expedition was given more column inches in *The Herald* than any feature of the autumn that was not directly related to the Civil War. Despite its length, the story about Hall was not written in a sensational style. In fact, there were no truly sensational stories of exploration in the major American press throughout the rest of the 1860s. And there are strong indications that following the Civil War sensationalism as a whole had been tempered.

There are two reasons commonly espoused for this decrease in sensationalism. First, the coverage of the Civil War was so sensational and graphic (not because of the techniques of presentation but due to the subject matter and thoroughness with which it was covered) that Americans became horrified by the use of sensationalism. Second, the theory of the normal course of newspaper improvement suggests that sensationalism initially attracted readers and advertisers, generating a revenue that in turn financed advances in news-gathering, transmission, reporting, and technology. With these improvements, sensational papers began to attract wider audiences that demanded better products and thus the sensational newspapers began to compete both with each other and with the more conservative penny press such as *The New-York Times*. By the 1860s, the best of the sensational papers had eliminated much of their invective and salaciousness. They had become among the most informative, best-written, and most influential papers in the world.

Despite the decrease in sensationalism in the daily press, it was still popular in the weekly market. In 1855 Frank Leslie, who had been an engraver for *The Illustrated London News*, started the first successful illustrated news weekly in America, *Frank Leslie's Illustrated Newspaper*. Like its model, Leslie's 16-page, 10¢ cross between a magazine and news-paper carried only semi-fresh information, but demonstrated the demand for news pictures. The key to its success, as opposed to its American predecessors, was the number and size of its illustrations and its emphasis on sensational current events rather than on literature. Two years later, the Harper's Publishing Company, which since 1850 had published *Harper's Monthly*, America's outstanding literary magazine, began to produce *Harper's Weekly*, a rival to Leslie's newspaper. In 1858 Leslie dropped the price of the *Illustrated Newspaper* to 6¢, and its circulation rocketed to 140,000.

Thus, at the end of the Civil War, the English and American press had a very important similarity: in both cases, the weekly papers were more sensational than the dailies. But sensationalism was about to take an entirely new turn in the Anglo-American press, a turn that could trace its twisted roots to an obscure German missionary who, in 1848, made the remarkable claim to have seen snow on mountains located near the equa-tor in the highlands of East Africa. With this vision, he opened the way for a new investigation of the sources of the Nile and the solving of the mysteries surrounding the Mountains of the Moon.

4

Dark sensations

The initial report of Johann Rebmann of the Church Missionary Society, that on 11 May 1848 he had glimpsed snow on the summit of an East African mountain called Kilimanjaro, was met with great skepticism in Europe. However, the next year another missionary, Johann Ludwig Krapf, also journeyed inland from Mombasa and reported a second snow-capped peak, Mount Kenya. A third missionary, James Erhardt, produced a map of the interior of East Africa; based on information from Arab slave and ivory traders, it showed a vast inland lake that he called the Sea of Uniamesi, but that came to be called, because of its shape, "the monster slug."

These and other reports helped lead the Royal Geographical Society to sponsor a systematic exploration of East Africa, with particular interest in this inland sea. In 1856 the RGS and the East India Company selected for this task a 35-year-old romantic, polymath, and officer of the Indian Army who was already a renowned traveler, Richard Francis Burton. An extraordinary linguist and Arabist, Burton had become a popular hero in 1853 when, in the disguise of a Moslem pilgrim, he had journeyed to Mecca and Medina, cities closed to non-Moslems. The next year he made a trek through Somaliland to the forbidden city of Harar. Perhaps the most erudite of all Africanists, Burton not only made detailed observations about botany, geology, geography, meteorology, and the anthropology and linguistics of local tribes, he recorded them with as much acumen, humor, and élan as any explorer of the nineteenth century.

When Burton left Zanzibar for the interior of Africa in June 1857, he was accompanied by a fellow Indian Army officer, John Hanning Speke, who had been a member of the Somaliland expedition, although he had not accompanied Burton to Harar and had, in fact, accomplished remarkably little on his own survey. On 13 February 1858 Burton and Speke became the first Europeans to reach Lake Tanganyika, although they were unable to determine with any certainty whether a river at its northern end flowed into or out of the lake, and therefore whether it had any relation to the Nile. While returning to the coast, Speke made a side-trip to the north to investigate rumors of a larger lake, and on 3 August 1858, at Mwanza, he beheld the southern reaches of the largest lake in Africa, which he named in honor of Queen Victoria. He did not question for a moment the importance of his discovery: "I no longer felt any doubt that the lake at my feet gave birth to that interesting river, the source of which has been the subject of so much speculation and the object of so many explorers" (Speke 1864: 307).

Almost from the moment Speke rejoined Burton, the two disagreed about Lake Victoria. While Speke confidently asserted that it was the source of the Nile, Burton dismissed his claims as unsubstantiated. It was much better, according to Burton, to report only what they knew rather than what they theorized. He, in fact, believed that Lake Victoria could well be a series of smaller lakes, and that it was more likely the sources of the Nile were located either in the Lake Tanganyika region or near Mount Kilimanjaro and Mount Kenya.

This debate exploded onto the British scene when Speke arrived back in England two weeks before Burton in May 1859. The young explorer immediately went to Murchison, who quickly saw that Speke's opinions were widely publicized and that the RGS received a full share of the glory (Maitland 1971: 99). By the time Burton reached England, Speke was being lionized by much of the English scientific and political establishment, which preferred this abstemious, conservative, prosaic model of Victorian values to Burton, the eccentric, unorthodox, Anglo-Irish rebel. Burton's objections to the claims about Lake Victoria were set aside by the hero-hungry press and public, as well as by Murchison, who saw in these discoveries the corroboration of his structural theory (Stafford 1989: 169).

With the backing of Murchison, Speke was sent back to Africa in the company of James Grant, with the goal of proving that Lake Victoria was the source of the Nile. They returned to England in 1862 after reaching Ripon Falls, where the Nile flows out of Lake Victoria, and following the river north for much of its course to the Mediterranean. According to Speke, the age-old mysteries were solved. The RGS agreed, awarding both Speke and Grant medals in honor of their journey. But Burton, with the aid of the popular press, had not had his last say.

The press begins to change

When one scans the most popular English and American daily newspapers in the years immediately following the American Civil War, it becomes apparent that they had important traits in common. The most obvious was the unrelieved grayness of the pages, with small type and little consideration for a lively format. In the US, headlines were smaller than during the Civil War, and there were far fewer illustrations. In England, crossheads to break up columns were not yet respectable, nor had paragraphing been introduced. Although *The Daily Telegraph* had for a brief while broken with typographical orthodoxy – using up to five decks during the Crimean War – it had soon returned to the accepted style.

Another similarity between the press of the two countries was its conservative nature. In England, newspapers were published with the assumption that the typical reader was male, privately educated, property-owning, and the possessor of enough income to support servants. It was also assumed that he was interested primarily in political news, and that he was prepared to set aside at least two hours per day to read a paper from beginning to end if it were closely argued, elegantly phrased, and liberally sprinkled with Oxbridge jokes. Further, it was understood that he deplored illustrations or typographical devices to aid reading and enjoyed the most abstruse classical allusions or Latin phrases (Boston 1976: 16–17). The result of these assumptions was that the major newspapers – even those of the penny press – were written for the upper or middle classes.

The conservative nature of the major dailies in the United States was also brought about by an attempt to appeal to a middle-class audience. In fact, the very success of the great New York papers in improving both their quality and the class of their readership seemed to have bred timidity and dullness into them:

> No more conspicuous evidence of the fact exists than the *New York Herald*, with which the elder Bennett started to fight the whole world. On that principle he made his fortune. But when it was made he toned down to conservatism. For many years the *Herald* has ceased to be outspoken on any subject. . . . Here is Mr. Dana, in the sere and yellow leaf of manhood, with a son whom he wants to see well started in life before he himself passes away. And so he becomes conservative, easy and inoffensive in spite of his natural tendencies. . . . The sharp, personal, incisive and sometimes abusive *Sun* . . . exists no longer. . . . Whitelaw Reid has society aspirations which clog the wheels of his presses so that they turn out not a virile, strong, decided sheet as the paper used to be under Horace Greeley, but a molasses and water style of journalism that reads like the compositions written by pupils from an academy of young ladies. (*The Journalist* 17 May 1884)

However, many features of the press – both in the US and Britain – were about to change. One reason was the technological developments in the newspaper business. In 1863 William Bullock constructed the web-offset perfector press, which printed both sides of a continuous role of paper instead of requiring individually fed sheets. Modifications to the web-rotary meant that by the end of the century the machines could print, cut, insert sheets, and fold for shipment. By 1904 *Lloyd's Weekly News* was using seven Hoe double-octuplets, each producing 55,000 32-page papers an hour (Lee 1976: 56).

The mass communication of news was also facilitated by the improvement of time-saving machines: the first viable typewriter was developed in 1873; the linotype and intertype were adopted in the 1880s; and the straight-line press was developed in 1889 (Berry 1958: 683–714). The speed of international news-gathering was vastly improved when a transatlantic cable was laid between Europe and the US; both *The New York Herald* and the *New-York Tribune* claimed to have sent the first message via the cable on 28 June 1866, the day it was completed (Seitz 1928: 203).

The new technologies affected more than just the speed with which reports were received. It has been argued that the wire services caused the standardization of news, which, in turn, gave the news function of the press pre-eminence over the editorial function (Carey 1983). The need for clarity and simplicity also shaped a new telegraphic style of journalism. Because economy of expression saved money, sentences were compressed into phrases and single words were created to do the work of several. The telegraph also encouraged the use of unambiguous words and the simplest syntax: reports were written with a minimum of punctuation, and adverbial phrases at the beginning of sentences were avoided because they might be attached to the preceding sentence. One essayist concluded, "The delicacy, intricacy, nuance of language is endangered by the wires" (quoted in Kern 1983: 115).

Changes were also forthcoming in the US because a new generation of journalists entered the business. Within a five-year span, the leadership of all the major New York newspapers changed. On 22 April 1867 a new era at *The Herald* was introduced when James Gordon Bennett Jr became the paper's manager. In January 1868 *The Sun* was purchased by the financial backers of Charles A. Dana, who became the new editor. On 18 June 1869 Henry Raymond died at the age of 49, following which George Jones assumed control of *The New-York Times*. On 1 June 1872 James Gordon Bennett Sr died; on 29 November of the same year, Horace Greeley died, and the *New-York Tribune* was taken over by one of its senior editors, Whitelaw Reid.

Each change was significant. Reid, who had earned fame as a war correspondent for the *Cincinnati Gazette*, gave new vigor to the austere *Tribune*, the popularity of which had declined after the Civil War. As a result it came to appeal to scholarly, conservative, middle- and upper-class readers. Meanwhile, Jones and *The New-York Times* were among the first to show how powerful a role newspapers could play on behalf of the public. In 1871 *The Times* exposed the corrupt dealings of New York mayor William Marcy Tweed. Faced with efforts by Tweed to take over *The Times*, threats of physical violence, and bribes of $5 million, Jones persevered and revealed Tweed and dozens of his cronies to have defrauded New York of more than $200 million (Myers 1901: 252–98; Davis 1921: 81–116). Although *The Times* did not gain much circulation as a result of these revelations, it re-established itself as a champion of quality journalism, offering sober, solid reporting.

The top two New York newspapers in terms of circulation remained *The Herald* and *The Sun*. Immediately after the end of the Civil War, the circulation of *The Sun* plummeted, reaching a low of 43,000 at the beginning of 1868. But Dana turned its fortunes around, and the circulation had increased to 103,000 by 1870, and 132,000 by 1875.

There were a number of reasons for Dana's success. Despite being only four pages, *The Sun* attempted to include "all the news, foreign, domestic, political, social, literary, scientific, and commercial" (*The Sun* 27 January

1868). With this broad objective, Dana by necessity had to make his paper a model of brevity and clarity. But *The Sun* was more than comprehensive; it was breezy, witty, and filled with human interest. Dana's commentary could be vindictive, acerbic, and cynical, but he also added polished writing and editing to his paper, and helped encourage sensationalism by seeking new ways to integrate emotional appeal with his stories (Stone 1938; Fenton 1941). Dana also had the ability to recognize journalistic talent. *The Sun* was long regarded as the first "school of journalism," and Dana hired a remarkable number of promising writers and editors, including Arthur Brisbane, Richard Harding Davis, Will Irwin, Julian Ralph, Jacob Riis, Carr Van Anda, and Joseph Pulitzer.

James Gordon Bennett Jr had a similar eye for journalistic talent. *The Herald* employed Mark Twain, Walt Whitman, Charles Nordhoff, Charles Edward Russell, and perhaps the greatest staff of foreign correspondents ever assembled (Coleman 1924–25). Bennett Jr also displayed an unusual combination of hard work and originality. After only a few months as manager of *The Herald* (and two years after first joining its staff), he started an afternoon edition, *The Evening Telegram*. He filled his new product – which sold for a penny and was printed on pink paper – with coarse, sensational stories rejected by *The Herald*. At the same time, he initiated *The Herald*'s gradual return to his father's early journalistic characteristics. He gave it appeal to a mass audience by aggressive marketing; better make-up; use of larger, bolder, and more attention-grabbing headlines; innovative use of illustrations; and making the primary function not just presenting the news, but doing it in an exciting manner.

The Herald maintained the largest circulation in America for most of the two decades after the younger Bennett's accession. However, after Dana took over *The Sun* the two newspapers fought a lively circulation war. One method that both used to get ahead was to publish the most gripping stories they could find, spurring Reid to comment: "There is not an editor in New York who does not know the fortune that awaits the man who is willing to make a daily as disreputable and vile as a hundred and fifty thousand readers would be willing to buy" (quoted in Dicken-Garcia 1983: 299). To Bennett, this strategy meant the frequent publication of features about a subject that truly fascinated him – exploration.

During this period, *The Herald* and *The Sun* were, more than any other newspapers, the basis of American opinion and thought (Seitz 1928; Fenton 1941). Not only did they have the largest circulations, but what they printed and advocated was reprinted and discussed in other newspapers across the country, in weekly and monthly magazines, and in pulpits and other public platforms. Thus, as *The Herald* carried more and more stories about exploration, the interest it generated in new lands carried far beyond New York City.

Early English press sensations

Changes were also occurring in the English press, although not as rapidly as in the United States. The morning dailies printed news and headlines in a uniform fashion, and even when extraordinary news did make its way into print, it was merged with the rest of the text so that it seemed quite restrained compared to the American papers.

Certainly the British press did not follow the American lead in headlines. *The Daily Telegraph* initially broke from the British conventions of headline writing but, as its circulation increased, it followed the other London dailies, lapsing into the passive announcement, rather than the dramatization, of news. With rare exception – such as when *The Telegraph* used 10 decks with its first report of the Battle of Sedan in the Franco-Prussian War (6 September 1870) – few advances were made in news-display until the late 1880s (Morison 1932: 269).

The lack of sensation in English headlines is well demonstrated by the coverage of one of the most publicized stories of the early 1860s, the "Vidil affair," in which the French Baron de Vidil attempted to murder his step-son in London. On 13 July 1861 *The Daily Telegraph* and *The Morning Chronicle* each ran the same headline: EXTRAORDINARY ATTEMPT AT MURDER BY A FOREIGN NOBLEMAN. *The Times* was even less evocative: THE CHARGE AGAINST BARON DE VIDIL.

The actual stories were a different matter. The dailies had learned enough from their Sunday counterparts to mean they would not omit any sensational material that became available. For although they constantly claimed to deplore American sensationalism, what actually distinguished the English sensations from their American counterparts was not that they were opposed to unrestrained and graphic accounts of daily occurrences such as murder, mayhem, or lust (which even *The Times* exploited), but that they did not approve of the manner in which American papers actively hunted for such sensations. It was the investigative reporting of sensational stories that disturbed the English press establishment more than what was actually written.

The English acceptance of sensationalism was demonstrated by the news selection of *The Daily Telegraph*, which was aware that even its "respectable" audience was fascinated by the continuing saga of "the Northumberland Street affair," a love triangle that had exploded in attempted murder. The Telegraph's report about the death of one of the men involved stated:

> . . . a mutilated creature, whose head was a mass of blood-stained pulp, one of whose eyes was a mere lump of purulent jelly, who, living and gasping in what seemed the death agony, lay yesterday before us in the hospital ward, with his weeping wife by his side and a police officer at the bed's foot . . . ere these lines were committed to print . . . rendered up his soul to the Almighty. (19 July 1861)

The case kept the London press occupied much of July 1861 and produced such stirring writing that *The Daily News* commented, "All these incidents read marvellously like a column of graphic description from an American newspaper" (29 July 1861). In fact, the papers became so vividly written that they provoked the comment, "there began in England in the 1860s a sensation mania" (Altick 1987: 3–4).

One of the greatest sensations of the time was the expedition by Speke and Grant. For two years Murchison and his allies did their best to gain publicity for it with a continual flow of letters to *The Times*, and when the explorers returned in June 1863 they were met with a remarkable press fanfare. But in his own series of letters and articles, Burton clearly demonstrated that Speke had again jumped to conclusions. Burton showed that Speke had neither proven that the water he had seen at Mwanza was connected to that at Ripon Falls, nor indeed, since he had marched overland much of the way to Egypt, that the river emerging from those falls was actually the same as that which he had only occasionally seen on his journey north. Concurrently, in a series of reviews in *The Morning Advertiser*, James McQueen, a respected geographer and journalist, viciously attacked Speke's character and geographical scholarship. Some of what McQueen wrote was decidedly libellous, but there was enough logic in his and Burton's arguments to convince much of the scientific community that Speke had not fully resolved the mysteries of the Nile.

Eventually, a debate between Burton and Speke was scheduled to be held at a session of the British Association for the Advancement of Science meetings at Bath. But on the day before the explorers were to confront each other, Speke was killed by his own gun in a hunting accident. Despite the Burton-Speke confrontation's sensational aspects, sensations other than crime and immorality did not necessarily make for sensational articles:

It was understood that in this section a discussion would take place between Captain Burton and Captain Speke on that interesting subject, the sources of the Nile, and there was a great rush, therefore, to this section at an early hour. The shocking death of Captain Speke, however, became known to many; and although, probably, this sad intelligence did not diminish the attendance in Section E, it need scarcely be added that it cast a gloom over the whole assembly. (*The Times* 17 September 1864)

This general air of complacency was standard for the British press of the 1860s and 1870s. Although to today's reader, most of the writing in British newspapers of the time might seem rambling, tedious, mandarin, even oblique, there was then no recognition of the news function as the primary purpose of a newspaper, and many people considered simple reporting to be vulgar. Thus, a leader about Speke in *The Times* became not a factual obituary or even a personal eulogy, but a glorification of the role of the explorer-hero in Britain's imperial mission:

We cannot but feel an interest in the fortunes of the class of men among whom SPEKE was so eminent. They have been in all ages the pioneers who have gone before our merchants, our missionaries, and our colonists, and have pointed out to us new regions where we may make homes for the overflow of our populations, new provinces for our great Empire, new countries adapted to the conditions required for the spread of our language, our institutions, and our spirit of Anglo-Saxon freedom. There are undoubtedly greater names than the discoverer of the Nile among the adventurers who have gone out from among us, and have brought back to us the gift of new worlds for peaceful conquest. . . . We would not wish to exaggerate the merit even of having solved the great geographical problem of the source of the Nile, and we will not claim for SPEKE a precedence over the genius of STUART or BURKE or WILLS; but it was a brilliant exploit, and we were still proud of the bold adventurer. (19 September 1864)

The public and the press now demanded a resolution of the Burton-Speke controversy, and the man selected to bring back definitive proof of the course of the Nile was the same man who had already been built into a national hero by the efforts of Murchison and the press: David Livingstone. When Livingstone returned to Africa in 1865, the public was promised a thrilling conclusion to this tale of discovery.

Bennett creates the news

If thrills were what the public wanted, the man who could – and would – produce them was James Gordon Bennett Jr, who first took full advantage of the mating between the press and explorers. This was the final step in a process that began when explorers realized there were advantages to writing thrilling narratives rather than scientific papers or books taken directly from expedition journals. Explorers not only could obtain fame and wealth directly from the newspapers, the exposure gained could increase other sources of income, such as lecture audiences, book sales, and independent contributions. As Ernest Shackleton later explained to the Canadian anthropologist Vilhjalmur Stefansson, lectures sold books, books sold lectures, and newspapers sold both, "particularly when you come home from an expedition with a big hurrah" (quoted in Hunt 1986: 146). Conversely, the newspapers stood to benefit greatly from increased sales due to the reports from expeditions, especially if those accounts were exclusive.

This relationship between newspapers and explorers required more than ever that new lands be portrayed as tests for daring individuals who were willing to risk their lives to make gains for science, the flag, or mankind. The public now wanted heroes it could admire for perseverance in the face of difficulties and courage in the face of danger. A demand developed for triumph over obstacles, and the greater the difficulty, the more the danger, the longer and harder the journey, the better the public liked it.

One of the first polar explorers to seek the sponsorship of the popular press was Charles Francis Hall, who, before he entered the Arctic arena, had himself started two newspapers. Before his first expedition, Hall met with Horace Greeley and received assurances that he would be paid for stories sent home (Loomis 1972: 61). From this beginning, the connection grew so that, by the 1880s, most explorers attempted to establish links with major newspapers.

Although a variety of British and American newspapers paid returning explorers for their stories, no newspaper gave more coverage to exploration than *The New York Herald*, and no newspaperman was more interested in exploration than Bennett Jr. Shortly after assuming day-to-day control, he demonstrated what his unique contribution to the newspaper business was going to be: whereas his father had shown the world how to obtain the news, Bennett Jr proved to be a genius at creating it. He had carefully taken note of the benefits when his father had sent correspondents around the US to cover the Civil War. He believed that the descriptions of the areas from which the stories emanated were as important to the readers as anything that might be happening there; he therefore began to send reporters to cover not only events in strange places but the places themselves. Bennett also quickly realized the value of exclusive news, so it was a logical progression for him to send correspondents as members of expeditions and then to organize and send the expeditions himself. In that way, he could first create the popular desire for information, and then satisfy it with exclusive reports.

Bennett's interest in foreign places and events was not totally based on his assessment of the American public; it was also the product of his mother having taken him to France at a young age in order to avoid the open hostility directed towards his father during the "moral war" against *The Herald* (O'Connor 1962). Within a decade of taking over *The Herald*, Bennett returned to Paris, from where he ran his paper *in absentia*. His love of France and things French helps explain his founding of a Paris edition of *The Herald*, his lifelong dislike of the British, and his devotion to foreign news, which *The Herald* covered better than any other paper in the United States (Riffenburgh 1991).

Bennett made his first great attempt to create news in 1869 when he assigned one of his roving reporters, Henry Morton Stanley, to locate Livingstone in central Africa. Stanley was perfect for Bennett: a man who always wanted to be where the action was – preferably in areas little known to the New York audience. He came to Bennett's notice two years earlier, when, as a writer for *The Missouri Democrat* of St. Louis and a stringer for three New York papers (*The Herald*, *The Times*, and the *Tribune*), he had "the very large commission to inform the public regarding all matters of general interest affecting the Indians and the great Western plains" (Stanley 1895: I, v).

In December 1867 Stanley presented himself to Bennett in New York and proposed accompanying the British punitive expedition against Emperor Theodore of Abyssinia, who had taken a number of British subjects hostage in his mountain fortress of Magdala. Bennett refused to send Stanley at *The Herald*'s expense, but agreed to pay him a high rate for exclusive reports (Stanley 1909: 228). Stanley immediately sailed to Suez, where he bribed the telegraph operator to ensure that his copy would be forwarded to Bennett's offices in London before rival accounts would be sent to the London papers. He then sped to the Horn of Africa, where the British commander, General Sir Robert Napier, was assembling his forces. On 10 April 1868 Napier's troops scored a spectacular victory, Magdala was taken and burned, and Theodore committed suicide. Stanley traveled much of the way back to Suez alone in order to beat the other journalists, and on 6 June he sent his story (Stanley 1874).

It was a complete triumph not only for Stanley but for *The Herald*. Shortly after his story was relayed, the cable between Alexandria and Malta broke and was out of action for six days. Stanley's story was not only the first detailed news of the action at Magdala, it was the only source for a week. The other papers howled in indignation, and actually went so far as to accuse *The Herald* of fabricating the results of the expedition – all of which made *The Herald*'s triumph so much the greater when the other accounts did finally arrive. Bennett was so pleased that he put Stanley on *The Herald*'s regular payroll.

It was shortly after this that Bennett decided to have Stanley interview Livingstone. For a year or so after his departure from Zanzibar, Livingstone's letters to Murchison had been published in the London papers, but then a silence descended over central Africa and the explorer's whereabouts became a mystery. In October 1868 Stanley left for North Africa, where rumors said Livingstone would soon appear. By February it had become apparent that Stanley could wait forever, and he returned to London, from where he was sent to cover other stories. Bennett was not put off the search, however. Throughout 1869 he followed the frequent and agonized correspondence of *The Times* on the whereabouts of the "lost Dr. Livingstone." At this stage, Bennett actually wanted to give the assignment to another reporter, Rudolph Keim, but he could not contact him immediately in the United States and was too impatient to wait for him to cross the Atlantic (Hall 1974: 381). So on 27 October 1869 he met again with Stanley and handed out one of the most famous journalistic assignments of all time, ordering Stanley to make several stops in Asia and then to proceed to Zanzibar, where he would organize an expedition to the interior to find Livingstone (Stanley 1872: xvii–xviii).

In November 1871 at Ujiji on the shore of Lake Tanganyika, Stanley did find Livingstone, and his exclusive stories relayed back to *The Herald* made him an international hero, resulted in an increase in the paper's circulation (Tebbel 1976: 233), and convinced Bennett that he had indeed discovered the most effective way to create news and grab an audience. Bennett followed this success by sending out another expedition under Alvan S. Southworth to "find" Samuel Baker in the Sudan (*The New York Herald* 19, 30 January 1872, 26 March 1873; Southworth 1875). *The Herald* also started giving major coverage to other African expeditions.

However, despite the gains in both circulation and prestige that *The Herald* made out of Stanley's reports, Bennett was never partial to his star correspondent. Bennett was jealous that one of his employees, someone he had personally created by sending him on an errand for his newspaper, received the glory rather than *The Herald* or Bennett himself, even though Bennett had conceived the idea for the expedition and had then financed it. Bennett was particularly annoyed at Stanley's reception by Queen Victoria at Dunrobin Castle, which made Stanley the toast of Britain (Seitz 1928: 298–302; Driver 1991: 146). Bennett slowly took his revenge. After the

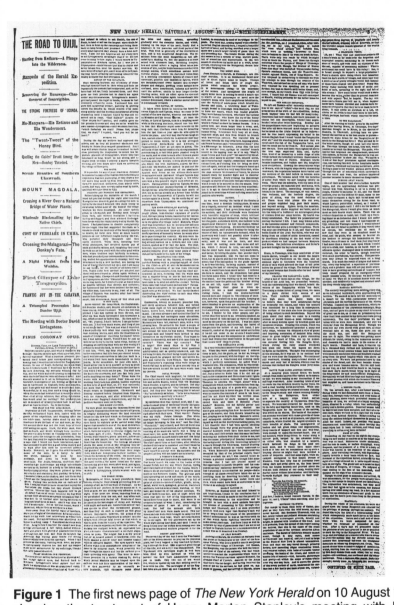

Figure 1 The first news page of *The New York Herald* on 10 August 1872, showing the treatment of Henry Morton Stanley's meeting with David Livingstone.

first of Stanley's lectures in New York in December 1872, *The Herald* pounced on its own man, claiming Stanley was "intolerably dull . . . his elocution is bad . . . [and] his anecdotes were spoiled in the telling." It went on to state that "Mr Stanley still betrays some of the vices . . . of the tyro. He speaks too fast in his eagerness not to bore his hearers, the consequence is that they sometimes fail to understand . . . what he has said . . . the subject matter was a trifle abstruse for his audience" (*The New York Herald* 4 December 1872). When *The Herald* admitted its own employee was a flop, there was little reason for anyone to attend, and the lecture series was quickly cancelled. Bennett continued to hold his grudge for years. In 1891 he sent one of his correspondents, Aubrey Stanhope, to Stanley's Swiss retreat to ask the explorer if his one-year-old marriage was on the rocks because he beat his wife (Stanhope 1914: 150–55).

Yet Stanley had hardly completed his trek to find Livingstone before he found that not only had he enemies other than Bennett, but that he had become a key pawn in an attack on *The Herald*.

The war against Stanley, Bennett, and *The Herald*

Upon Stanley's return from Africa at the end of July 1872, the English scientific and geographical communities were astonished and horrified that an American journalist, especially one from "that detestable newspaper" (*Saturday Review* 1872: 527) had upstaged the latest RGS expedition, led by Lieutenant L.S. Dawson, in locating Livingstone. A number of prominent officers of the RGS were not only critical, but openly antagonistic to Stanley. This hostility was based on three issues. The first mark against Stanley was his assumed nationality: although born in Denbigh, Wales, at this stage of his life Stanley was claiming to be an American. The second issue was his profession: as a reporter, Stanley not only lacked the credentials of a gentleman, he was certainly no scientist. Francis Galton, the chairman of the British Association meeting at which Stanley first lectured on his expedition, addressed this problem by commenting on Stanley's "sensational geography" (*The Standard* 17 August 1872). Yet what grated the English the most was Stanley's confident assertion that he was the personal representative of Livingstone. This drew howls of indignation from the establishment. Sir Henry Rawlinson, who had become President of the RGS on Murchison's death in 1871, clearly attempted to demean Stanley's achievement when he commented:

> There is one point on which a little *éclaircissement* is desirable, because a belief seems to prevail that Mr. Stanley had discovered and relieved Dr. Livingstone; whereas, without any disparagement to Mr. Stanley's energy, activity, and loyalty, if there has been any discovery and relief it is Dr. Livingstone who had discovered and relieved Mr. Stanley. Dr. Livingstone, indeed, is in clover while Mr. Stanley is near destitute. . . . It is only proper that the relative position of the parties be correctly stated. (*The Echo* 26 July 1872; *The Standard* 27 July 1872; *The Times* 27 July 1872)

The British scientific community quickly found an ally in the London press. But there was more to the English newspapers' involvement than just a dislike of Stanley. Just as the success of Bennett Sr had brought upon *The Herald* the "moral war" of the 1830s, the success of Bennett Jr in sponsoring and reporting exploration now caused considerable animosity from newspapers that were neither as innovative, nor as willing to spend large sums of money to create news.

The immediate response to Stanley's dispatches about Livingstone was the same as when he had reported about the Abyssinian campaign: disbelief of the accomplishment and an assessment that Stanley and Bennett were charlatans who invented stories. When the London papers had atacked Bennett and Stanley after the Abyssinian campaign, only to find that *The Herald* had simply out-performed them all, so great was Bennett's pleasure at the discomfort of his English rivals that he printed Stanley's dispatches without cuts. He then personally taunted the other papers with *The Herald*'s superiority: "Our readers will not fail to perceive the vast superiority in style of writing, minuteness of detail and graphic portrayal of events which *The Herald* correspondence possesses over the written accounts of the same matter in the London journals" (*The New York Herald* 26 June 1868).

Now the English press moved in for its revenge. *The Standard* declared that Stanley's claims would have to be proven by "African experts" and stated that it was obvious the letters purporting to be from Livingstone to Bennett had been forged. It questioned why Livingstone had not returned with Stanley, why the doctor had not communicated with anyone but *The New York Herald*, and how Livingstone could have such an extensive knowledge of American literature as the letters indicated (*The Standard* 3, 6, 8 August 1872). *The Echo* entered the fray when it commented that perhaps Livingstone's letters to *The Herald* had been written with the help of a spiritual medium (*The Echo* 4 August 1872). Such taunts were widespread, as almost every London paper took aim at Stanley.

But it was *The Herald* with which the English newspapers were actually at war, and they never missed a chance to attack it directly. *The Saturday Review* captured the essence of the English position when it commented, "The *New York Herald* has a world-wide reputation, but its reputation is not exactly for literal and prosaic accuracy of statement . . . daring romances are the staple of the *Herald's* news" (*Saturday Review* 1872: 527).

One of the few defenders Stanley or his proprietor had in England was *The Pall Mall Gazette*, which published Winwood Reade's withering critique of the vicious and inaccurate ways in which Stanley had been attacked (29 August 1872). Yet even this paper did not remain open-minded on the subject for long. By the time of Stanley's return from his next expedition, it was among the most vociferous in calling for his scalp (22, 30 January, 11 February 1878).

Even when the English papers were not directly antagonistic to Bennett or his star reporter, they were invariably supportive of attacks on them. Rawlinson delighted the London press with his cynical appraisal: "He [Stanley] had been sent out by our Transatlantic cousins, among whom the science of advertising has reached a far higher stage of development than in this benighted country" (Rawlinson 1872: 370).

Of course, the sniping was not unilateral. Stanley and *The Herald* were well able to take care of themselves. Stanley let the press know how he felt about one of his opponents when he mentioned him as, "Mr Francis Galton, F.R.S., F.R.G.S., and God knows how many more letters to his name." And he took his vengeance on another of his tormentors, Clements R. Markham, by releasing to *The Daily News* a copy of one of Markham's supercilious letters together with a running commentary mocking Markham's remarks (*The Daily News* 10 September 1872). He also attacked Rawlinson and the RGS, accusing the former of drawing maps of Africa to suit his own prejudices, and stating that most of the members of the latter,

> despite being in London, and never having been within two thousand miles of the spot, declare positively that Livingstone has not discovered the source of the Nile, whereas Livingstone who has devoted thirty-five years to Africa only says he thinks he has discovered it. I think if a man goes there and says "I have seen the source of the river", the man sitting in his easy chair or lying in bed cannot dispute this fact on any grounds of theory. (*The Times* 17 August 1872)

Bennett, sensing in the wake of the Alabama Claims dispute between the United States and Great Britain an anti-British sentiment almost as strong as his own, also took the offensive. Before Stanley's expedition had even been concluded, he claimed that his objective in sending Stanley was not a sensational story but the promotion of civilization, science, and humanity, and the enhancement of the prestige of the "fourth estate" (*The New York Herald* 23 December 1871). He argued that in sending Stanley he had shown more of an interest in Livingstone than had the British government (*The New York Herald* 13 February 1872), and he repeatedly attacked the RGS and English press, stressing their ingratitude, xenophobia, and curmudgeonly refusal to give Stanley his due (*The New York Herald* 4, 5, 10, 16, 18, 19, 23, 27 August 1872).

Thus it was that exploration provided one of the first forums for the competition between the American and English press. The two could easily attack each other through explorers while acting as if they were only discussing a third party. Yet the third party could perhaps see the entire situation more clearly than anyone. Stanley acknowledged in his journal that American editors might be bullies, but that their "English contemporary is in my mind more like an old shrew with his venom-laden pen and his effeminate malice . . . their propensity to nagging at a man marks the unmanliness to which their excess of laws have [*sic*] reduced them" (Stanley 1872–74: Journal 25 August 1872).

But it was not only the English that attacked *The Herald* and its correspondent. On 24 August 1872 Dana released his thunderbolt. Under the headline HENRY M. STANLEY, VILLAIN, FORGER AND PIRATE, *The Sun* printed a long letter from Lewis Noe, one of Stanley's former associates. Noe detailed several episodes from the 1860s when Stanley had broken the laws of various countries in which he had traveled, and gave numerous examples of his cruel and unscrupulous behavior. Four days later, *The Sun* was back on the offensive, with a story headlined IS THE ALLEGED DISCOVERY OF DR. LIVINGSTONE BY HENRY STANLEY ANYTHING BUT AN ENORMOUS FRAUD? The article vehemently declared: "No one can compare the LIVINGSTONE letters of the *Herald* with STANLEY'S letters to NOE without being impressed with the opinion that every word and every line of these are the work of the same hand, and that this hand is STANLEY'S own." *The Sun* further stated that Stanley's claims were the "most gigantic hoax ever attempted upon the credulity of mankind" (28 August 1872). The next day *The Sun* printed an interview with Noe, in which he enlarged on some of the details of his letter (*The Sun* 29 August 1872). During the following days, *The Sun* contained further editorials and articles challenging the character of Stanley and his reports about Livingstone.

The *Herald* quickly defended Stanley and itself, printing a response on 29 August. It then published an interview with Edward J. Morris, who had been the Minister to Turkey from 1861 to 1870, and from whom, according to Noe, Stanley had borrowed £150 that he never repaid. Morris, not wanting to risk attack by *The Herald*, concocted a story about a repayment (*The New York Herald* 7 September 1872). However, skilful questioning by a reporter for *The Sun* showed beyond doubt that Morris really had been swindled. The charges and denials continued for well over a month before dying out.

The growth of English sensationalism

The attacks on Bennett and Stanley were only one example of the English press adopting American methods. Another was the increase in sensational presentation in the evening papers. Most evening papers, such as *The Courier* and *The Globe*, traditionally had been produced in the same spirit and with the same contents and typographical style as those in the morning. But 1865 marked the founding of the first notable breakaway from this mid-Victorian journalism: *The Pall Mall Gazette*, edited by Frederick Greenwood. *The Pall Mall Gazette* was something different: its leaders contained paragraph breaks, it had witty causerie, and it had a distinct typographical look featuring only three columns per page. It also included stories and leaders that were shorter and of more diverse subject matter. Designed for when the reader presumably had more leisure for reflection, it was the first evening journal to take on the aspects of a daily review (Schults 1972: xv).

These features did not immediately impress potential readers, however, because within 11 months of its founding, *The Pall Mall Gazette* was on the verge of insolvency. What Greenwood did to set it on its feet was to publish a series of sensational exposés by his brother James, writing under the byline "The Amateur Casual." The first of these series, "A Night in a Workhouse," appeared in four installments, 12–15 January 1866, and exposed the conditions found by Greenwood and a friend when they stayed overnight in a Lambeth workhouse. Even then the story was not splashed across page one as it would have been two decades later, but was quietly placed on page nine. Nevertheless, it helped guarantee the paper's success; the circulation doubled in three days. Although the circulation was admittedly small (less than 2,000), it was still a remarkable journalistic success.

Greenwood would never have used the term sensational for the articles in *The Pall Mall Gazette*. Nevertheless, it was his combination of typographical innovations and investigative exposure that made his paper seem sensational to his contemporaries. Consciously looking for information to satisfy the appetite for sensation was a novel step for a newspaper in Britain. All in all, Greenwood combined the elements of sensationalism, social commitment, and business sense as none of his predecessors in Britain had done. Although it is common to credit W.T. Stead with the "Americanization" of British journalism, Greenwood was in essence the English precursor of the New Journalism.

The Pall Mall Gazette was not the only evening paper to break with morning traditions. December 1868 saw the founding of *The Echo*, which sold for the sensational price of one-half penny. Yet in its substance, *The Echo* was not sensational in the American style. Its success was based on providing evening reading matter for intelligent business folk unable to spend the time or money reading the morning press. For the next seven years, *The Echo* was the best-selling evening paper in London (Boston 1976: 19).

Yet, in part because of their greater size and in part because they concentrated more on hard news and less on commentary and review, the foremost English dailies in the presentation of foreign and travel writing remained the morning papers, particularly *The Daily Telegraph*, *The Standard*, and *The Daily News*. Although *The Daily News* was noted for generally having the best foreign coverage in the 1860s, each of the major papers made important contributions in the 1870s. On 22 October 1870 *The Times* published William Howard Russell's interview with Bismarck, the first formal interview in an English newspaper. The same year, *The Daily News* began a contract that called for a regular exchange of foreign dispatches with the *New-York Tribune*. In 1871–72, *The Standard*'s reporters Frederick Boyle and G.A. Henty topped the field in reporting the Ashanti War, and during the Russo-Turkish War of 1877–78, an arrangement was made for reports from J.A. McGahan and Archibald Forbes to go to both *The Daily News* and *The New York Herald* (Hohenberg 1964: 119–20).

But the greatest coup of the decade in the field of foreign reporting was made by *The Daily Telegraph* in 1874. Shortly after the state funeral of Livingstone, Edwin Arnold, the editor of *The Telegraph*, persuaded his proprietor, Edward Levy-Lawson, to put up £6,000 for an expedition that not only would resolve the questions about Lake Victoria and its relation to the sources of the Nile, but that would follow the mysterious Lualaba River to its mouth, thus determining whether it flowed into the Nile, the Congo, or the Niger. Arnold recruited Stanley as the leader and then invited Bennett to match his offer, making it an Anglo-American venture.

Bennett did not want to advance Stanley's career, but to refuse would have meant to lose the story, which probably would have been offered to *The Sun*. He therefore tersely agreed (Stanley 1909: 297–8). However, when Stanley visited Bennett in New York prior to departing for Africa, the proprietor snubbed him and turned him over to an editor who conveyed the deep unhappiness at *The Herald* about the "enforced" collaboration with *The Telegraph* (Stanley 1872–74: Journal 11 July 1874).

The crossing of Africa

Few expeditions were ever more successful in attaining their goals than Stanley's trans-Africa expedition. Not only was Stanley remarkably efficient, determined, and ruthless, but his generous funding gave him advantages none of his predecessors had. When Stanley left Zanzibar in November 1874, he took with him three white assistants, 356 native bearers and laborers, eight tons of stores, and a 40-foot boat, *Lady Alice*, that had been built in sections so that it could be carried across the savanna and through the jungles.

Stanley made for Mwanza and upon arriving there in March 1875 assembled *Lady Alice*. In the next two months, he and his crew sailed more than 1,000 miles and proved not only that Lake Victoria was a single body of water, but that it had only one major outlet: Ripon Falls. Speke had been vindicated. Next was Lake Tanganyika. In June 1876 Stanley launched *Lady Alice* from Ujiji, and within two months he had deflated Burton's theories by showing that there was no major river running to the north that could possibly be the source of the Nile.

Now Stanley and his party turned first west to the Lualaba and then north to areas completely unknown, regions of such dark and frightening legend that even the Arab slavers had never entered them. They followed the course of the Lualaba to where it joined the Congo, and then charted that river's great sweeping arch to the north and back south again, reaching Stanley Pool and the falls that had stopped both Cão and Tuckey. In August 1877, after 999 days, the expedition reached the Atlantic with only 114 of the 356 followers remaining.

Stanley had thus answered all the essential remaining questions about the major rivers and lakes of central Africa; the blank space on the map was blank no longer. Despite his success, however, Stanley again found himself criticized and condemned by large sections of both the press and the public. Part of the reason was that there was still great envy and dislike of *The New York Herald*, and even of *The Daily Telegraph*, since it had proven to be similarly innovative and successful. But, in addition, Stanley was now a target on his own merits; his very success engendered jealousy and antagonism, and his negativity about any who might be considered his equal only added fuel to the flame. An example was his contemptuous remarks in a letter to Edward Levy-Lawson about Verney Lovett Cameron, who, two years before Stanley, had himself completed a crossing of central Africa, having turned south down the Lualaba where Stanley had gone north:

> We have obtained a signal triumph over Cameron, the protégé of the RGS, whose attainments were said to be vastly superior to those of Burton, Speke, or Livingstone and Baker – if Markham was to be believed. At the Lukuga, he simply sounded the water at the end and then vanished from the scene, only taking the chief's word that the "River went to Rua." Possibly he would have been more careful had he expected a "damn penny a liner" for a successor in that locality. (quoted in Bennett 1970: 465)

Stanley's comments were a great injustice to Cameron, who had not only produced accurate maps of Lake Tanganyika, but had showed that its main outlet, the Lukuga, flowed west, making it part of the Lualaba drainage system. When he reached the Lualaba, Cameron had been prevented from going north by the great Arab slaver Tippu Tip, and had instead headed southwest to Benguela, which he reached in October 1875.

Stanley also antagonized the British geographical community by his continued attempts to appropriate Livingstone's reputation and to establish himself as his successor. The English mediator of the Livingstone myth, Horace Waller, had been very carefully selected by Livingstone's son, the RGS, and the publisher John Murray. An old friend of Livingstone's, Waller first edited the Scottish explorer's journals from his final expedition, and then devoted the remainder of his life to carefully creating the Livingstone myth that would popularize the British anti-slavery movement at the same time as justifying Britain's territorial and commerical expansion into Africa (Helly 1987).

But much more important to the English public was Stanley's remorseless acknowledgement that he had gone out of his way to attack the natives of the Bumbire tribe on Lake Victoria for having earlier opposed his passage. There was widespread outrage in England when it was learned that 42 tribesmen were slain and more than 100 wounded as Stanley's men fired on them with elephant rifles loaded with exploding bullets, ammunition that had been forbidden in "civilized warfare" (*The Daily Telegraph* 10 August 1876; *The New York Herald* 10 August 1876; Stanley 1878: II, 218–23). In February 1878, when Stanley was honored by the RGS, not only did several members resign over this issue, but the press went into a frenzy (Galton 1878; *Saturday Review* 1878). *The Pall Mall Gazette* and *The Standard* in particular published numerous critical articles, the former commenting, "Exploration under these conditions is, in fact, exploration plus buccaneering, and though the map may be improved and enlarged by the process, the cause of civilization is not a gainer thereby, but a loser" (11 February 1878). *The Standard* was even less charitable, remarking:

> It cannot be seriously contended that in judging an explorer's achievements in geographical discovery no account should be taken of his acts from a moral point of view. If a traveller were to secure a free passage through Central Asia by poisoning whole tribes of Turkomans by prussic acid, he would hardly expect a welcome in England. The line must be drawn somewhere. We allow explorers a large latitude; but there are some extravagances of zeal against which a protest ought to be made. (9 February 1878)

Map 2 Sub-Saharan Africa
Key to routes: ·—·— Burton and Speke (1857–8)
····· Stanley (1874–7)
– – – Cameron (1873–5)

Stanley attempted to justify his actions by calling upon the memory of Livingstone, but the English press would not, of course, accept it. At a dinner of the RGS, he defended himself with the statement, "What I have done at Bambireh and other places on the Victoria Nyanza and on the Kwango-Lualaba has been done to satisfy justice. Where I have failed to make peace Livingstone would have failed, and where I have made friendships with natives I made firmer and more lasting friendships than even Livingstone himself could have made" (quoted in Yule and Hyndman 1878: 38–9). But the English would have none of it, as *The Saturday Review* made clear: "He has no concern with justice, no right to administer it; he comes with no sanction, no authority, no jurisdiction – nothing but explosive bullets and a copy of the *Daily Telegraph*" (1878: 208).

Detesting the English press even more than he did Stanley, Bennett again came to his reporter's defense, taking every opportunity to abuse "the howling dervishes of civilization . . . safe in London." When Stanley reached the Atlantic, *The Herald* unleashed its full fury against those who had condemned the killing of the Bumbire tribesmen: "This will greatly depress the philanthropists of London . . . [whose] impractical view it is that a leader in such a position should permit his men to be slaughtered by the natives and should be slaughtered himself and let discovery go to the dogs, but should never pull a trigger against this species of human vermin that put its uncompromising savagery in the way of all progress and all increase of knowledge" (17 September 1877). As before, Bennett kept up a constant barrage at the English press and establishment, although it was more for his own interests than to come to the aid of Stanley.

As earlier in the decade, it was not only the English newspapers that attacked Stanley, although he was not nearly such a popular target as he had previously been in the US. Stanley's violent progress through Africa did not seem to disturb the New York press as it did its London counterparts, but both *The New-York Times* and *The Sun* jibed the explorer over his failed relationship with Alice Pike, whom he had expected to marry upon his return (*The New-York Times* 4 November 1877; *The Sun* 5 November 1877).

Despite the broad spectrum of attacks on Stanley, his second expedition marked more than a major opportunity for newspapers to fall upon either each other or their rivals' correspondents. It represented more even than the first major British press-sponsored expedition of exploration. Much more important than either was the style of the reports Stanley filed. By submitting to *The Daily Telegraph* the same kind of thrilling accounts he had become famous for at *The New York Herald*, Stanley had made sensational coverage of exploration an active part the English press.

5

James Gordon Bennett discovers the Arctic

When Bennett first sent Stanley to Africa, the owner of *The Herald* was in some ways going into an area as uncharted as the unexplored lands themselves. Exploration had received very little attention in the American press since the beginning of the Civil War, with the exception of the return of Charles Francis Hall in 1862. When Hall came back from his second expedition in 1869, it was to negligible interest, and even *The Herald* ran only a small note on page seven (27 September 1869). The most complete coverage of Hall's expedition was given by the *New-York Tribune* (27, 29, 30 September 1869). Meanwhile, the English press had become more interested in the exploration of Africa than in that of the far north, at least in part because much of the former was carried out under the aegis of the RGS, whereas most Arctic journeys were by central Europeans and Scandinavians, particularly Norwegians hunting for seal and walrus.

The first Scandinavian to become well known to the English and American publics for his Arctic work was Adolf Erik Nordenskiöld, who initially led a scientific expedition to Svalbard in 1864. By 1868, Nordenskiöld had recognized an important new development in Arctic exploration: to obtain funding it was becoming desirable to produce more than scientific results. Certainly, science validated expeditions in the public mind, but discovery or the potential for commercial gain brought the necessary financial backing. Nordenskiöld's 1864 expedition had been backed by the Swedish government and the Swedish Academy of Sciences, but four years later the government was losing interest in the study of the north and had begun to dry up as a source of funding (Nathorst *et al.* 1909).

Nordenskiöld's plans were saved by the contributions of a wealthy Göteborg businessman, Oscar Dickson. The goals of the 1868 expedition were to penetrate as far north as possible from Svalbard and to carry out scientific programs on the way. The expedition made Nordenskiöld an international celebrity not only because his ship *Sofia* reached a new farthest north (for a ship) of 81° 42' (*The Standard* 6 October 1868; *The Daily News* 6 October 1868), but also because his work appealed to a public fascinated by the newly defined branches of science. Thus *The Daily Telegraph*, in an article the next spring about James Lamont's impending hunting trip to the Barents Sea and Svalbard, recalled Nordenskiöld's scientific work: "It will be remembered that the Swedes made a great discovery last year. They ascertained that Spitzbergen was connected with Scandinavia by a submarine bank, with a maximum depth of 500 fathoms, whereas the sea to the west of that bank deepened to 2,600 fathoms" (3 April 1869).

Nordenskiöld made two more Arctic expeditions (1870 and 1872–73) emphasizing both geographical exploration and science, before adding a commercial element to his ventures (Leslie 1879). In 1875 and 1876, with the sponsorship of Dickson and Aleksandr Sibiryakov, a Russian merchant, he made expeditions to the Yenisey River to demonstrate the feasibility of a trading route between Sweden and Siberia via the Kara Sea (Kish 1973). Then in 1878–80, sponsored by Dickson, Sibiryakov, and King Oscar II of Sweden and Norway, he led an expedition that was the first to navigate the Northeast Passage. Although the voyage had an important commercial component, and certainly was a symbolic act of conquest, the enormous amount of scientific data collected indicated that Nordenskiöld's primary interest remained the collection of scientific data (Nordenskiöld 1881).

Despite the great success of Nordenskiöld's work over a long period, he did little before the completion of the Northeast Passage that made a major impact on the British and American publics. Nordenskiöld, Dickson, and Sibiryakov were not interested in planning or participating in heroic tales. Nordenskiöld and Dickson both wanted to understand the Arctic – how it was formed, what lived there, what secrets of science it could explain (Nathorst 1897), while Sibiryakov was dedicated to opening up trade with his native Siberia (Hesselman 1933: 447). Therefore, although Nordenskiöld published many articles detailing the scientific results of his work, he did not write an account for the general public until after the voyage of *Vega*. Even then, it was not a story of adventure, but "a description of the voyage itself, of the nature of the northern coast of Siberia, of the animal and plant life there in existence, and of the tribes with which we met during the voyage" (Nordenskiöld 1885: 267).

Nordenskiöld's *The voyage of the Vega* was widely acclaimed, and his prudent and patient management of the expedition was noted with admiration (*Century Illustrated Magazine* 1882: 304). However, the typically Scandinavian thoroughness and accuracy in planning that allowed the voyage to be completed so easily and successfully – as well as the book's seriousness of tone and ponderous attention to detail – meant that the account itself did not captivate the masses to the same degree as others that were presented in sensational fashion. In fact, the greatest interest in Nordenskiöld in America was generated by fanciful stories in *The New York Herald* expressing concern over his supposed disappearance during his voyage (6 February, 16 March 1879). *The Herald*'s presentation to the

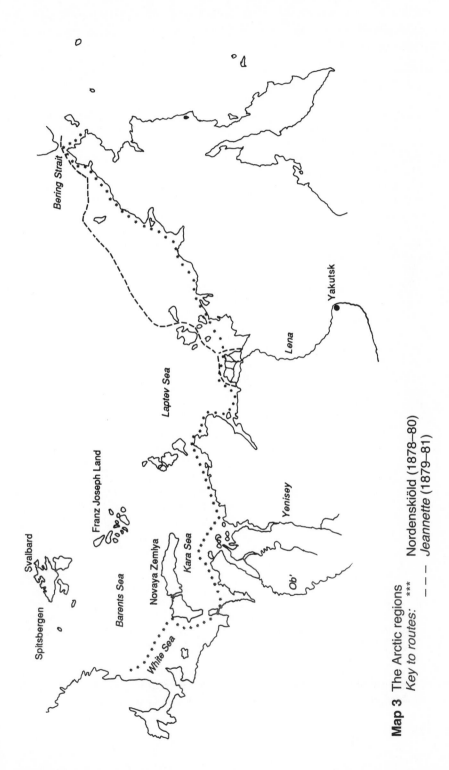

Map 3 The Arctic regions
Key to routes: ***   Nordenskiöld (1878–80)
  – – –   *Jeannette* (1879–81)

public of what was actually a scientific expedition had been reduced to the status of a thriller.

Bennett and the Arctic

Having discovered through his association with Stanley the financial rewards of creating news and presenting it in a sensational manner, Bennett surrounded himself with investigative reporters who could make exciting stories out of his wealth of ideas. One such reporter was Januarius Aloysius MacGahan, who has been described as America's first great foreign correspondent (Tebbel 1976: 234). MacGahan initially made a reputation filing reports from the Franco-Prussian War (1870–71) and the Paris Commune; in fact, it was primarily the efforts of MacGahan during the Franco-Prussian War that reconfirmed *The Herald*'s position as the nation's top source of foreign news. His reports in September 1870 about the Battle of Sedan were widely considered the best in either England or the US (Bullard 1914: 115–54).

MacGahan received his first exposure to the Arctic when Bennett sent him to Geneva for the sitting of the Alabama Claims Arbitration Commission. At this the United States was awarded damages from Great Britain, which was ruled to have breached its neutrality in the American Civil War by allowing Confederate naval vessels to be built and equipped on British territory.

Bennett's own fascination with the north convinced him that topics such as the navigation of the Northwest Passage and the attainment of the North Pole could be of great interest to the public. One of his earliest attempts at creating news in the Arctic was to send reporters with the US relief effort searching for the members of Hall's North Pole expedition (1871–73). A reporter accompanied each of the two relief ships, Martin T. Maher on *Juniata* and Frank Y. Commagere on *Tigress*. In August 1873 Maher served under George Washington De Long in the steam-launch *Little Juniata*, which searched the treacherous reaches of Melville Bay for traces of Hall's *Polaris*. Maher's report back to *The Herald* was perhaps the first Arctic account ever written specifically for immediate publication in a newspaper. His thrilling tale established the pattern later press reports followed:

> There was a terrible sea running and the spray danced into the air to a great height and could be seen overleaping icebergs of one hundred feet high, and the waves, lashed to fury by the hurricane, burst against those mountains of ice, breaking off ponderous-looking, solid masses which fell into the sea with a rushing, deafening sound. The destruction of the boat and all on board, now seemed imminent. (*The New York Herald* 11 September 1873)

After continuing the search for 36 hours under these conditions, De Long turned back, but his determination under stress gained him the praise of Maher, who wrote in the same story: "Our expedition was well managed, proving that the commander was a skilful and courageous officer, and worthy of honorable mention on the record of Arctic heroes."

Tigress unsuccessfully continued trying to locate *Polaris* even after *Juniata* had returned to New York. Although Commagere did not have such hair-raising experiences, he did create an impression on his ship-mates. An account of the expedition later stated: "Mr. Commagere was one of those energetic correspondents of the *New York Herald* who are ever ready to do and dare in any field where reportorial honors are to be won" (Blake 1874: 347).

The stories by Maher and Commagere demonstrated the completion of the transition from the sublime to the sensational in the presentation of the Arctic. This transition was subtle because it did not involve a major adjustment of the cognitive element in the physical image of the north; rather, it influenced the affective element, that is, the interpretation of that physical image. According to Boulding (1956), images incorporate three related features – the cognitive, affective, and behavioral characteristics – that influence responses to objects and situations. The cognitive element comprises awareness, knowledge, and information; the affective component embodies feelings about and interpretations of the cognitive element. Thus, although the wordings of many descriptions of the Arctic beginning in the 1860s were not significantly different from those written earlier, the underlying image transmitted became decidedly different: whereas before it was mysterious and sublime, it now became an area of excitement and tension, an adversary to be conquered.

Despite Bennett's growing interest in the Arctic, he turned down an opportunity the next year to have a correspondent accompany a voyage into the Russian north. This was by way of Joseph Wiggins who, in 1874, began to revive the centuries-old British interest in the commercial viability of the Northeast Passage. He chartered Lamont's steamship *Diana* in an attempt to become the first man since the sixteenth century to reach the mouth of the Ob' from western Europe via the Kara Sea, and a few days before he left, Wiggins invited Stanley to join him. As Wiggins related the incident:

> I said to him: "Stanley, if you ascend these rivers and go over Asia home, you will be the first man to do it, after the fashion of what you did in Africa." Stanley said: "You have the right track; if Bennett will let me go, I will go with you." I said: "I am nearly ready to sail. I will give you a week." He replied: "Three days will do. I'll telegraph." He cabled Bennett, and Bennett replied with the monosyllable: "No." (Johnson 1907: 24)

Regardless of Bennett's lack of foresight, Wiggins made a successful voyage that inspired Nordenskiöld's first expedition to the same area the following year (Johnson 1907: 22–53). Financed in part by Sibiryakov, Wiggins did more in the next two decades to open up the Kara Sea route than even Nordenskiöld's completion of the Northeast Passage.

In 1875 Bennett was again involved in the north, when he helped finance Allen Young's expedition in the barque *Pandora*. The primary object of the journey was to navigate the Northwest Passage in one season, but it had as subsidiary goals the exploration of King William Island for relics of Franklin's expedition, the gathering of news about the British Arctic Expedition (1875–76) under George S. Nares, and, from Bennett's stand-point, the selling of newspapers featuring the first-hand accounts of MacGahan, whose adventurous disposition and facility as a vivid descriptive writer with an eye for drama made him the perfect reporter for Bennett's "Arctic beat." Perhaps more than any of his predecessors, MacGahan emphasized not just the thrill of the expedition, but the feel of the Arctic, and his vivid descriptions were credited with increasing *The Herald*'s sales:

> For hundreds of miles in every direction it is the same. The whole north coast of America, from Behring's Straits to Hudson's Bay, with the great Archipelago north of it, is nothing but stone and rock and ice, not only without a tree or shrub, or blade of grass, but without even a handful of earth to hide its savage nakedness. The water is ice, the land is rock; the sea a frozen corpse, the earth a bare, grinning skeleton, that meets you everywhere, that seizes you by its bony clasp, and will not let you go; the skeleton of a dead world. (MacGahan 1876: 226)

Pandora was plagued by heavy ice almost from the beginning of its passage through Lancaster Sound, and although the expedition continued down Peel Sound, the ice in Franklin Strait proved impassable, so Young did an about-face. Even the return was full of tension and danger, and MacGahan's story was used throughout England with the permission of Bennett:

> The race through and out of Peel Strait in a heavy gale, with snow and sleet, proved to be a slow one. Ice following from the south and also coming down from the north next day we were nearly jammed between them. Just off Cape Rennel the fog lifted one morning, and we found a high rocky coast on the starboard two or three lengths off, while the pack on the port beam scarcely allowed room to put the ship about. We succeeded and were driven back into Peel Strait. Ice was rapidly closing the outlet, and young ice was forming on the waves like oil, and rising and falling without breaking. At last we found a "lead," closed at the further end by a broadneck of ice. This we charged and got through, and finally made our escape. . . . (*The Times* 18 October 1875)

Within a year of the voyage, MacGahan's account of the expedition was published in England. *Under the northern lights* not only brought McGahan's Arctic directly to the English public, it helped him establish such a reputation that he was hired as a correspondent for *The Daily News*, after he left *The Herald* due to a disagreement with Bennett (Bullard 1933: 46).

In 1878 Bennett continued his use of the Arctic to gain readership. At the beginning of the year, a report appeared indicating that he had finally decided to allow Stanley to head north: "I am assured by a journalist who ought to know that Mr. Stanley has really declared his readiness to undertake the discovery of the North Pole. If he has, there will be an end of that old secret; if the problem is within the compass of mortal man to unravel it" (*The New-York Times* 22 February 1878). However, Bennett's jealousy and unwillingness to commit the financial resources the free-spending Stanley felt he needed, led not only to the termination of the project but to Stanley's resignation from Bennett's employment (McLynn 1991: 16).

But Bennett simply found another correspondent who could excite the readers of *The Herald* – William Henry Gilder. Bennett's plan was to send out a party to search for the records and journals of the Franklin expedition. Although ultimately the American Geographical Society sponsored the search (1878–80), which was led by Lieutenant Frederick Schwatka of the US Army, Gilder was the second-in-command.

After being landed near Daly Bay on the northwest shore of Hudson Bay, the party of five men spent a winter learning the lifestyle and traveling techniques of the local Eskimos. In the spring of 1879 they sledged to King William Island, where they found skeletal remains and relics that had not been discovered by McClintock in 1859, and that made sensational material for Gilder: "there is little doubt that they were in desperate condition; in fact, as we subsequently learned from other witnesses, there were almost unmistakable evidences of their being compelled to resort to cannibalism until at last they absolutely starved to death at this point" (*The New York Herald* 25 September 1880).

The party then sledged back to Camp Daly in the midst of the winter of 1879–80, only to find that the expected provisions had not been left for them. They proceeded to Marble Island, where they boarded a ship back to the US. This sledge journey of 3,251 miles was the longest by any white men at that time, and was accomplished without any deaths or serious illnesses. But Gilder indicated that it was yet more significant. As he stated in his book *Schwatka's search* (taken directly from his accounts to *The Herald*): "It was the first expedition which relied for its own subsistence and for the subsistence of its dogs on the game which it found in the locality. It was the first expedition in which the white men of the party voluntarily assumed the same diet as the natives" (Gilder 1881: xi).

Gilder's claims about the "firsts" of the Schwatka expedition ignored the earlier achievements of Rae and Hall, among others. However, no previous Arctic adventurer had written at such length or in such detail for newspapers. Immediately after the return of the expedition, Gilder's accounts appeared in *The Herald*, frequently taking an entire page or more of the 12–16-page paper, and running each day from 23 September to 6 October 1880. In fact, the expedition was given considerably more coverage than the election of James Garfield as US President a month later or even than Garfield's assassination the next year. Bennett might not have been the first to realize that a story that takes several days or weeks to reach a climax is more exciting, and sells more newspapers, than one that can be reported in a single issue, but he certainly understood it. Earlier, the bulk of Stanley's reports about his expedition to find Livingstone were spread out over more than a month.

Much of Gilder's account was wrapped in sensationalism, especially the headlines and decks. On 27 September one of the decks read "Eight Days Between Meals." It was only well into the story that the reader learned that it was the dogs that had to go that length of time without eating. However, on the same day another deck was not an exaggeration: "One Hundred and One Degrees Below Freezing Point" referred to the party's traveling in the midst of winter during the lowest temperature recorded in the Canadian Arctic to that time.

Gilder's account emphasizing the excitement and danger of exploration thrilled the New York reading public, helped him become a celebrity, and, once again, was credited with boosting sales of *The Herald* (Guttridge 1986: 285). But he also gave a more enlightening record of Arctic travel than had virtually any of his predecessors. Certainly Gilder mentioned the desperate conditions the party found itself in: "Sometimes we would sink to our waists and then our legs would be dangling in slush and water without finding bottom. The sled would often sink so that the dogs could not pull it out" (*The New York Herald* 25 September 1880). But he also discussed not-so-simple day-to-day life and distresses:

> It is one of the great discomforts of Arctic travel that the exercise of walking wets one's fur stockings with perspiration. At night they freeze, and it is anything but an agreeable sensation to put bare feet into stockings filled with ice, which is a daily experience in winter traveling. But it is astonishing how soon one gets accustomed to that sort of thing and how little he minds it after a while. The warmth of the feet soon thaws the ice and then a wet stocking is nearly as warm as a dry one except in the wind. (*The New York Herald* 24 September 1880)

Gilder's accounts had hardly appeared in *The Herald* when he was off on another Arctic adventure, one that would raise the sensationalization of the far north to new heights.

The *Jeannette* expedition

Bennett's last great attempt to create exclusive news in the Arctic was also the press' most obvious and disastrous meddling in polar exploration. Following the theories of August Petermann, Bennett's *Jeannette* expedition (1879–81) under George Washington De Long initially aimed to reach the North Pole via Bering Strait.

One of the most-highly respected geographers of the nineteenth century, Petermann, the "Sage of Gotha," was the last major advocate of the theory of an ice-free polar sea. Scientific theories about an open polar sea around the North Pole had long been popular. Barrow had been influenced by them, as had Kane and Hayes (Barrow 1846; Kane 1854; Hayes 1867). Petermann initially argued that the best route to the North Pole was not through Smith Sound but between Spitsbergen and Novaya Zemlya (Petermann 1852). After the Austro-Hungarian Exploring Expedition (1872–74), Petermann revised his theory, incorporating those of American oceanographers Silas Bent and Matthew Fontaine Maury into his own, and determined that the way to reach the open polar sea was to start even farther east. He concluded that if the thermal current known as the Kuro Siwo (the

"Black Steam of Japan") were followed through Bering Strait, it would lead to a hole that it cut in the paleocrystic sea, a great ring of pack ice around a warm polar basin that was formed by the meeting of the Kuro Siwo and the Gulf Stream (Maury 1859; Wright 1953).

There was confusion about goals from the very start of the *Jeannette* expedition, because it was funded by Bennett (who purchased Young's *Pandora*, which was renamed *Jeannette* after Bennett's sister) but placed under the auspices of the US Department of the Navy. Yet Bennett could still count on his whimsical orders being followed by Richard Thompson, the malleable Secretary of the Navy. Before *Jeannette* even left San Francisco, Bennett changed the mission's directives. He envisaged a sequel to Stanley's African adventure, with De Long playing the part of Stanley, and Livingstone being portrayed by Nordenskiöld, who was currently wintering north of Siberia during his navigation of the Northeast Passage. Although Nordenskiöld did not require assistance, Bennett decided he needed rescuing, and attempted to involve the American public by running stories in *The Herald* about the importance of the voyage of Vega and the dangers the expedition faced (*The New York Herald* 6 February, 16 March 1879). Fanning the flames of interest in a subject *The Herald* was going to cover in the near future was nothing new to Bennett; while Stanley was first awaiting Livingstone in North Africa, *The Herald* printed stories about the accomplishments of and fears for the Scottish missionary (for example, 9, 23 April 1868).

When *Jeannette* sailed on 8 July 1879, De Long's orders were to give relief to Nordenskiöld before attempting to reach the Pole. In anticipation of one, and possibly two, major series of stories, Bennett assigned Jerome Collins, a *Herald* writer, to the ship's company. In fact, *Jeannette* never came close to finding *Vega*, and De Long proceeded north. After being beset by ice in September, *Jeannette* drifted north of Siberia for almost two years before being crushed. The crew lived for several months on the ice, then headed for the Lena delta in three open boats. One of the three boats, under Lieutenant Charles W. Chipp, was never seen again; one, under Engineer George W. Melville, reached the delta safely on 16 September 1881, and the crew made its way up river to Yakutsk; and the third, under De Long, reached the delta on 17 September, but all except two of the members died before help could reach them. In early 1882 Melville – who had first earned a reputation in the Arctic in 1873 while searching for Hall as an officer on *Tigress* – returned north from Yakutsk, found and buried the bodies of De Long and his party, and sent messages about his searches to the Secretary of the Navy (Melville 1885: 283–366).

In June 1881, the same month that *Jeannette* was crushed, a relief expedition, sponsored in part by Bennett and including Gilder as the representative of *The Herald*, had been sent out under Lieutenant Robert M. Berry. However, the ship, the USS *Rodgers*, caught fire in St Lawrence Bay (Zaliv Lavrentiya) in eastern Siberia. Berry ordered Gilder to sledge approximately 2,500 miles across northeast Siberia and make his way to Irkutsk to telegraph news of the loss of *Rodgers* and the desperate condition of its survivors. The trip not only illustrated that Gilder was one of the most accomplished of Arctic travelers, but provided unique commentary for readers of *The Herald*. For example, in one dispatch, Gilder wrote about travel difficulties in Siberia, discussing what the Russians call *rasputitsa* (the season of bad roads, a term that focuses on the total elimination of travel):

> "Like the breaking up of a hard winter" is an expression frequently used, but I doubt if any one knows what "the breaking up of a hard winter" really is like unless he has had the misfortune to travel in Northern Siberia during the spring time. I thought I had seen hard winters and pretty hard breakings up in the northern portion of North America, but they were nothing like the affair in this country. To get the real thing in all its force and significance you must be near one of the great north-flowing rivers of Siberia about the time of the spring floods, when whole districts are covered with water and swift moving ice, and no land is to be seen for miles in any direction, but occasional forests apparently growing right up out of the water. To travel over roads where for hundreds of yards your sled is entirely under water and you only maintain a position upon it by half standing up and clinging to the side pieces until the whole concern is dumped into an unexpected hole – this is what you must expect. (*The New York Herald* April 1882)

In Verkhoyansk, Gilder learned about the loss of *Jeannette* and about Melville's search. He intercepted a courier carrying Melville's dispatches, obtained the messages, and used them as the basis for a report to *The Herald* about the *Jeannette* disaster. He returned the documents with his own copy – so that *The Herald* would receive the news as quickly as would the Department of the Navy – and went to find Melville, who had continued his search in the hope of finding Chipp (Gilder 1883: 198–216).

Meanwhile, as soon as he heard of Melville's arrival in Yakutsk, Bennett dispatched *Herald* correspondent John P. Jackson to Siberia, not only to get the story of *Jeannette*, but to send back travel articles (17, 27 April 1882). In late February and March 1882 Jackson interviewed John Danenhower, one of the survivors, who, on his way back to the US, had reached Irkutsk. The glimpses Danenhower volunteered of the incompetence, intransigence, and infighting, involving not only De Long and the officers but the crew, created an uproar in the US (Guttridge 1986: 271–3). *The Herald* featured Danenhower's account for more than a week (26 April to 5 May 1882), including a report on the sinking of *Jeannette*:

> Thus the ship lay for two hours and a half, the pressure of the ice relaxing at times and the ship almost righting. Then again she would be hove over to twenty-three degrees, and we felt sure there was no longer any hope for her, for she would not lift. . . . Each officer kept his knapsack in his room, and most of us thought it was time to have them on deck; but we would not make the move until ordered for fear of attracting the attention of the crew, who were at work on provisions and boats. . . . Feeling that the moment had arrived I went for mine, and at the head of the ladder on my return, the Doctor said to me: – "Dan the order is to get the knapsacks." It seems that he had stepped below and found water in the wardroom, which he then reported to the captain, and the order was then given to abandon the ship. The national emblem was hoisted at the mizzen. . . . The ship in this condition was like a broken basket, and only kept

from sinking by the pressure of the ice, which at any moment might relax and let her go to the bottom. (*The New York Herald* 2 May 1882)

The next day *The Herald*'s readers learned of the crew's attempts to reach the Lena delta, of the gale that separated the three boats, and of the arrival on land of Melville's party:

> The gale was now at its full force, and the seas were running high and spiteful. Leach was steering admirably, but we had to keep four balers going all the time to prevent the boat from filling and sinking. . . . So we stood up stream and were fortunate enough to make a landing. . . . We had been 108 hours in the boat. . . . We had a cup of tea and a morsel of pemmican, having been on quarter rations since we separated. We went to sleep with our feet toward the fire, and several of the men passed the night in agony, as if millions of needles were piercing their limbs. (*The New York Herald* 3 May 1882)

After concluding his interviews with Danenhower, Jackson went north, first finding Melville, and then traveling to where De Long and his comrades had been buried. Jackson and his men exhumed the bodies in order to sketch pictures of them and to discover whether letters to Bennett were present on Collins' corpse (*The Illustrated London News* 7 October 1882).

Although the articles by Jackson and Gilder made sensational reading, they were the source of bitter charges and debates. Jackson's interviews with Danenhower began a furor at both public and official levels. A naval court of inquiry was followed by a Congressional investigation. Both, fearing a scandal that would have negative effects on the Department of the Navy, whitewashed the affair and issued findings indicating that the expedition had been efficiently planned, provisioned, and conducted (Guttridge 1986).

Concurrently, Melville objected strenuously to Gilder having opened his dispatches, and he was even more critical of Jackson's violation of the mass grave (Melville 1885: 370). Gilder was just as critical of Melville. On 6 May 1882, the day after the last interview with Danenhower, *The Herald* published the report from Gilder that De Long and his party had been found dead. The story included a commentary about Melville that stated:

> He had, so far as I can learn, succeeded in finding the route taken by the party – was, indeed, in their very footsteps – yet he turned back, alleging that the natives refused to go any further, and that the snow drifts were at that time forty feet deep in places. This last assertion we must refuse to believe at present, but must await patiently his own explanation of his search. There does not appear to have been the slightest necessity for his leaving Bulun, giving the natives charge of the search, while he went to Yakutsk in order to send dispatches home.

The entire affair highlighted a conflict between the interests of the press and the interests of the government or expedition members. Melville wanted to keep many aspects of the expedition and search secret, at least until the Department of the Navy and other governmental agencies were made aware of them. But Gilder and Jackson quickly made public everything they learned. As it turned out, both the Navy and, to a certain extent, the public thought Jackson had overstepped the bounds of good taste in exhuming the bodies of De Long and his party.

Figure 2 Illustrations accompanying the story about the finding of the bodies of De Long and his party in *The Illustrated London News*, 14 October 1882.

At the same time, Gilder and Jackson contributed enormously to the American public's awareness of the Arctic. Gilder was not only a reporter but an accomplished Arctic traveler. His newspaper features and books alike accurately portrayed life in the Arctic. Gilder wrote with more understanding than most of his contemporaries about sledge travel, dogs, native populations and their customs, and living off meager Arctic resources. Although at times his accounts inclined toward the sensational, his writing was remarkably accurate, especially that about the environment:

> The Lena, for the thousand miles or so down which I passed, was monotonous in the extreme, and monotony ten times monotonous after all the dangerous places had been passed in safety. High, sloping, wooded mountains on either side that irritate you by their sameness and continual presence, that seem to look sullenly at you as you sink down under your wraps for the night, and as sullenly at you in the morning when you awake before the sunshine has dissipated the chill and the gray sadness of everything. And whenever you look ahead, morning, noon, or night, the road seems to be barred by a big, frowning mountain, that never seems to change. . . . (*The New York Herald* 19 June 1882)

New national expeditions

In contrast to *The Herald*'s involvement with the *Jeannette* expedition, English newspapers did not begin to sponsor polar expeditions until the 1890s. Press coverage of the Arctic was not extensive in England in the 1860s and 1870s, perhaps because of the paucity of British expeditions at the time, and perhaps because most of those that did take place were relatively minor affairs carried out for sport or scientific research. Many of the press accounts of the foreign expeditions appear to have been taken directly from American newspapers. The exception to this lack of coverage was the British Arctic Expedition of 1875–76, the first British national polar expedition since the start of the Crimean War.

In the mid-1860s a movement to re-enter the Arctic gained momentum, and in 1865 Sherard Osborn read an exhaustive paper to the RGS in which he advocated a renewal of Arctic exploration by the Smith Sound route. Osborn pointed out the gains that had been made in scientific research in the Arctic, and discussed the work still to be done. He harkened back to John Barrow's arguments when he stated: "The Navy needs some action to wake it up from the sloth of routine, and save it from the canker of prolonged peace. Arctic exploration is more wholesome for it, in a moral as well as a sanitary point of view, than any more Ashantee or Japanese wars" (Osborn 1865: 52). But his most misleading argument indicated that service in the Arctic was not dangerous because, "more sailors have been thrown to the sharks from the diseases incident to service in China and the coast of Africa, within the last four years, than ever fell in thirty years of Arctic service" (Osborn 1865: 43).

Despite strong opposition, notably from *The Times* (24, 26, 28 January 1865), Osborn's proposal appeared likely to be accepted until two letters from August Petermann – in which he argued that such exploration should take place via Spitsbergen – created enough dissension to cause the project to collapse (Markham 1874: 85).

For almost another decade, Osborn and Clements R. Markham kept working for the renewal of Arctic exploration. In 1873 Markham published *The threshold of the unknown region*, a best-seller that ran to four editions, in which he stated: "in the light of former experience, there is no undue danger in Arctic service; provided that the expedition is under naval discipline and Government control" (Markham 1873: 282). He also dismissed scurvy as a problem of the past. But when the British Arctic Expedition actually was approved by the government, it was not as much because of the pressure from Osborn and Markham as because William Gladstone had been succeeded as Prime Minister by Benjamin Disraeli, an imperial expansionist. Disraeli declared that the expedition had been sanctioned because of "the scientific advantages to be derived from it, its chances of success, as well as the importance of encouraging that spirit of maritime enterprise which has ever distinguished the English people" (*Nature* 1874: 55). Interpreted, this meant that it was an enterprise for commercial and naval benefit and to enhance Britain's reputation. In other words, it was not unlike the British expeditions of the 1820s.

Ostensibly, the scientific role of the expedition was to be important. George S. Nares, the commanding officer, was recalled from the command of HMS *Challenger*, a ship then being used as a floating laboratory by a group of civilian scientists in the Antarctic (Nares 1878). In addition, the officers were widely publicized as having been selected for their scientific qualifications. In reality, however, the expedition was for geographical exploration, with science second, as shown both by the scientific personnel being naval officers with limited scientific backgrounds and by relegation of science to paragraph 26 of the Admiralty's orders.

Behind the government's rhetoric, there were three motives for the expedition, none pertaining to science. First, it was to help the British whaling industry by emphasizing the British presence in and rights to the rich fisheries of northern Baffin Bay. Second, the Royal Navy was beginning to lose the polar expertise that had been gained early in the century, and realized that the only way to maintain it was to re-enter the Arctic. Third, Britain was losing its prestige in the Arctic. The success of the Austro-Hungarian Exploring Expedition of 1872–74 had been an embarrassment to the country that formerly had dominated Arctic exploration. The British Arctic Expedition, which was actually simply an effort to attain the farthest north, would serve all three purposes.

Unlike its lack of attention to recent polar events, the English press seemingly could not write enough about the British Arctic Expedition. Even *The Times*, which regularly opposed northern exploration, wrote optimistically about the chances of reaching the North Pole. *The Illustrated London News* and the journal *The Navy* in particular oversold both the importance of the expedition and its chances of success.

Thus, there was enormous disappointment in October 1876 when, due primarily to scurvy, the expedition returned home a year early. Although a sledge party under Albert H. Markham had indeed established a new farthest north (83° 20′), the expedition generally was a failure, and its scientific and commercial values were nominal. The English press was merciless. *The Navy* (1876: 441) declared, "Verily the expedition of 1875–76 has but little of which to boast. It went out like a rocket, and has come back like the stick."

In direct contrast to the British Arctic Expedition was that of the Austrian Empire. Like the *Jeannette* expedition, this effort was in part prompted by Petermann's theories. It was financed by Graf von Wilczek, who was motivated by his keen interest in polar science and the area itself (Barr 1987: xxix). The stated goal of the expedition was to examine as large an area as possible of the unknown region in the vicinity of Novaya Zemlya (Payer 1876: I, 114–16). In this, the expedition, sailing in *Tegetthoff*, was an unqualified success, and it not only carried out scientific investigations, it discovered and partially explored and mapped Franz Joseph Land (Zemlya Frantsa-Iosifa).

Perhaps the most impressive quality of the expedition, however, was the work produced by its co-commanders after its return. Few if any other expeditions could claim both the literary achievement of Julius Payer's *New lands within the Arctic circle* and the scientific accomplishments of Karl Weyprecht. Payer's account was an enormous success in both England and America, at least partly because of the attendant publicity. The expedition's return precipitated Nares' departure, and the book's publication coincided with his return. But it was also successful in its own right.

Perhaps the strongest appeal of Payer's narrative was its simplicity; at no point did Payer bombard the reader with scientific accomplishments or heroic efforts. But even in calm, simple terms without embellishment, the saga of *Tegetthoff* was spellbinding. And Payer's account brought to the Anglo-American public its first real exposure to the Arctic efforts of other Europeans, who had been all but ignored in both the English and American press.

Weyprecht also indirectly – and unintentionally – helped sensationalize the Arctic. After the Austro-Hungarian exploring expedition returned, he concluded that the era of independent expeditions aimed primarily at geographical exploration and with little interest in science was over. In a speech to the RGS in 1875, Weyprecht stated:

> The key to the many secrets of nature . . . is certainly to be sought for near the Poles. But as long as Polar Expeditions are looked upon merely as a sort of international steeplechase, which is primarily to confer honour on this flag or the other, and their main object is to exceed by a few miles the latitude reached by a predecessor, these mysteries will remain unsolved. (quoted in Baker 1982: 276)

Weyprecht proposed that a co-ordinated, international program of intensive scientific investigation be established, one that would benefit not only individual nations, but mankind. The ultimate realization of his ideas was the International Polar Year, 1882–83, for which 14 scientific stations were planned with the goal of making simultaneous scientific observations, using comparable means and methods, and with the desired result of discovering fundamental laws and principles of nature (Barr 1985: 2–5). However, although the International Polar Year expeditions were designed for the exclusive purpose of science, one of them was to make Arctic exploration a favorite topic of the sensational press throughout England and America.

The spread of sensationalism

Although *The New York Herald* was the first newspaper to sponsor exploration and for several decades featured the most thorough and sensational coverage of geographical discovery in the English-speaking world, even in the 1870s it was not the only paper to turn to sensationalism or to show an interest in exploration. *The Sun* could compete on sensational terms with *The Herald*, although it did not have either the interest or the expertise of *The Herald* in exploration. But Dana was a brilliant salesman as well as journalist, and he had not so forgotten Day's example that he allowed *The Sun* to ignore stories of obvious powerful interest. When the people of New York wanted to read about one of Bennett's creations, Dana gave it to them.

Coverage of exploration in *The Herald* and *The Sun* was sensational not only by comparison with most of the rest of the press, but with the treatment of other subjects in those papers themselves. Exploration received special coverage, with larger and bolder headlines, more prominent placement of stories, greater length of articles, and higher frequency of appearance than most other topics.

A comparison of *The Herald* in 1870 and 1875 testifies to Bennett's exploitation of exploration. In October 1870 no story on any topic received as much as a half-page on the first news page of *The Herald*. For most of Bennett's reign over *The Herald*, the first two pages of his newspaper, and sometimes the first four, were devoted to classified advertisements. The first news page, either page three or five, was usually devoted to sections titled WASHINGTON, POLITICAL, NEW YORK CITY, or NEWS FROM ALL PARTS OF THE WORLD. Each section was from one to two columns (out of six on the page) in length. By comparison, in October and November 1875 Stanley's trans-Africa expedition received at least the entire first news page on four occasions (11, 12, 13 October, 29 November) and at least one-third of a page twice more (10, 15 November). Reports about Young's expedition in *Pandora* received virtually the entire first news page twice (31 October, 6 November) and more than one-third of a page six times (17 October, 4, 5, 9, 15, 18 November).

By the time of the *Jeannette* expedition, exploration had become one of the main staples of *The Herald*. Apart from the reports sent back by Gilder and Jackson, the paper printed articles about Russia, Siberia, or exploration in Asia; "expert commentary" and other speculation on the missing ship and crew members; and official reports. This continued even after the saga of the search for the missing crew had ended. Throughout the last three months of 1882, the Jeannette Board of Inquiry met almost daily. The hearings were given at least a full column each day in *The Herald*, as well as receiving a great deal of attention in *The Sun* and *The New-York Times*. The coverage by *The Times* indicated that even if the reputedly quality press was not as sensational as *The Herald*, it was interested in some of the same topics.

Dividing the American press of the nineteenth century into strict categories based on sensationalism, as is frequently done, can be misleading. The writing styles of the sensational or quality papers were not mutually exclusive. The range of variation within these groups was so great that there was a distinct overlap among the groups; some papers considered sensational were in fact closer to the style and content of the quality papers than to that of the most sensational ones.

In fact, a difference in the style of writing was one of the prime demarcations between the two great sensational papers. Dana's *Sun* was only four pages, so it emphasized a quick, clever, biting prose. In contrast, the 12–16-page *Herald* frequently used a leisurely, plodding style; this was inordinately effective for exclusive and lengthy reports on new areas and experiences. An example of *The Herald*'s treatment was a feature on the midnight sun and snowblindness written by Gilder after his return from the Schwatka expedition, but before he left on *Rodgers*:

> It might be supposed that in the utter barrenness of the Arctic landscape flowers never grow there. This would be a great mistake. The dweller in that desolate region after passing a long, weary winter, with nothing for the eye to rest upon but the vast expanse of snow and ice, is in a condition to appreciate beyond the ability of an inhabitant of warmer climes the little flowerets that peep up almost through the snow when the spring sunlight begins to exercise its power upon the white mantle of the earth. In little patches here and there, where the dark-colored moss absorbs the warm rays of the sun and the snow is melted from its surface, the most delicate flowers spring up at once to gladden the eye of the weary traveller. . . . Thoughts of home, in a warmer and more hospitable climate, fill his heart with joy and longing as meadows filled with daisies and buttercups spread out before him while he stands upon the crest of a granite hill that knows no footstep other than the tread of the stately musk ox or the antlered reindeer, as they pass single file upon their migratory journeys. . . . He is a boy again, and involuntarily plucks the feathery dandelion and seeks the time of the fair one, who is dearer to him than ever in this hour of separation, by picking the leaves from the yellow hearted daisy. Tiny little violets, set in a background of black or dark green moss, adorn the hillsides, and many flowers unknown to warmer zones come bravely forth to flourish for a few weeks only and wither in the August winds. (*The New York Herald* 17 May 1881)

The article continued at the same pace, taking several paragraphs before it finally reached its basic point – how to avoid snowblindness when traveling in the Arctic. But the very success of such an article, like that of *The Sun*'s human-interest stories, was based on the author's ability to see the most minute detail and to convey the feelings that the average man would have felt. Although the experience of a journalist who "has seen it all" is an advantage in writing straight news stories that require facts be set down accurately and succinctly, it can be a disadvantage for the writer who is trying to draw tears or gasps or sighs from an audience. One of the reasons Gilder remained perhaps the most effective writer about the Arctic was that despite his professionalism he never lost his innocence, his fresh vision, his inquiring attitude.

This type of article also built a comfortable relationship between the writer and his audience, so that when the writer produced a shocking or sensational feature, its power was enhanced. This was the device used in *The Herald* when Gilder copied a letter from William Nindemann, one of the two survivors from De Long's party, which was run as part of Gilder's account about the death of De Long:

> [The party] remained a few days on the seacoast on account of some of the mens [*sic*] feet being badly frost bitten, leaving behind the ship's log and other articles, not being able to carry them, started to travel south with five days [*sic*] provisions. Erickson, walking on crutches a few days after made a sled to drag him, came to a hut on the 5th of October. On the morning of the 6th the Dockter [*sic*] cut off all his toes, the Captain asked me if I had strength to go to one of the settlements with one of the men to get assistance, as he was gowing [*sic*] to stay by Erickson. While talking about it Erickson *died*. (*The New York Herald* 6 May 1882; emphasis Nindemann's)

It has been shown that a sensational style of writing produces greater interest from the reader than a non-sensational style (Sasser 1967). No such research had been conducted in the nineteenth century, but the fact was apparent to astute journalists. Therefore, even the supposedly sedate *New-York Times* at times engaged in somewhat sensational writing, as when it forecast what Hall and his comrades could expect while wintering on *Polaris*:

> The voyager will undergo almost incredible suffering in his first long Winter, or prolonged night, confined in the narrow, dank atmosphere of a ship's forecastle or cabin. Damp blankets, fetid woollens, odoriferous furs, filthy Esquimaux, and myriads of unpleasant insects, who seem to have a particular affinity for the Polar Indians, and who will swarm the ship night and day, are among the number of unpleasant experiences with which his Arctic life will be marked. Weeks before the long night has passed the ennui will be almost unbearable. Inside he will see his companions, a group of unhealthily fattened faces, pale and dejected, worn out with long confinement, if not by the dread destroyer, scurvy. Outside, he will be met by the repulsive features of the Esquimaux, their still more repulsive and disgusting modes of life, and the never-ending line of ice and snow – vistas of dazzling whiteness – whose monotony alone becomes truly insupportable. If the voyager wanders far from the vessel he is liable at any moment to encounter a sudden northerly gale, or arctic sirocco which sweeps with the most impetuous fury across the vast expanse of snow and ice, and if not accompanied with a trusty guide he inevitably perishes with cold, or falls a victim to prowling bears and ravenous wolves. Most of these, indeed, are among the least of the perils which Capt. HALL and his fellow voyagers will be called upon to undergo. . . . (*The New-York Times* 7 May 1871)

It is evident that based on their actual articles, rather than on their reputations alone, some of the quality papers were a great deal closer in style to the sensational papers than is usually acknowledged. In fact, by the 1880s, *The Herald* served as a model for a growing number of papers on the east coast of the United States, including *The World* of New York, *The Boston Daily Globe*, the *Philadelphia Record*, and *The Washington Post*.

Perhaps the most powerful newspaper in what was considered the west of the US was *The Chicago Daily Tribune*. First issued on 10 June 1847 and named after the *New-York Tribune*, it was taken over by Joseph Medill and five partners in 1855 and became a cornerstone for the Republican Party and Abraham Lincoln (Kinsley 1943–46). *The Daily Tribune* (which went through at least eight name changes by 1890) could be extremely sensational, especially when exposing local corruption (Wendt 1979: 200). It also showed a strong interest in new places, particularly the American west and the Arctic. Like most papers, *The Daily Tribune* did not have a large foreign staff and had to pick up much of its material from elsewhere (Kinsley 1943–46). In *The Daily Tribune*'s case, this seems to have caused an uncommonly high number of inaccurate stories, such as one, under the headline THE NORTHEAST PASSAGE, reporting Nordenskiöld's completion of the Passage – four years before it actually occurred (28 October 1876).

In the following years, another paper that showed interest in Nordenskiöld, although not exploration in general, was the *St. Louis Post-Dispatch*, which, during the navigation of the Northeast Passage, printed brief, but accurate, accounts of the expedition (3 June, 19, 22 October 1879, 17 May 1880).

However, it was not for its Arctic coverage that the *Post-Dispatch* became known. Rather, it was because the paper was the proving ground for one of the great journalists of the nineteenth century, Joseph Pulitzer. In 1864 the Hungarian-born Pulitzer came to the United States at the age of 17 to fight in the Union army. After the Civil War, he moved to St Louis and began his career in journalism as a reporter for the German-language daily *Westliche Post*. He later served as a reporter for Dana's *Sun*. On 9 December 1878 Pulitzer purchased *The St. Louis Dispatch*, and three days later his new paper merged with the *St. Louis Evening Post*.

In the next five years, Pulitzer and his managing editor, John Cockerill, experimented with the techniques that they would perfect after moving to New York when Pulitzer purchased *The World*. Pulitzer initiated the kind of urban and moral crusading that he would make famous in New York, although in St Louis he appealed to, and crusaded for, a middle-class audience rather than one composed of immigrants and the labor force (Rammelkamp 1967: 207–283).

It was also in St Louis that Pulitzer and Cockerill first developed their sensational style of journalism. As had Bennett Sr, Pulitzer and Cockerill exploited not only murder, sex, and public hangings, but social scandal and gossip-mongering. The paper's editorial page was equally sensational, attacking politicians and society figures with a seeming disregard for the consequences (Rammelkamp 1967: 163–206).

The story that showed the *Post-Dispatch* at its most sensational was the murder in April 1882 of Jesse James, a famous outlaw whose gang had worked in western Missouri for years and who had emerged with a personal reputation as a kind of Robin Hood. For more than two weeks, the *Post-Dispatch* ran articles about James; his brother Frank; James' killer, Bob Ford; Ford's trial for murder; and Missouri Governor Crittenden's "complicity" (for offering a reward for James, dead or alive). As the first article on the murder recounted the events:

> Even in that motion, quick as thought, there was something which did not escape the acute ears of the hunted man. He made a motion as if to turn his head to ascertain the cause of that suspicious sound, but too late. A nervous pressure on the trigger, a quick flash, a sharp report, and the well-directed ball crashed through the outlaw's skull. (*St. Louis Post-Dispatch* 5 April 1882)

The controversy over the killing of James increased the circulation of the *Post-Dispatch* by more than 30 per cent (Rammelkamp 1967: 178) and provided a stimulus for the man who would later try to "out-Bennett Bennett" (Fermer 1986: 312).

6

New Journalism and new lands

A new man in town

When, in May 1883, Joseph Pulitzer purchased *The New-York World* from financier Jay Gould, most people had never heard of the owner of the *St. Louis Post-Dispatch*. Nor did many of them care much about his new newspaper, which appeared to be in its death throes.

Pulitzer's acquisition had been founded in June 1860 as *The World*, a penny daily with an emphasis on religion, full of church notices and messages to uplift its audience. Despite a price increase to 2¢, heavy losses forced the sale of *The World*, which was run for a number of years by Manton Marble, who changed it to an organ of the Democratic Party, and then by Gould, who changed the name to *The New-York World*. Under Gould, it lost about $40,000 per year, and by 1883 it had a daily circulation of less than 15,000.

Pulitzer wasted no time in making alterations. In his first edition he changed the name back to *The World*. He eliminated the news summaries that occupied the left-hand column of page one. In his own words, his paper was to be "not only cheap but bright, not only bright but large, not only large but truly Democratic – dedicated to the cause of the people" (*The World* 11 May 1883). Making *The World* inexpensive was no problem. It continued at 2¢ for eight pages. By comparison, *The Herald* cost 3¢ for 12 to 16 pages, *The Sun* was 2¢ for four pages, and the *Tribune* and *The Times* each were 4¢ for eight pages.

To help make *The World* bright, Pulitzer filled the blank space around the nameplate with "ears," boxes for self-advertisement, such as the announcement of circulation increases or exclusive stories. The ears initially proclaimed "Only 8-page Newspaper in the United States sold for 2 cents," but they later featured such slogans as "Spicy, Pithy, Pictorial."

Pulitzer also changed the position of the lead story. On the assumption that the eyes of the readers moved across the page from left to right, most American editors had traditionally run the main feature in the first column, with the second-most-important story in the right-hand column. Pulitzer suspected that when readers quickly glanced at a newspaper, they started on the right, so he switched the positions of the top stories, leading to the format most papers follow today (Juergens 1966: 28–9).

Making *The World* large and Democratic were factors closely related in Pulitzer's formula. He was aware that four out of five New York City residents were either immigrants or children of immigrants, and that few of them had any effective spokesman (Juergens 1966). This is exactly what he became. Within a week of taking over *The World*, Pulitzer published a 10-point program for which his paper would campaign: tax luxuries, tax inheritances, tax large incomes, tax monopolies, tax the privileged corporations, institute a tariff for revenue, reform the civil service, punish corrupt office-holders, punish vote buying, and punish employers who coerce their employees in elections (*The World* 17 May 1883). Pulitzer thus made his new paper a high-minded crusader and public defender, much like the *Post-Dispatch* was in St Louis, except that *The World* represented the poorer classes rather than the middle class (Seitz 1924a; Rammelkamp 1967).

A mass circulation was needed for the success of *The World*'s liberal ideology. "If a newspaper is to be of real service to the public," Pulitzer commented, "it must have a big circulation, first because its news and its comments must reach the largest possible number of people, second, because circulation means advertising, and advertising means money, and money means independence" (Ireland 1938: 98).

That Pulitzer's audience included the mass of people near the lowest level of literacy meant that, like Day and Bennett Sr before him, he would create a sensational journal. Yet it was a new blend of sensationalism and idealism. On page one, *The World* adopted a combination of sex, scandal, and corruption, but the editorial page comprised well-reasoned expressions of Pulitzer's intellectual idealism. Though unusual, this combination was comprehensible: Pulitzer understood that sensationalism sold newspapers, and that to succeed he had to challenge Bennett Jr and Dana on their own ground.

To achieve his goals, Pulitzer quickly revamped *The World*'s staff, bringing in a number of his better writers and editors from the *Post-Dispatch*, including John Cockerill. The handsome, dynamic Cockerill was one of the most capable journalists in the US, a fact he had proven earlier as the managing editor of the *Cincinnati Daily Enquirer*, *The Washington Post*, and the *Post-Dispatch*. Cockerill became responsible for much of the day-to-day control of *The World*, because Pulitzer was both slowly going blind and suffering from an increasingly severe nervous affliction that compelled him to retire from on-the-spot management in 1887. As managing editor of *The World*, Cockerill made substantial contributions to the sensationalism for which Pulitzer gained much of his fame.

The sensationalism of Pulitzer and Cockerill at *The World* was unlike that of their predecessors because technological advances meant that *The*

World could obtain more information, present it in a more sensational manner, and distribute it more widely than had been possible in the first half of the nineteenth century.

Pulitzer's sensationalism was also different in that its goal was to achieve more than just financial success. The sensations on page one were to attract readers so that the editorials on page four could educate, uplift, and crusade for them. If crime and scandal were needed to bring them to the editorial page, then crime and scandal they would receive. "Of course newspapers are 'made to sell,'" Pulitzer responded when attacked about *The World*'s news selection. "In that respect they resemble the highest works of art and intellect as well as sermons" (*The World* 6 May 1884).

Pulitzer believed that the sensational press was the most important agency in the moral betterment of the nation: "the newspaper, whether printed on Sunday or on week days, is a great aid to the preservation of peace and order. Sinners do not shrink from vice, but they are awfully afraid of exposure in the newspapers. No pulpit orator can reach the evil-doer like a Sunday newspaper with a quarter of a million readers" (*The World* 27 May 1884).

Sensational or not, Pulitzer believed the press should obey the dictates of good taste (Juergens 1966: 73). Rather than compare his paper to the scandal sheets of the day, he saw it more akin to that symbol of high moral tone, *The Evening Post* of E.L. Godkin. Pulitzer simply argued for a broader definition of good taste than did Godkin:

Now about this matter of sensationalism: a newspaper should be scrupulously accurate, it should be clean, it should avoid everything salacious or suggestive, everything that could offend good taste or lower the moral tone of its readers; but within these limits it is the duty of a newspaper to print the news. When I speak of good taste and of good moral tone I do not mean the kind of good taste which is offended by every reference to the unpleasant things of life, I do not mean the kind of morality which refuses to recognize the existence of immorality – that type of moral hypocrite has done more to check the moral progress of humanity than all the immoral people put together. What I mean is the kind of good taste which demands that frankness should be linked with decency, the kind of moral tone which is braced and not relaxed when it is brought face to face with vice. (Ireland 1938: 96–7)

Pulitzer also agreed with Godkin that the press had a responsibility to serve the public. Again, the major difference was not in basic doctrine, but in the response to it. Pulitzer believed sensational articles helped fulfill this responsibility:

We are a democracy, and there is only one way to get a democracy on its feet in the matter of its individual, its social, its municipal, its State, its National conduct, and that is by keeping the public informed about what is going on. There is not a crime, there is not a dodge, there is not a trick, there is not a swindle, there is not a vice which does not live by secrecy. Get these things out in the open, describe them, attack them, ridicule them in the press, and sooner or later public opinion will sweep them away. (Ireland 1938: 97–8)

So of what, then, did *The World*'s sensationalism consist? It was an unusual *mélange* brought about because Pulitzer was not only innovative but willing to learn from his predecessors and competitors. The influence of Day and Bennett Sr was shown by an abundance of stories about crime and scandal. From Bennett Sr, Jones, and Leslie, *The World* inherited a tradition of investigative journalism. Human-interest stories were attributable to Dana. And from Bennett Jr, *The World* learned another of its specialties – stunts.

As he had in St Louis, Pulitzer showed a decided preference for local news, but this did not mean he did not understand Bennett Jr's success. His point was not indiscriminately to play down every item of foreign intelligence, but to use discretion in deciding which ones appealed to his audience.

Pulitzer's assessment of what his readership wanted was reflected in his efforts to create news. In these, he was no Bennett, and he had no Stanley or Gilder. But then he did not want to be just an imitator of *The Herald*; in fact, he told one of his reporters, "that I could do anything on behalf of the paper except hunt for the North Pole" (Seitz 1924a: 296). Pulitzer's stunts aimed at generating excitement rather than at true exploration.

The best known of *The World*'s special correspondents was Nellie Bly, whose real name was Elizabeth Cochrane, and who first impressed Cockerill when she barged into his office and demanded an assignment. Her first task was to feign insanity so that she could write an inside account of the asylum on Blackwell's Island in New York (Cochrane 1887). She later reported on poor working conditions in factories, mistreatment of female prisoners, and unfair labor practices. But her most ambitious effort was traveling around the world in an attempt to beat Phileas Fogg's record set in Jules Verne's *Around the world in eighty days*. Her trip of 72 days, 6 hours, 10 minutes, and 11 seconds (14 November 1889 to 25 January 1890) by steamship, sailboat, train, horseback, and foot fascinated the audience of *The World*, as did the contest to predict her exact time of completion (Rittenhouse 1956). However, the entire stunt was totally ignored by *The Herald*, *The Sun*, *The Times*, and the *Tribune*.

Another of *The World*'s special correspondents was Thomas Stevens, who initially earned a reputation from a 31-part series of stories in *Outing* magazine based on his experiences while trying to ride a bicycle around the world (Stevens 1887). He was later sent by Cockerill to ride horseback 1,100 miles from Moscow to the Black Sea and to report back on the conditions, manners, and customs of the people of European Russia (Stevens 1891).

Pulitzer's use of illustration

Pulitzer's efforts to attract readership led to his innovative use of illustration. *The World* was certainly not the first newspaper to use pictures: illustration dated back at least to 20 December 1638, when the *Weekly News* in England printed a full-page engraving of "the places where the fire burst out" after a volcanic upheaval on Saõ Miguel in the Azores (Jackson

1885: 42–3). Illustration took on a much more important role in 1842 when Herbert Ingram founded *The Illustrated London News*, the intent of which was to use pictures to assist in the understanding of news and to reveal information difficult to place in verbal context.

The first daily newspaper to make frequent use of illustration was *The New York Herald*. Bennett Sr printed pictures of murder victims, crime scenes, and other sensational topics. During the Civil War, maps were regularly featured, and drawings of battle scenes were not uncommon. Bennett Jr frequently used maps and drawings of unusual scenes to go along with his travel or exploration accounts. *The Herald* did not have exclusive use of illustrations, however. On 31 March 1860 *The Press and Tribune* of Chicago printed its first map, of the Pike's Peak gold regions. The first illustrations in *The New-York Times* – two caricatures of Bennett Sr – were printed in 1861.

However, it was not a daily that most directly influenced Pulitzer's use of illustration, but *Frank Leslie's Illustrated Newspaper*. *Leslie's* was not only one of the earliest American newspapers with a fighting social conscience – the most famous of its crusades was the "swill milk campaign" of 1858–59 – it established the editorial methods for dealing with pictures that were followed by American editors for the rest of the nineteenth century (Huntzicker 1989).

Yet because of Pulitzer's and Cockerill's innovative techniques and extensive use of the new medium, *The World* is associated as much as any newspaper with the development of illustration. These two did not view illustration simply as an art form admirable for its own sake, as did the early picture dailies, nor as a way to spice up a dull page, but as an unexploited medium of sales. Pulitzer commented:

> They call me the father of illustrated journalism. What folly! I never thought of any such thing. I had a small paper which had been dead for years, and I was trying in every way I could think of to build up its circulation. I wanted to put into each issue something that would arouse curiosity and make people want to buy the paper. What could I use for bait? A picture, of course . . . .(Barrett 1941: 81–2)

Actually, it was Cockerill, even more than Pulitzer, who was the force behind the continued use of illustration:

> When Joseph Pulitzer went to Europe he was a little undecided about the woodcuts. He left orders to gradually get rid of them, as he thought it tended to lower the dignity of the paper, and he was not satisfied that the cuts helped it in its circulation. After Pulitzer was on the Atlantic, Col. Cockerill . . . found, however, that the circulation of the paper went with the cuts, and, like the good newspaper general that he was, he instantly changed his tactics. (*The Journalist* 22 August 1885)

From then on, *The World* printed large numbers of news pictures, both multi-column illustrations and halfsticks of local people. Just as Pulitzer assumed that local features meant more to his readers, he determined that they would be more interested in pictures of people or places with which they were familiar than in drawings of famous strangers or faraway, unknown areas, such as were printed in *The Herald*.

As he did with sensationalism, Pulitzer argued that illustrations served a high moral purpose. His point was proven in 1884 when two criminals were arrested in Canada on the strength of portraits run in *The World*: "While some of our esteemed, aesthetic contemporaries assume to censure the frequent illustrations in the *World* as sensational," Pulitzer crowed, "we are subserving the cause of public justice by presenting faithful portraits which enable the officers of the law, here and abroad, to arrest criminals" (*The World* 11 December 1884).

The true significance of Pulitzer's adoption of illustration is how it influenced the press as a whole. Pulitzer's success quickly attracted the attention of his rivals, and in a short period of time not only the New York press but papers throughout the US were printing more pictures than they had ever previously considered.

The World's victory

Within several months of arriving in New York, Pulitzer had shown his major rivals that this liberal spokesman and his newspaper were serious competition. *The World* steadily gained readers until those rivals took steps to protect themselves. In September 1883 the *Tribune*, *The Times*, and *The Herald* cut their prices, the first to 3¢, the latter pair to 2¢. The day after *The Times* dropped its price, Pulitzer proclaimed it needed to go further than that to challenge *The World*: "If our neighbor will imitate us in style and tone, now, it may hope to amount to something" (*The World* 19 September 1883).

Pulitzer was even more satisfied with Bennett's price cut, which was promptly followed by the unprecedented act of *The Herald* taking out full-page advertisements in *The World* for a week to announce it (*The World* 27 September to 3 October 1883). Pulitzer pointed out to his readers that Bennett thereby conceded not only *The World*'s increase in circulation, but its effectiveness as an advertising organ: "To-day we surrender our fifth page to Brother Bennett, who, though far away across the ocean, understands the value of advertising in a newspaper with a large and growing circulation" (*The World* 27 September 1883).

Pulitzer frequently claimed that Bennett's move indicated *The Herald* had lost its position as the dominant American newspaper. It was easy thereafter to treat it in the same cavalier manner that he did the rest of the press. For example, when Bennett's paper followed some of *The World*'s leads in illustration, Cockerill boasted:

> There is no flattery so sincere as imitation, and the *World* feels a sense of pride in noting the care with which the *Herald* follows in its wake. . . . But until the *Herald* equips itself with sound principles, a few bright ideas and a collection of fresh brains, we shall not regard it as a formidable journalistic adversary. (*The World* 2 May 1884)

By May 1884, one year after Pulitzer had purchased *The World*, its circulation had grown fourfold to almost 60,000. Although *The Herald* and *The Sun* still dominated the field, with circulations of around 190,000 and 150,000, respectively, that too was about to change.

In 1884 Dana grew disenchanted with New York governor Grover Cleveland, the leading Democratic candidate for President. By backing Benjamin Butler, the candidate of the National (or Greenback) Party, Dana left *The World* as the only major New York paper supporting the Democrats and drove thousands of his subscribers into the arms of Pulitzer, with the result that *The Sun* lost some 40 per cent of its readers, most of which it never recovered (Rosebault 1931: 228). Readership losses by *The Sun* were closely matched by the gains of *The World* (Juergens 1966: 331). By May 1885, when *The Sun* had fallen to a circulation of about 90,000, *The World* had risen to more than 150,000. Soon only *The Herald* could compete with Pulitzer's daily, which became even more powerful when *The Evening World* was founded in 1887 to challenge Bennett's *Evening Telegram*. By 1890, despite a price increase to 3¢ on 29 November 1887, *The Herald*'s circulation had grown to about 212,000. But *The World* had attained a readership of 246,000, the largest in the United States.

The triumph of sensationalism in the United States

While *The Herald* and *The World* fought for supremacy in New York, a third paper also made a national reputation for both its use of sensationalism and its coverage of exploration and other foreign news. This was *The Chicago Daily News*, founded in December 1875 by Melville Stone. Although Stone wrote that the four-page *Daily News* published "no so-called sensational and exaggerated or scandalous material for the purpose of making sales" (Stone 1922), and it did not emphasize common crime, sex, or human-interest stories, it nevertheless quickly developed its own style of sensationalism, what Stone called "detective journalism."

In 1881 Stone and his partner, Victor F. Lawson, started a morning edition, *The Chicago Morning News*, and in 1885 the combined morning and evening circulation passed 100,000. By the time Stone sold his interest to Lawson in May 1888 the combined circulation trailed only *The World* and *The Herald*; by 1894 the evening edition had reached 200,000, making it the largest evening paper in America. Because he considered it a public service, Lawson emphasized foreign news (Dennis 1935), and his papers had some of the best and most complete coverage of exploration in the American press. They also sponsored two North Polar expeditions under the leadership of Walter Wellman in the first decade of the twentieth century.

Meanwhile, almost unnoticed in the national picture were the developments at *The Examiner* of San Francisco. Founded in June 1865 as *The Evening Examiner*, it was acquired in 1880 by George Hearst, who changed it to a morning edition and, seven years later, turned it over to his 24-year-old son William Randolph, who had closely studied the sensational techniques of both *The Boston Daily Globe* and *The World* (Winkler 1928: 59–63; Swanberg 1961: 36).

Even Pulitzer's sensationalism was exceeded the next decade by Hearst, who was interested in increasing circulation not as a means of serving the people, but to gain money and power (Lundberg 1936). Hearst admired Pulitzer's methods of running a newspaper, and he particularly approved of *The World*'s front page. But Hearst was neither an intellectual nor a social reformer, so the editorial page meant little to him (Tebbel 1952: 78–82). Hearst was the heir to a huge fortune, and he spent continuously to build his paper into a power of western journalism. By the end of his first year, *The Examiner* had doubled its circulation to 30,000. Five years later it had increased to 72,000, surpassing the long-time west-coast leader, *The San Francisco Chronicle*.

As the dailies emphasized sensational aspects of exploration, some of the monthly magazines followed to a lesser degree. *Scribner's Monthly*, one of the great American middle-class magazines of the day, broke away from Scribner's book-publishing company in 1881, was renamed *The Century Illustrated Monthly Magazine*, and came under the editorship of Richard Watson Gilder. For 28 years under Gilder, *Century Illustrated* remained one of America's most-respected and thought-provoking publications, although the focus widened from literature to include wars, travel, and exploration – events similar to those Gilder's brother, William Henry Gilder, publicized for Bennett (Mott 1930–68: III, 457–80).

Five years after the name change, Scribner's book-publishing company re-entered the magazine business, and *Scribner's Magazine* was born with a format not unlike that of *Century Illustrated*. The new magazine had more interest in Africa than its predecessors, and featured travel articles by both H.M. Stanley and Theodore Roosevelt (Mott 1930–68: IV, 717–32).

Conversely, *Frank Leslie's Illustrated Newspaper*, which had long been the weekly leader in scandal, thrills, and adventure – featuring accounts of expeditions such as Kane's to the Arctic, Livingstone's to Africa, and Matthew Perry's to Japan – lost its sensational qualities and most of its widespread appeal after Leslie's widow sold it in 1889. *Frank Leslie's Popular Monthly* (founded in 1876) also suffered a large drop in circulation after it stopped concentrating on tales of adventure (Mott 1930–68: II, 452–65; III, 510–12).

American-style sensationalism also spread to Europe. On 4 October 1887 Bennett published the first number of the Paris edition of *The New York Herald*. Although this new paper was never very successful financially under his guidance, two years later he began publishing another edition in London.

W.T. Stead and the New Journalism

Even before Bennett made his entry into the English market, his influence, and that of Pulitzer, Dana, and the other proponents of sensationalism, had begun to be felt there. What the great radical editor H.W. Massingham later referred to as "the Americanization of the press" was beginning in England (Massingham 1892: 182). In fact, in 1883, the year that Pulitzer took control of *The World*, an event of equal significance occurred in British journalism: W.T. Stead became the editor of *The Pall Mall Gazette*.

Despite the efforts of Frederick Greenwood, *The Pall Mall Gazette* had never been an economic success, and in 1880 George Murray Smith passed the paper to his son-in-law, Henry Yates Thompson. The new owner wished to change the paper to a Liberal viewpoint, which led Greenwood to resign in May 1880 and to establish a competing evening paper, *The St. James's Gazette* (Scott 1952: 4). One of the first moves of his successor, John Morley, was to hire Stead, the editor of the *Northern Echo* of Darlington, as his assistant.

Stead was a liberal firebrand, a man who believed the press was "the greatest agency for influencing public opinion in the world . . . the only true lever by which Thrones and Governments could be shaken and the masses raised . . ." (quoted in Baylen 1972: 369). He made the *Northern Echo* – which in 1870 had become the first successful halfpenny morning daily in England – the noisiest advocate of social reform in the provinces, supporting the Liberal Party, compulsary universal education, equal opportunities for women, women's suffrage, collective bargaining, and Irish home rule, while inveighing passionately against gambling, immorality, the Poor Law, and trade union discrimination (Schults 1972: 1–28). Gladstone was so impressed by Stead that when he became Prime Minister he urged Morley to hire the young crusader. In August 1883 Morley became a Member of Parliament, and Stead was made the editor of *The Pall Mall Gazette*.

For the next seven years *The Pall Mall Gazette* reflected Stead's convictions that a revitalized press could shape and voice the desires and opinions of the newly enlarged and literate British electorate, and that public opinion could be utilized by the press to determine government policy and to compel the government to reverse unpopular decisions.

Before Stead could fulfill his mission, however, he needed to keep his paper alive. Despite Morley halving the price from 2*d*. in 1882, *The Pall Mall Gazette* still had a circulation of only 8,000. So Stead set about on a "revolutionary programme" to make it "vigorously alive" (Stead 1893: 152–3). First, he gave it a face-lift, introducing bold headlines, multi-line heads, crossheads, maps, and diagrams, all relatively new to the British press. He also experimented with illustrations and political cartoons.

In addition, the content changed. Eschewing traditional anonymous journalism, Stead developed the signed leader, featuring famous individuals such as Oscar Wilde, Cardinal Newman, and John Ruskin. He also published interviews, the first with W.E. Forster about the condition of the Ottoman Empire (*The Pall Mall Gazette* 31 October 1883). Ignoring those who scoffed at this technique, Stead printed 137 interviews the next year (Schults 1972: 61).

The most significant of Stead's interviews was with General Charles

George Gordon (*The Pall Mall Gazette* 9 January 1884), who had first become a popular hero in 1863 when he had suppressed the Taiping Rebellion in China. He had later served the khedive of Egypt as governor-general, first of Equatoria and then of the Sudan (1877–79), where he had helped curb the slave trade. However, he had not had an active commission for several years when, in January 1884, he came to England to resign from the army so that he could join Stanley in his work in central Africa for King Leopold II of Belgium.

The day after Stead interviewed Gordon, the headline of *The Pall Mall Gazette* blared out: CHINESE GORDON FOR THE SOUDAN. Stead insisted that Gordon should immediately be appointed governor-general with full power to crush the Mahdist uprising that had started in 1881 and to relieve the besieged Egyptian garrisons. With the backing of Reginald Brett (later Viscount Esher), an imperialist cabal in the War Office, Sir Samuel Baker, and Gordon himself, Stead followed his initial interview with almost daily commentary (Baylen 1988: 110–15). Soon virtually every London newspaper had started demanding the government avail itself of Gordon's services before he left for the Congo. At the end of January, under intense pressure, Gladstone dispatched Gordon to Khartoum.

But Stead's involvement did not end there. Throughout 1884 he carried on a campaign that first supported Gordon's erratic conduct and then helped compel the reluctant Gladstone to dispatch a relief expedition. When Khartoum fell to the Mahdists and Gordon was killed, Stead excoriated Gladstone for doing too little, too late (*The Pall Mall Gazette* 5, 7, 9, 11, 19 February 1885).

On the domestic front, Stead's investigative stories attempted to open the eyes of the British nation to moral, political, and economic injustices and inequalities. The combination of Stead's crusades and his sensational techniques led one assistant editor, Alfred Milner, to call him "a compound of Don Quixote and P.T. Barnum" (quoted in Mills 1921: 60).

Stead's most famous crusade, known as "The Maiden Tribute of Modern Babylon," was an attempt to compel an indifferent Parliament to enact the Criminal Law Amendment Bill, raising the legal age of consent for girls from 13 to 16. Stead undertook a personal investigation of child prostitution in London and published his results in a sensational series of articles (*The Pall Mall Gazette* 6–10 July 1885). He shocked his readers with revelations of the sale, purchase, and violation of children; the procurement of virgins; the international slave trade in girls; and unnatural crimes perpetrated on women. The uproar that occurred culminated with the passage of the bill (Whyte 1925: II, 159–86; Schults 1972: 128–68), and proved that *The Pall Mall Gazette* "had an influence out of all proportion to the number of copies sold" (Scott 1950: 3). However, the paper's regular circulation only increased to 12,250, despite it rocketing to more than 100,000 during the week the series actually appeared (Wadsworth 1955). The series also meant a three-month prison term for Stead, who had purchased a 13-year-old girl from her mother, simply to prove that it could be done. He had never touched the child and had turned her over directly to representatives of the Salvation Army, but he had still broken the law, and, after his sensations, the authorities were not inclined to view him favorably.

Stead considered his term in Holloway Gaol a martyr's triumph (Stead 1913). While there, he expounded more clearly than ever his theories about the power and importance of the press, writing,

> the editorial pen is a sceptre of power, compared with which the sceptre of many a monarch is but a gilded lath. . . . In a democratic age, in the midst of a population which is able to read, no position is comparable for permanent influence and far-reaching power to that of an editor. . . . In him are vested almost all the attributes of real sovereignty. (Stead 1886: 661)

Matthew Arnold attacks the New Journalism

As they had been when developed in the United States, Stead's typographical innovations, investigative reporting, and interviews were the cause of much sniping about sensationalism within the journalistic community. However, what had been a small-time gentlemanly discussion turned into a mud-slinging contest when the scholar-poet Matthew Arnold vented his feelings in *The Nineteenth Century*, at the same time coining the term "New Journalism":

> We have had opportunities of observing a new journalism which a clever and energetic man has lately invented. It has much to recommend it; it is full of ability, novelty, variety, sensation, sympathy, generous instincts; its one great fault is that it is *feather-brained*. It throws out assertions at a venture because it wishes them true; does not correct either them or itself, if they are false; and to get at the state of things as they truly are seems to feel no concern whatever. (Arnold 1887: 638; emphasis Arnold's)

Following Arnold's lead, critics of the New Journalism argued that Stead's campaigns were disturbing the fabric of Victorian society by promising the lower classes more than was constitutionally possible. They insisted his crusades were conducted in a sensationally vulgar, morally offensive manner that concentrated solely on commercialism. They charged that the New Journalism catered to the emotions, to triviality, and to public whim, while lacking persuasive political commentary.

Actually, Stead's motives were humanitarian rather than commercial. His journalism was not injurious to the working class, it was uplifting. It was read not because it was sensational but because it was radical, entertaining, and ennobling at the same time. Nevertheless, *The Pall Mall Gazette* was damned by most critics because its New Journalism resembled that of the United States, "fit only for the servants' hall . . . raw, crude and sensation-mongering" (Arnold 1888: 490). *The Times* reflected this distaste when it declared: "It is strange that a moralist, when moved to speak stern truths, should stoop to . . . the arts of fourth-rate Transatlantic journalism. In the unnatural alliance of true philanthropy and sensational journalism, the former is apt to suffer" (9 November 1885).

In his defense, Stead berated those unable to see the crusading aspect of

THE
PALL MALL GAZETTE
An Evening Newspaper and Review.

No. 6336.—Vol. XLII.　　　　MONDAY, JULY 6, 1885.　　　　Price One Penny.

"WE BID YOU BE OF HOPE."

THE Report of our Secret Commission will be read to-day with a shuddering horror that will thrill throughout the world. After this awful picture of the crimes at present committed as it were under the very ægis of the law has been fully unfolded before the eyes of the public, we need not doubt that the House of Commons will fi...d time to raise the age during which English girls are protected from inexpiable wrong. The evidence which we shall publish this week leaves no room for doubt—first, as to the reality of the crimes against which the Amendment Bill is directed, and, secondly, as to the efficacy of the protection extended by raising the age of consent. When the report is published, the case for the bill will be complete, and we do not believe that members on the eve of a general election will refuse to consider the bill protecting the daughters of the poor, which even the House of Lords has in three consecutive years declared to be imperatively necessary.

This, however, is but one, and that one of the smallest, of the considerations which justify the publication of the Report. The good it will do is manifest. These revelations, which we begin to publish to-day, cannot fail to touch the heart and rouse the conscience of the English people. Terrible as is the exposure, the very horror of it is an inspiration. It speaks not of leaden despair, but with a joyful promise of better things to come. *Wir heissen euch hoffen!* "We bid you be of hope," CARLYLE'S last message to his country, the rhythmic word with which GOETHE closes his modern psalm—that is what we have to repeat to-day, for assuredly these horrors, like others against which the conscience of mankind has revolted, are not eternal. "Am I my sister's keeper?" that paraphrase of the excuse of CAIN, will not dull the fierce smart of pain which will be felt by every decent man who learns the kind of atrocities which are being perpetrated in cool blood in the very shadow of our churches and within a stone's throw of our courts. It is a veritable slave trade that is going on around us; but, as it takes place in the heart of London, it is a scandal—an outrage on public morality—even to allude to it. We have kept silence far too long. There are a few devoted workers who have been labouring for years endeavouring to save those who might well address GORDON'S homely reproach to the "majority of us : "While you are eating and drinking and "resting on good beds, we, and those with me, are watching by night and by day"—working against this great wrong—happy, indeed, if they escaped obloquy and abuse for endeavouring to remind us of our duty. No longer will good men be able with easy conscience to join in that indignant "Hush !" by which the evil-doers have hitherto silenced every attempt to make articulate the smothered wail that rises unceasing from the woeful under-world. There is now an end to that conspiracy of silence by which, after every inquiry, " the door was each time quickly closed upon "the question, as the stone lid used to be shut down, in the "Campo Santo of Naples, upon the mass of human corpses that "lay festering beneath." That "stone lid " is raised now, never again, we may hope, to be closed until something has been done. Under the ruthless compulsion of publicity even those but indifferent honest will do more good than many of the most virtuous when the evil could be hidden out of sight.

That much may be done, we have good ground for hoping, if only because so little has hitherto been attempted. A dull despair has unnerved the hearts of those who face this monstrous evil, and good men have sorrowfully turned to other fields where their exertions might expect a better return. But the magnitude of this misery ought to lead to the redoubling, not to the benumbing of our exertions. No one can say how much suffering and wrong is irremediable until the whole of the moral and religious forces of the country are brought to bear upon it. Yet, in dealing with this subject, the forces upon which we rely in dealing with other evils are almost all paralysed. The Home, the School, the Church, the Press are silent. The law is actually accessory to crime. Parents culpably neglect even to warn their children of the existence of dangers of which many learn the first time when they have become their prey. The Press, which reports verbatim all the scabrous details of the divorce courts, recoils in pious horror from the duty of shedding a flood of light upon these dark places, which indeed are full of the habitations of cruelty. But the failure of the

Churches is, perhaps, the most conspicuous and the most complete. CHRIST'S mission was to restore man to a semblance of the Divine. The Child-Prostitute of our day is the image into which, with the tacit acquiescence of those who call themselves by His name, men have moulded the form once fashioned in the likeness of GOD.

If Chivalry is extinct and Christianity is effete, there is still another great enthusiasm to which we may with confidence appeal. The future belongs to the combined forces of Democracy and Socialism, which when united are irresistible. Divided on many points they will combine in protesting against the continued immolation of the daughters of the people as a sacrifice to the vices of the rich. Of the two, it is Socialism which will find the most powerful stimulus in this revelation of the extent to which under our present social system the wealthy are able to exercise all the worst abuses of power which disgraced the feudalism of the Middle Ages. Wealth is power, Poverty is weakness. The abuse of power leads directly to its destruction, and in all the annals of crime can there be found a more shameful abuse of the power of wealth than that by which in this nineteenth century of Christian civilization princes and dukes, and ministers and judges, and the rich of all classes, are purchasing for damnation, temporal if not eternal, the as yet uncorrupted daughters of the poor? It will be said they assent to their corruption. So did the female serfs from whom the seigneur exacted the *jus primæ noctis*. And do our wealthy think that the assent wrung by wealth from poverty to its own undoing will avert the vengeance and the doom?

If people can only be got to think seriously about this matter progress will be made in the right direction. Evils once as universal and apparently inevitable as prostitution have disappeared. Vices almost universal are now regarded with shuddering horror by the least moral of men. Slavery has gone. A slave trader is treated as *hostis humani generis.* Piracy has disappeared. Intestine war is now almost unknown. Torture has been abolished. May we not hope, therefore, that if we try to do our duty to our sisters and to ourselves, we may greatly reduce, even although we never entirely extirpate, the plague of prostitution ? For let us remember that—

　　Every hope which rises and grows broad
　　In the world's heart, by ordered impulse streams
　　From the great heart of GOD.

And if that ideal seems too blinding bright for human eyes, we can at least do much to save the innocent victims who unwillingly are swept into the maelstrom of vice. And who is there among us bearing the name of man who will dare to sit down any longer with folded hands in the presence of so great a wrong ?

THE MAIDEN TRIBUTE OF MODERN BABYLON.—I.

THE REPORT OF OUR SECRET COMMISSION.

IN ancient times, if we may believe the myths of Hellas, Athens, after a disastrous campaign, was compelled by her conqueror to send once every nine years a tribute to Crete of seven youths and seven maidens. The doomed fourteen, who were selected by lot amid the lamentations of the citizens, returned no more. The vessel that bore them to Crete unfurled black sails as the symbol of despair, and on arrival her passengers were flung into the famous Labyrinth of Dædalus, there to wander about blindly until such time as they were devoured by the Minotaur, a frightful monster, half man, half bull, the foul product of an unnatural lust. "The " labyrinth was as large as a town and had countless courts and galleries. " Those who entered it could never find their way out again. "If they "hurried from one to another of the numberless rooms looking for " the entrance door, it was all in vain. They only became more hopelessly " lost in the bewildering labyrinth, until at last they were devoured by " the Minotaur." Twice at each ninth year the Athenians paid the maiden tribute to King Minos, lamenting sorely the dire necessity of bowing to his iron law. When the third tribute came to be exacted, the distress of the city of the Violet Crown was insupportable. From the King's palace to the peasant's hamlet, everywhere were heard cries and groans and the choking sob of despair, until the whole air seemed to vibrate with the sorrow of an unutterable anguish. Then it was that the hero Theseus volunteered to be offered up among those who drew the black balls from the brazen urn of destiny, and the story of his self-sacrifice, his victory, and his triumphant return, is among the most familiar of the tales which since the childhood of the world have kindled

---

Figure 3 The first page of *The Pall Mall Gazette* on 6 July 1885, featuring the first installment of 'The Maiden Tribute of Modern Babylon' by W.T. Stead.

his New Journalism, commenting: "Sensationalism in journalism is justifiable up to the point that it is necessary to arrest the eye of the public and compel them to admit the necessity of action" (Stead 1886: 653). Although he felt no admiration for the Bennetts, whom he saw as exploiters of the public, Stead consciously emulated Greeley (Stead in *Northern Echo* 5 December 1872).

Yet the American journalist to whom Stead undoubtedly was most similar was Pulitzer, who was also one of Stead's strongest supporters and one of the most vocal opponents of the criticisms of Arnold. Pulitzer regularly attacked the hypocrisy of the British press, which consistently decried American newspapers, only to follow slavishly in their tracks:

> Matthew Arnold tells the Chicago reporters that our newspapers contain too much about the woman who married the skeleton and the woman who turned out to be a man and all that sort of thing, you know, with racy headlines. Still he says he laughs at the racy way in which these sensational and trivial things are written about. Like everybody else, Matthew buys and reads the newspapers that are racy. (*The World* 25 January 1888)

T.P. O'Connor and *The Star*

The very month that Pulitzer wrote about racy newspapers, the raciest yet – *The Star*, a four-page, half-penny, politically Radical evening paper – was founded in London. From the beginning, editor T.P. O'Connor was inspired by Stead's break with tradition. He was also influenced by Bennett, having worked for the London office of *The New York Herald*. O'Connor initially came to Bennett's personal attention for his handling of the first letter received from Stanley after the explorer left Zanzibar in search of Livingstone. Wanting to save money, O'Connor promptly mailed the letter to New York, much to the disgust of Bennett, who had wanted it cabled, regardless of cost (Fyfe 1934: 64).

O'Connor made crimes, crusades, and gossip integral parts of *The Star* and also followed Stead's lead in investigative reporting. The appearance of *The Star* also screamed of the New Journalism: it experimented with illustrations, introduced a "Stop Press" section, and was the first British paper to extend its headlines across two columns, to vary the position of its subheads rather than centering them, and to use lower-case type for its crossheads and subheads (Morison 1932: 289–91).

Unlike Stead's paper, however, *The Star*'s blatant use of the New Journalism and its adoption of American-style sensationalism, in conjunction with its price, quickly attained it a mass audience: the first day of publication brought 142,600 readers, and the first fortnight averaged more than 125,000 (Goodbody 1988: 147–8). Within a short time, it regularly proclaimed: "Largest Circulation of Any Evening Paper in the Kingdom," and, spurred by the sensational coverage of the "Jack the Ripper" murders in the autumn of 1888, its circulation climbed to more than 300,000 (O'Connor 1929: II, 257; Fyfe 1934: 172–3).

Meanwhile, Yates Thompson had become disenchanted with Stead due to the ridicule and loss of advertising suffered by *The Pall Mall Gazette* following the "Maiden Tribute." Even though none of Stead's later crusades produced such results, the tension between the two men never disappeared, and in 1888 their relationship further degenerated because of a circulation loss due to the success of *The Star* (Schults 1972: 233–49). On 1 January 1890 Stead left *The Pall Mall Gazette* to become the editor of George Newnes' new monthly *Review of Reviews*. Within three months he had bought out Newnes, and the magazine remained his primary work for more than two decades.

Despite Stead's departure from *The Pall Mall Gazette*, by 1890 he and O'Connor had changed the look of British journalism forever. Stead had introduced the New Journalism, and O'Connor had shown that it could pay on a day-to-day basis. It only remained for Alfred Harmsworth to demonstrate that even greater triumphs could be achieved by the morning papers.

The spread of the New Journalism

The success of *The Star* pushed many of the other English papers more or less reluctantly into the practices of the New Journalism. The Sunday papers did not need any encouragement. By the mid-1880s more than 51 per cent of the content of *Lloyd's Weekly Newspaper* dealt with murder, sex, and other sensational events (Berridge 1978: 256–258).

The daily that most quickly followed *The Pall Mall Gazette* and *The Star* was the halfpenny, four-page *Evening News*, which had been founded in 1881, printed on eye-catching blue paper. It later was released on yellow or green paper, but there was more to its sensationalism than its color. *The Evening News* ignored politics for gossip, crime, and sex. As Frank Harris, its editor in the early 1880s, commented: "Kissing and fighting . . . were the only things I cared for at thirteen or fourteen, and those are the themes the English public desires and enjoys today" (quoted in Wiener 1988: 54). *The Evening News* also was one of the first dailies to concentrate on sports and became the first London paper to introduce a Saturday sports edition. By 1890, having merged with *The Evening Post* to become *The Evening News & Post*, it was a direct challenger to *The Star*, and even claimed on its front page, that it "Has, Beyond All Question, the LARGEST SALE of any Evening Paper in London," a claim similar to those made by *The Star*, *The Echo*, and *The Evening Standard*.

Adventurous practices also began to filter into the morning press. In 1892 *The Morning*, founded by former Bennett employee Chester Ives, became the first London daily regularly to print news on its front page in place of the smalls, or advertisements. Even *The Times* began to adopt some of the practices of the New Journalism, such as the interview. Nevertheless, the mainstream morning papers were still distinguishable from their American counterparts, as Pulitzer noted to his English secretary:

You mustn't think that because you've written articles for the London *Times* you are competent to write for *The World*. It's a very different matter. The American people want something terse, forcible, picturesque, striking, something that will arrest their attention, enlist their sympathy, arouse their indignation, stimulate their imagination, convince their reason, awaken their conscience. . . . *The World* isn't like your *Times*, with its forty or fifty thousand educated readers. It's read by, well, say a million people a day. . . . (Ireland 1938: 55–6)

One year after he took control of *The World*, Pulitzer was given the virtually perfect story with which to elicit all of these responses from his readers. For in 1884, the American public was exposed to the most sensationalized exploration account yet.

The Lady Franklin Bay expedition

When Karl Weyprecht initially proposed the ideas that led to the International Polar Year, he planned to strip the glamour and romance from polar exploration and to concentrate exclusively on scientific matters (Barr 1985: 2–5). Thus it is one of the inconsistencies between design and result so often observed in history that of the 14 expeditions ensuing from Weyprecht's concepts the sole one about which the Anglo-American public received much information was that marked by the greatest hardship, adventure, and tragedy.

The most remote of the Arctic stations set up for the International Polar Year was at Fort Conger on the north coast of Lady Franklin Bay on north Ellesmere Island, near where Nares' *Discovery* had wintered in 1875–76. Here a US Army party of 25 men under the command of Lieutenant Adolphus W. Greely was to spend two years making scientific observations. The expedition left in June 1881 so that its outpost could be fully operational by the time measurements were to be started in 1882.

From the beginning, it should have been obvious that science was not the only purpose for the Lady Franklin Bay expedition. Although half of Greely's command were officers or non-commissioned officers – an indication that the US Army placed a great deal of importance on the expedition – none had any expert scientific training. Even the scientific leader and doctor of the expedition, Octave Pavy, appears to have been less interested in science than in the possiblity of reaching the North Pole.

Greely was by no means immune to a similar ambition. At the very least, he wanted one of his sledge parties to pass the farthest north set by Albert H. Markham in 1876. This goal was achieved in May 1882, when a party consisting of Lieutenant James B. Lockwood, Sergeant David Brainard, and the Eskimo dog driver Fred Christiansen reached 83° 24' North, besting Markham's record by nearly four minutes (Greely 1886: I, 295–350).

Despite such accomplishments, what little harmony there was on the expedition did not last long. Greely, a humorless, aloof puritan, was constantly at odds both with Lieutenant Frederick Kislingbury, who resigned his commission after a brief time at the post and then refused to work or co-operate, and with the ambitious, condescending, and jealous Pavy (Greely 1888: I, 7–8, 112–14). One winter together was bad enough, but when the supply ship that had been expected in the summer of 1882 – bringing provisions, news, and personnel to replace various members of the expedition – did not arrive, the disharmonious company had to spend another gloomy winter cut off from civilization.

In 1883 sledge parties charted the interior of Ellesmere Island and discovered the vast Agassiz Glacier, but the party sent north did not come close to the latitude of the previous year. Moreover, once again the supply ship did not arrive, and on 9 August, in two open boats and a steam launch, the expedition set off south through the pack ice of Kennedy Channel and Kane Basin.

The orders Greely had received were remarkably vague other than to direct him to leave Fort Conger if the relief ship failed to appear. Although he did not know what was being done to relieve his command, he assumed that supplies had been left for him at specific points, including Cape Sabine on south Ellesmere, and Littleton Island, off Greenland. It was an unfortunate assumption.

In 1882 a relief expedition under the command of Private William M. Beebe had been hopelessly bungled. Faced by heavy ice, Beebe had returned south after depositing only two small food caches. The next year, two ships, *Proteus* and her escort vessel *Yantic*, sailed north. However, flawed planning, contradictory orders, and the inexperience of the commanding officer, Lieutenant Ernest A. Garlington, were the recipe for another calamity. Proteus stopped at Cape Sabine where a substantial cache was to be left, but nothing was deposited before Garlington demanded the ship steam north, where he thought he saw a lead of open water. Within hours, *Proteus* was caught in the ice, was crushed, and sank. Garlington and his crew retreated south in open boats to meet *Yantic*, which unknowingly passed them in the fog. At Littleton Island, Frank Wildes, the commander of *Yantic*, learned that Garlington's party had turned south. Without depositing any supplies, he followed them, but the two parties narrowly missed each other at a series of rendevous points before being reunited a month later at Upernavik, from where they returned to the US (Schley and Soley 1885: 35–94).

Meanwhile, the Greely party slowly moved south, augmented by the supplies from a cache that had been left by Nares at Cape Hawkes in 1875. They were at the mercy of the ice, which carried them alternately south and back north again. Finally, on 29 September they reached land, only to find that Cape Sabine, which was supposed to be a peninsula, was in fact an island (Schley and Soley 1885: 9). Here, on Pim Island, they used their waning energy to build a three-foot-high hut with stone walls and a roof of the whaleboat and oars. The food was almost gone, so Greely cut the rations first to 14 ounces per man per day and then to 10. The party began to fall apart: the ravenous men, cramped into the small hut, grew quarrelsome. Joseph Elison was so badly frostbitten that his feet and hands had to be amputated. Greely realized that Pavy and Charles Henry were stealing food, but there was little he could do.

The problems caused by the lack of food were compounded by a brutally cold winter, and in January Sergeant William Cross died of starvation and scurvy. A similar fate for the rest of the party was only averted by the bagging of a small bear, a remarkable feat because that area of Ellesmere was virtually devoid of animal life. With the return of the sun in March, Sergeant George Rice started fishing for shrimp. They were no bigger than a grain of wheat, with three quarters of their bulk hard shell, and 700 were needed to produce an ounce of meat. But they were a Godsend to the starving men. In April five men, including Lockwood and Rice, died within a week. The others were sustained only by the capture of a seal.

The party continued to dwindle, existing on shreds of saxifrage, shrimp, and sealskin boots and coats. When Jacob Bender saw a caterpillar, he swallowed it whole, exclaiming, "This is too much meat to lose." Brainard, who had taken over the shrimping, was the only man able to work regularly until Pavy, in a surprising burst of energy, began to go to the lake to chop ice for water.

In May, the 14 survivors abandoned the hut when melt water made it uninhabitable, and they moved into a tent meant for no more than five. At the beginning of June, Henry, who had been caught stealing food time and again, was executed (Greely 1888: 90). The other thieves, Bender and Pavy, died shortly thereafter, Pavy apparently from an overdose of ergot, which he believed to be iron. Then, on 22 June 1884, the horror ended. The seven remaining men were discovered by a relief expedition under the command of W.S. Schley. When Greely was found under the collapsed tent, he left no doubt about the relative importance of the scientific research: "Here we are – dying – like men," he gasped. "Did what I came to do – beat the record" (Powell 1961: 298). Although Elison died shortly thereafter, the other six, including Greely and Brainard, returned home as heroes.

The sensation

The press had paid little attention to the departure of Greely in 1881 or to the failure of Beebe the next year. Garlington's failure caused great concern, however, and as Schley's expedition was readied in 1884, it received a similar amount of coverage in the American newspapers as the sending of Gordon to Khartoum. Then in July 1884, when the first message was received from Schley, all hell broke loose.

On 18 July all of the major American papers led with the rescue of Greely's party. *The New-York Times, The Chicago Daily Tribune,* and *The Washington Post* each devoted the entire first page (except for advertising columns in the last two) and at least two columns of page two to the Lady Franklin Bay expedition, but even that fell short of *The Herald*, which gave it three full pages. *The New-York Tribune* gave half of page one and two-thirds of page two to the story, a similar amount as in *The World*. The stories were virtually as long for the next two days, with reports from correspondents who accompanied the relief expedition and comments by "knowledgeable" Arctic sources, such as George Kennan, Danenhower, and Nares. Certainly no paper had an exclusive on thrilling writing or presentation. *The New-York Tribune*, *The Washington Post*, and *The Chicago Daily Tribune* each carried part of the same story word-for-word:

> The story told by Connell from his recollection of their starving experience is heartrending: how they burned the hair off their sealskin boots and coats, cut them into strips, boiled them into a stew and ate voraciously of them till the stomach rebelled, and nausea and weakness ensued in several cases. Nature gave no call for twelve, fifteen, and even eighteen days, and then hemorrhage and consequent weakness ensued, prostrating the victims for several days. The difficulty of keeping heat in the body was great. The rule of the camp was to permit no one to sleep longer than two hours. He was awakened roughly and called upon to shake himself, beat his hands, and pound his feet and restore circulation. This was found absolutely necessary to prevent torpor and possible death, the usual accompaniments of intense cold. (19 July 1884)

During the next several weeks, the expedition was reviewed intensely by the press, and prominent coverage was given to the homecomings and the funerals of its members. *The Washington Post* was typical:

> Amid the strains of mournful music and followed by sorrowing relatives and thousands of sympathizing friends the mortal remains of Sergt. William H. Cross, one of the noblest of the unfortunate victims of the Greely Arctic expedition, were yesterday borne to their final resting place in the city of his nativity. . . . The floral tributes were many and beautiful, the largest and handsomest offering being a huge white pillow resting at the foot of the casket of white flowers, the gift of the Signal Corps, of which the deceased was a member. In the center of the pillow was the floral representation of two crossed signal flags with purple outlines and white grounds, each inclosing a small square of red. . . . Among the floral offerings was the floral design of a heart composed of white flowers, on which was the touchingly suggestive word "Papa," the tribute of little Charlie, a youth of thirteen, the only child of the deceased. (11 August 1884)

The early accounts of the Greely expedition included virtually everything the American public craved: hardship, scurvy, a farthest north, a desperate retreat by boat and sledge, three winter ordeals, suicide, insanity, and death. Then *The New-York Times* broke a story with even more sensational aspects: execution and cannibalism.

For a number of days, reporters for *The New-York Times* had prowled around the docks where the rescue vessels *Thetis* and *Bear* were stationed. The resultant story appeared under the headline HORRORS OF CAPE SABINE, and not only first drew attention to the execution of Henry but stated:

> It has been published that after the game gave out early in February they lived primarily on sealskins, lichens, and shrimps. As a matter of fact, they were kept alive on human flesh. . . . The bodies were dug from their graves in the little hill, just back of the permanent camp. . . . Most of the blankets contained nothing but heaps of white bones, many of them picked clean. . . . It is reported that the

only men who escaped the knife were three or four who died of scurvy. The amputated limbs of men who afterward perished were eagerly devoured as food. (12 August 1884)

The Times followed up with even more graphic accounts, based on gossip and innuendo, and garbled and exaggerated in the telling. The response to the tale by *The Times* was varied. *The Herald*, the *Tribune*, *The Boston Daily Globe*, *The Washington Post*, and *The Chicago Daily News* gave page-one coverage to the story, but tried to play down its sensationalism and questioned its accuracy. *The Washington Post*, under the headline THE CANNIBAL CANARD, ran extensive denials (13 August 1884). *The Herald* commented, "It has been discovered that there is a basis for the charges, though the circumstances of the case are by no means so horrible or so sensational as the published story indicates" (14 August 1884).

Alternatively, the normally conservative *Chicago Daily Tribune* directly picked up the report of *The Times*, inaccurately stating, "Yet of Private Henry, who died only sixteen days before the relief party arrived, there was nothing left but skin and bones. The head had . . . been thrown into the sea to prevent identification" (14 August 1884).

But no paper was as extreme as *The World*, which, under the headline EATING DEAD COMRADES, commented about an unidentified survivor:

He would give years from his life to forget it, but, he said, that first taste, the sensation of having between his teeth the flesh of one who had been once his friend, was with him always. Waking or sleeping, he seemed to feel his lips pressing the smooth, flabby meat that must be choked down somehow if he would live. And then the inhuman, savage way of getting it! Each feeder upon such food must cut off his own shreds of flesh. No friend could be found to perform the horrible office. Every man, if he would eat, must of necessity be his own butcher. And these cannibalistic orgies, these midnight feasts, were secret. The little beaten path, worn smooth between the graveyard and the wretches' tent, told its own tale. . . . Body after body was stripped of flesh, but none of those that trod that little path dared speak of this. No man asked a question at the too common sight of a starving wretch, creeping up to the only fire at midnight, carrying in his hand a strip of flesh. As he thrusts this into the flame on the end of a pointed stick, no one of his companions says a word. And when tearing the smoking flesh with his teeth, he lies down and another of the would-be sleepers rises up and goes silently down that mysterious path, knife in hand, it is easy to guess his horrid purpose. (15 August 1884)

Predictably, the English coverage of the rescue and subsequent charges of cannibalism was considerably less sensational, although the initial story certainly was page-one news. *The Times* even gave details missing in some of the American papers:

Lieutenant Greely was just able to support himself on his hands and knees. He was dressed in fur, with a red knitted hood, which added to his haggard appearance. His long hair and beard, his wasted form and deep, sunken eyes, which shone through his glasses with increased brilliancy, and his feeble voice, which he strove to control, but which revealed his overwhelming feelings, brought moisture to the eyes of the strongest of the relief party. (19 July 1884)

The charges of cannibalism caused as wide a division in the English papers as there was in the American press. *The Manchester Guardian*, *The Daily Telegraph*, *The Illustrated London News*, and *The Daily News* dismissed the charges, with the first commenting, "A doctor who handled the bodies declares they bore no appearance of mutilation, and there was nothing to suggest that flesh had been eaten" (14 August 1884), and the last stating, "The testimony fortunately is dubious and disputable. The ravings of a delirious man are certainly not evidence" (14 August 1884).

The Sunday papers were considerably more sensational, however. The *Sunday Times*, which picked up the story directly from *The New-York Times*, commented, "It is inferred that the earlier cannibalism was more frightful than it is possible to describe . . . The body of Lieutenant Kislingbury has been exhumed, and it was found that the flesh had been cleanly stripped off" (17 August 1884).

Eventually the furor died down. Despite several exhumations, which showed that at least some of the flesh on some of the bodies had been stripped away, the American public – reminiscent of its English counterpart 30 years previously – seemed to want to believe that Greely, Schley, and the living members of the party knew nothing about cannibalism.

Recent assessments assume that there was at least some cannibalism. It was pointed out in *The New-York Times* that the flesh had been removed "by a hand skilled in dissection" (13 August 1884), and that flaps of skin had been used to conceal the neatly cut and systematic wounds. It also was later recalled that Dr Pavy, who was normally uninspired to work, had frequently gone to the lake near Cemetery Ridge to chop ice for fresh water. These facts, in conjunction with Greely's assessment that Pavy appeared to be in better condition than the others (Greely 1888: I, 85), have led some scholars to indicate that Pavy was engaged in cannibalism. Whether anyone else was involved is unknown.

One result of the Lady Franklin Bay tragedy was a renewal of protests against what *The Philadelphia Inquirer* called "the monstrous and murderous folly of so-called Arctic exploration" (15 August 1884). In an editorial reminiscent of the post-Franklin attitude in Britain, *The Washington Post* pleaded:

> And now let us, in the name of decency and humanity, have no more investigations of Arctic voyages. Let us pay all honor to the living and the dead, to the rescued and their rescuers, but may the country be spared the affliction of such investigations as we have had in the case of more than one disastrous Arctic expedition. (18 July 1884)

A week later *The Illustrated London News* captured the attitude of most of the English press when it stated:

> Why then should any more Arctic expeditions be sent out, either from England or America? The only result is much suffering, terrible loss of life, and the amendment of maps and charts which are of no general utility. Apollyons are too many and Greathearts too few for us to regard with equanimity this waste of men, money, and energy. (26 July 1884)

After the cannibalism story, the opposition to exploration grew even stronger. While accepting that the survivors had engaged in cannibalism, *The World* suggested that not only the expeditions, but the discussion of them be terminated:

> The whole country is convinced that the poor wretches constituting the Greely party were compelled to eat each other in order to subsist, and there is no further need of breaking open tombs. It is not proposed to prosecute the survivors, and no sensible people condemn the cannibalism under the circumstances. We have had enough of these sickening revelations to make Arctic exploration rather unpopular for some years. So let the matter drop. (20 August 1884)

But the matter did not drop. Explorers would not consider abandoning the Arctic. "I shall be ready to try to carry the Union Jack further north than the Stars and Stripes whenever I am wanted," stated Sir George Nares. "I regret as deeply as any can the loss of the gallant men who went with Greely . . . but battling with northern ice is like any other warfare, and some must fall" (*The Standard* 19 July 1884).

Another man who intended to continue his explorations was Frederick Schwatka, who favored privately sponsored expeditions over those of the government:

> I think polar expeditions by our Government should be stopped. Disaster is inherent in all of them. After a lot of preliminary gush by politicians and boards of this and that, an expedition is sent out under a totally inexperienced man, who is bound by instructions of a rigid character, so that he has scarcely any option in the whole affair. If military and naval men are sent they should go out under the patronage of private individuals or societies. (*The New-York Times* 17 August 1884)

To prove his belief in the private sector, Schwatka tendered his resignation to the US Army, effective 31 January 1885, and set his eyes on the north.

The spread of Arctic sponsorship

Within a year of the return of the Greely expedition, Schwatka had joined with the first newspaper to rebut the call for an end to Arctic exploration – *The New-York Times* – to show that the Arctic could still be an area of active participation for the press. The notion caught on almost immediately, as a number of dailies worked out a combination between stunting and news to create an impression of aggressive newsgathering. Sponsoring adventurous trips became a popular pastime.

Schwatka was a natural for such expeditions. He had first made a reputation as the leader of the American Geographical Society's Franklin search (1878–80). In 1883 he was sent by the War Department on a military reconnaissance of Alaska. Traveling through an area that was hardly charted, he crossed the Chilkoot Pass to a lake that he named "for James Gordon Bennett, a well-known patron of American geographical research" (Schwatka 1885a: 100). Following an overland journey of more than 2,800 miles, in which they reached the headwaters of the Yukon in Canada, Schwatka's group built a large raft and commenced a voyage of 1,829 miles to the river's mouth (Schwatka 1885b).

When Schwatka left the army, he turned to writing and that year published three books, two on his Yukon journey and one general travel account of the Arctic (1885c). He also started writing for *The New-York Times*, which, between May and November, published about a dozen articles under his byline. These dealt with various aspects of the Arctic, including the 71-degree-below-zero temperatures encountered in the Franklin search (25 May 1885), facts about the Eskimos and their lifestyles (13 July, 3, 10 August 1885), the northern lights (31 August 1885), and the planning of expeditions (8, 15 November 1885). They also showed Schwatka to be, like Gilder, not only a talented writer but a keen observer:

> One of the worst features of walking in this country was the disposition of the small clay stones, reduced oftentimes to the thinnest and razor-edged slates, and these were again and again turned on end over areas many acres in extent. Our sealskin boots were wet nearly all the time, and when they were in this condition these sharp-edged rocks left a feeling in the foot as if there was only a piece of mosquito net between the foot and the burning stones beneath. Add 60 to 75 pounds on a person's back, just enough to make them hesitate about attempting to avoid these stoney places by long detours, and some of the miseries of Summer foot marching in the Arctic, or at least this part of it, can be imagined. (23 August 1885)

The series also served as a prelude for the first expedition ever sponsored by *The New-York Times* (Berger 1951: 167–8), in which Schwatka was sent to Alaska to climb Mount Saint Elias, then thought to be the highest peak in North America. In the tradition of *The Herald*, from June to November 1886 *The Times* gave continuing page-one coverage to Schwatka's reports about what it called "THE TIMES expedition to Alaska."

On 20 September 1886 *The Times* proudly announced that Schwatka had discovered a "second Mississippi," a river "not thought to be rivaled by any Alaskan River" and named after the proprietor of *The Times*, George Jones, "in compliment to a gentleman whose relations to the expedition justly entitle him to the distinction." The next day, *The Times* indicated just how in favor of Arctic exploration it had become:

> These considerations furnish a complete answer to the suggestion that such explorations as THE TIMES has sent out under the command of Lieut. SCHWATKA are of no "practical value." This might as well have been said of the voyage of COLUMBUS. It is not until regions as remote as Alaska have been brought to the notice of the public . . . that the commercial "prospector" is stimulated to see what can be done toward developing the resources. (21 September 1886)

Throughout October and November, *The Times* published article after article by Schwatka, most of them more than half a page long. The features virtually ignored that Schwatka and his companions never reached the top of Mount Saint Elias, but they did reveal his ability to captivate an audience with sensational stories:

> When one, in the deep recesses of a dark forest, suddenly hears a terrible roar right before him that lowers the temperature of his blood about a dozen degrees, a crashing of underbrush that sounds like the breaking up of his own bones, and has a paw measuring 8 by 14 inches dropped thoughtlessly on his shoulder accompanied by a huge open mouth bristling with huge spikes of ivory that closes over the head, the sorrowing friends . . . are fully justified in attributing any amount of ferocity to such an animal. (*The New-York Times* 5 October 1886)

The series also helped establish Schwatka as one of the first mercenaries of exploration, a man who would travel anywhere, if he had sufficient financial incentive. The next year, *The World* sponsored Schwatka's attempt at the first winter crossing of Yellowstone National Park (Johnson *et al.* 1984: 12). In 1888–89, *The Chicago American* sponsored his expedition to the Sierra Madre Mountains of Mexico (Schwatka 1893). And in 1891 a consortium of more than 50 newspapers sent Schwatka back to Alaska to explore the valley of the White River and the route of the Copper River (Hayes 1892).

By this time Schwatka had become such a well-known figure that his sudden death received a full column on the front page of *The New-York Times* under the headline LIEUT. SCHWATKA IS DEAD (3 November 1892). The morning before, in Salem, Oregon, Schwatka had accidentally taken an overdose of laudanum, which he had been prescribed to relieve acute gastric pain.

In the same year that Schwatka made his attempt on Mount Saint Elias, his old companion, William Henry Gilder, started another expedition to the Arctic under the sponsorship of Bennett. Gilder's plan to travel to Greenland on whaling ships, to recruit Eskimo dog drivers, and thence to dash north was spelled out in an interview the night before he was due to leave New York:

> Lockwood could have easily gone 100 miles further, so Greely states, if he had had better sleds and good drivers. But he was directed to return as soon as his supplies were exhausted and to run no risk. I shall be hampered by no instructions, and I have experience in this kind of work, too, and I have full confidence of being able to reach a much higher latitude. . . . I would be able to add to the maps of the land to the immediate northwest [of Greenland] which is believed to exist but has never been seen. . . . I shall try to reach the Pole. (*The New York Herald* 12 July 1886)

The enterprise was a fiasco from the beginning. Due to legal complications, Gilder missed his ship. But he simply adjusted his plans and started from a different place – Winnipeg, 2,300 miles from the Pole. The expedition struggled from the outset and in January 1887, four months after leaving Winnipeg, was still bogged down just north of York Factory. Gilder finally turned south so he could regroup in New York, but once he was back in the United States, he never returned to the Arctic. Yet the expedition was not a total loss. As on his other northern journeys, Gilder

111

wrote with great insight about travel conditions, the life of the local people, and the beauty and danger of nature.

Gilder never lost his interest in the Arctic, and he continued to publish articles about the north. In 1892 the *Scottish Geographical Magazine* first mentioned his plans for an expedition to ascertain the exact position of the Magnetic North Pole, something that had not been done since 1831 (*Scottish Geographical Magazine* 1892: 445). A year later, Gilder wrote about these aims in great detail (Gilder 1893). The proposed expedition never got off the ground, however, and again Gilder did not go farther north than Canada. As had Stanley, MacGahan, James Creelman, and many other of Bennett's correspondents, Gilder ultimately tired of his cantankerous owner and left *The Herald* (*The New York Times* 6 February 1900).

In the ensuing years, the direct role of the press in exploration and adventure continued to grow. In 1887, with money donated by (among others) *The Daily Telegraph*, *The Daily News*, *The Standard*, *The Manchester Guardian*, and *The Scotsman*, Stanley was sent on a trans-Africa expedition beginning in the Congo, to rescue Emin Pasha, the governor-general of Equatoria, who was believed to have been trapped near Lake Albert by the continuing Mahdist uprising (Stanley 1890). Two years later, both Bennett and Pulitzer sent out correspondents to "find" Stanley, who had not been heard from since disappearing into the previously unexplored Ituri Forest of the northern Congo. In late November 1889, just a few miles from the coast of east Africa, both correspondents, Edward Vizetelly of *The Herald* and Thomas Stevens of *The World*, found Stanley and Emin comfortably enjoying glasses of champagne. Stevens obtained the first interview (Stevens 1890: 267–71), but Vizetelly scooped his rival by offering Stanley £2,000 for the first *published* interview, and by spending $3,500 to cable his 1,400-word story to New York (*The New York Herald* 5 December 1889; Vizetelly 1901: 445–53).

The press was even more active in the Arctic. In 1890–91 *Frank Leslie's Illustrated Newspaper* sent a five-man party – three of whom were reporters or artists – to explore the upper Yukon River. *Leslie's* did not need lessons to know how to present the story in an exciting manner. "It is not unlikely that the result will be second only to that of Stanley's explorations in Africa," it stated on 5 April 1890. To try to insure such success, it sent as executive officer and expedition artist E.J. Glave, who had worked under Stanley setting up trading stations in the Congo (Stanley 1885). Glave and one companion soon parted from the other members of the expedition and discovered the Alsek River, which they descended to the Pacific. Glave's report was published in nine parts (*Frank Leslie's Illustrated Newspaper* 15, 22, 29 November, 6, 13, 20, 27 December 1890, 3, 10 January 1891), and the explorations of the entire expedition were reported in 44 issues. Although the geographical and scientific results of the expedition were limited, the regular coverage by *Leslie's* did much to stimulate public interest in Alaska.

The *Leslie's* expedition also stimulated further interest from publishers. In 1892 the relief ship sent to give assistance to Peary's North Greenland expedition included editors and artists for three different newspapers or magazines, as well as Angelo Heilprin, a member of the sponsoring Philadelphia Academy of Natural Sciences, commissioned to write an article for *Scribner's Magazine* (Heilprin 1893). And in 1894 Walter Wellman, a Washington correspondent for *The Chicago Herald*, led an expedition to reach the North Pole from Svalbard. This was the first of five unsuccessful attempts on the North Pole for Wellman, who had come to the public's attention in 1891, when he claimed to have located the exact place where Columbus first landed in San Salvador (*The Chicago Herald* 4 July 1891).

Wellman's expedition actually did not receive a great deal of attention in the American newspapers. However, it was much maligned in the English press after news was received that its ship had been crushed by the ice near Waldenøya. The contempt of the English for Wellman is accentuated by comparing two articles from *The Standard* of 24 July 1894. One on Wellman commented, "that such a hair-brained expedition, based entirely on the placid theories of a Chicago newsman, without the least Arctic experience, should come to grief can surprise no one." The other noted with high hopes: "Mr. Pinkert, the inventor of a land and water tricycle, left Cape Grisnez yesterday morning to cross the English Channel on his machine."

The crossing of Greenland

While the English newspapers reproached Wellman, they showed considerable concern for the plight of another explorer. This man, the first European explorer to capture British hearts in nearly half a century – since Joseph René Bellot – was Fridtjof Nansen, a Norwegian.

The Nansen story had begun more than a decade before. In August 1883, the same month that Greely abandoned Fort Conger, a Swedish Arctic expedition in northwest Greenland admitted defeat and turned for home. Sponsored by Oscar Dickson and the Swedish government, it had been sent to conduct scientific studies, seek traces of Norse settlements on the east coast, and determine whether the ice cap covered all of inland Greenland. Under the leadership of Adolf Erik Nordenskiöld, the expedition accomplished its scientific goals, but was unable to cross the ice cap.

After a quarter of a century of exploration, the expedition was Nordenskiöld's last in the Arctic. But just as Sven Lovén had inspired Otto Torell, who was in turn the mentor of Nordenskiöld, when the conqueror of the Northeast Passage wrote of his attempt to cross Greenland, it helped persuade Nansen to attempt a similar venture (Kish 1973: 256).

Although Nansen had, the previous year, gone to East Greenland for his first Arctic experience, it was 1888 before Nansen was ready for his assault on the Greenland ice cap. He had, in the interim, made himself thoroughly familiar with every aspect of Arctic travel and living, become the curator of the oceanographic museum at Bergen, and submitted his doctoral thesis, one of the pioneering studies about the neuron theory (Nansen 1887).

Many explorers had attempted to cross Greenland, including Nordenskiöld, the English mountaineer Edward Whymper, and, only two years previously, a young American civil engineer on his first polar journey, Robert E. Peary. Because they all had failed, Nansen did not receive much support, and his plan was ridiculed in the press (Nansen 1890: I, 12–14). However, Augustin Gamél, a Danish philanthropist, ultimately provided the necessary funding.

Nansen's plan was in itself remarkably innovative. Instead of starting from the inhabited west coast, as had previous expeditions, his party was dropped near the sparsely populated east coast of Greenland. This not only meant that it had to cross the ice cap only once, but that there was no turning back: salvation in the form of additional supplies was only to be reached by the successful completion of the journey. Nansen's party left the sealer *Jason* by boat on 17 July 1888, and, after drifting with the ice, landed 12 days later. The six men made their way north to Umivak, from where they set out on 15 August. They reached the west coast on 26 September, built a small boat from wood and canvas, and two of them (Nansen and Otto Sverdrup) rowed to Godthåb (Nuuk), arriving on 3 October. Because the captain of the last ship back to Europe – coincidentally *Fox*, which, after McClintock's voyage had become a transport vessel for kryolite – would not sail north to pick up Nansen's companions before departing, the entire party wintered there (Nansen 1890).

Nansen's success marked the beginning of the domination of polar exploration by the Norwegians, who, during the next quarter of a century, virtually turned polar travel into an art. The essence of their success was an understanding of the Arctic and a willingness to adapt to it, to attain a oneness with the environment. Nansen and his fellow Norwegians started a step ahead of the British, Dutch, Austrian, and American explorers because, as Ludvig Schmelck wrote in an article in the Christiania (Oslo) newspaper *Morgenbladet*: "Norway lies closer to the Polar Regions than any other country. . . . If a Norwegian North Pole expedition were to be organised, we could provide an elite corps of experienced and tough men, used to travel in ice and snow, on ski or snowshoes" (*Morgenbladet* 12 December 1888). But the Norwegians had more of an advantage than just their vast experiences in Arctic travel and living. They were not limited in outlook by nationalist superiority as were Britain or the US. From their very entrance into the Arctic, the Norwegians respected the native peoples of the north. The Lapps, the Greenlanders, the Chukchi, and the North American Eskimos all had superior knowledge and experience in Arctic travel, and the Norwegian explorers were willing to learn from them. An example occurred that winter in Godthåb where Nansen and Sverdrup spent their time learning the techniques of Eskimo travel and living (Nansen 1890, 1894).

Nansen's crossing of Greenland galvanized the Norwegian school of exploration. His most conspicuous achievement was the application of skis to polar exploration. Nordenskiöld had already introduced skis on Arctic expeditions, but, when crossing Greenland, Nansen gave the first proof that they would function at the altitude and under the conditions of the

Greenland ice cap. He also improved on Nordenskiöld's techniques by using waxless telemark skis, innovative steel edges, advanced bindings with a heel grip rather than just a toe hold, and a new type of skiing that has since become known as the telemark style. Moreover, while wintering in Godthåb, Nansen first realized that a man skiing at the correct pace goes the same speed as dogs pulling a sledge. The technique of driving a sledge while skiing next to it was later used for the first time by Nansen and then improved upon by Sverdrup (Nansen 1897; Sverdrup 1904).

Nansen also broke new ground elsewhere. He replaced the traditional, heavy, narrow-runnered sledge with a prototype of the modern one – lighter, flexible, and running on skis. He personally designed special clothing, tents, sleeping bags, and cooking equipment, including the "Nansen cooker," a saucepan that conserved heat and fuel. He was one of the first people to apply scientific principles to the calculation of the dietary needs of expedition members. He popularized what came to be called the "sportsman's method" of Arctic exploration. This meant that whereas most previous expeditions had featured a large number of participants, working in a clumsy and frequently inefficient manner, Nansen selected a small, trained, paid party able to achieve the greatest possible degree of physical stamina and to keep pace with each other (Huntford 1980: 24–6). Nansen also was the first polar explorer to recognize the psychological implications of groups, and he attempted to select a group that was mentally and emotionally compatible.

When Nansen returned to Europe in 1889, he found that he had become a celebrity. The news of his success, sent in a letter with the captain of *Fox*, made him a figure of enormous proportion, even in England. *The Pall Mall Gazette* was particularly partial to Nansen, giving front-page coverage to his expedition on 10 November 1888, the same day that the major story – covering virtually the first two and a half pages of the paper – was about the eighth of the "Jack the Ripper" murders. Two days later, Stead's paper described Nansen in tones one would expect to hear applied to a beauty contest:

> Dr. Nansen, who has just crossed Greenland in snow shoes, is about twenty-seven years of age, and considerably over six feet in height. He is a 'hardy Norseman' every inch of him. He has a magnificent breadth of chest, and a well-proportioned figure, which shows to advantage in his tight-fitting blue woollen suit. His face is long, his brow broad; his eyes are blue, and his moustache and closely cropped hair fair in colour. (12 November 1888)

One might accuse *The Pall Mall Gazette* of sycophancy were it not for the fact that most of the major newspapers were equally enraptured with the young explorer: "Throughout the length and breadth of his country, Dr. Nansen has long been recognized as a man of singular strength, daring, intellect, and grace. Now he has added achievement to that already impressive list" (*The Standard* 14 November 1888). "His tall and well built figure, with the Norse head and fair hair, was easily discernible in the midst of any crowd" (*The Manchester Guardian* 26 May 1889). "Dr. Nansen and his companions have, in short, performed a feat which renders them worthy descendants of their Viking forefathers" (*The Times* 25 May 1889).

115

Conversely, Nansen did not receive such praise in the US. This was in part because his achievements coincided with the making of a great American hero – Robert E. Peary. Peary had first come to national attention in 1887 when *The New-York Times* and *The New York Herald* had followed his progress as second-in-command, or sub-chief engineer, of the project responsible for the survey of the course of the proposed canal to be cut through Nicaragua.

It was two years previously, however, that Peary had first turned his attention to the north: "My interest in Arctic work dates back to 1885, when as a young man my imagination was stirred by reading accounts of explorations by Nordenskjold [*sic*] in the interior of Greenland" (Peary 1910a: 25). In 1886 Peary had attempted to cross Greenland, reaching a point some 100 miles inland (Peary 1898). His lack of success had been followed by a lack of interest from potential future sponsors, and he had taken the position in Nicaragua. But in 1888, with the irrational feeling that Nansen had stolen both his route and his glory, he decided to return north: "This forestalling of my work was a serious blow to me . . . and I could only fall back upon the other northern route" (Peary 1898: xxxvii).

That northern route across Greenland, and the exploration of the north-western parts of the island, occupied Peary for the next decade, before his explorations turned even farther north. In 1891–92, sponsored primarily by the Philadelphia Academy of Natural Sciences and the American Geographical Society, but also with financing from *The New York Herald* (which sent along reporter A.C. Kenealy for the first part of the expedition), Peary and a party of seven, including his wife Jo, overwintered in northern Greenland (Peary 1893). Between May and August 1892, Peary and Eivind Astrup crossed to the previously unexplored northeast coast of Greenland and discovered Independence Fjord. The journey made Peary's reputation, despite the fact that one member of the expedition, John Verhoeff, disappeared while on a geological survey. The papers were effusive in their praise of the new hero and quite willing to overlook the tragedy accompanying the expedition:

> Rarely has so distinguished a success in poleward exploration been accomplished with so little cost in money, exertion, and suffering, so that the skillful explorer may well try once more the method of arctic travel, of which he has become the most conspicuous master. . . . The fate of young VERHOEFF, whatever it may be, is really not chargeable to the expedition. (*The New-York Times* 26 September 1892)

Once again, it was *The Herald* that made the most of the story, including publishing Mrs Peary's exclusive accounts (13–16 September 1892). *The Herald* also ran other stories about the expedition, one of which commented: "Lieutenant Peary has done in a magnificent manner what he proposed to do and has made the most remarkable journey on the inland ice, far excelling the work of Nansen and his predecessors in that direction" (13 September 1892).

Two months later, however, even *The Herald*, which had steadfastly ignored Nansen for four years, carried a news item about him. He had

presented to the Royal Geographical Society an audacious and controversial enterprise – a drift across the polar basin. The idea had first
occurred to Nansen eight years before, when he read that wreckage from
Jeannette had been found near Julianehåb (Qaqortoq) on the southwest
coast of Greenland, where it had apparently drifted with a polar current.
Nansen immediately saw the possibility of using the current to carry him
to, or at least near, the North Pole, and he explained to both the international polar community and the general public his intention to build a
ship designed so that it could not be crushed by the ice and then intentionally to enter the ice-pack for a ride north (Nansen 1893a, 1893b).

A number of Arctic experts were skeptical of Nansen's ideas (Greely
1894; Nansen 1897: I, 41–53), but most of the English press sprang to his
defense. *The Times* commented, "Of all the Arctic explorers of our day,
none has shown greater daring and originality than this young Norwegian,
whose views and methods have always been his own" (15 November 1892),
and unyieldingly took his side against the argument of Nares that the
primary dictates of Arctic exploration were to keep as close to civilization
as possible and to insure a line of retreat:

> DR. NANSEN would probably answer that those axioms are inconsistent with
> the only method that, in his belief, can be followed with any prospect of success.
> So he treats the Polar regions as STANLEY and LIVINGSTONE treated the
> Dark Continent; he means to plunge in . . . and trust to PROVIDENCE and
> pluck to bring him through. Twenty years ago the dangers and uncertainties of
> traversing Africa were thought to be as great as those which DR. NANSEN is
> now about to encounter; we trust that he may live to see a time when a trip down
> the Polar currents will be thought as ordinary an achievement as we now think a
> journey along the shores of the Zambesi. (15 November 1892)

Not only did most of the English papers that had not previously been
pro-Nansen support his new plan (for example, *The Echo* 15 November
1892), even the American press wrote admiringly (*The New-York Times* 13
November 1892; *The Sun* 15 November 1892).

But, as usual, the strongest support came from *The Pall Mall Gazette*,
now under the editorship of E.T. Cook. A story entitled A CHAT WITH
DR. NANSEN and covering much of pages one and two, showed Nansen
as both romantic and realist. When asked what was most vivid when he
thought about the Arctic, Nansen replied:

> I think of the Arctic summer rain. I think of the sunshine, reflected from
> mountains of snow and ice, shining upon little lakes of clear, rippling water,
> where hundreds of seals playfully splash the water into glistening sprays of
> rainbow hues. What is the charm of the Arctic? Health, glorious health! Your
> muscles twitch with a desire for action. You eat like a horse, and sleep twelve or
> fourteen hours without a dream. Before you is the vast unknown: all around you
> is silence and solitude. . . . In winter the scene is almost as beautiful as in
> summer. The nights are clear, the moon and stars shine brightly upon the sea of
> soft white snow. (17 November 1892)

But when asked how long he would be away, Nansen replied: "I really
cannot say. Perhaps six years, perhaps only two years. We ram ourselves

into the ice, and there we stay and drift with the current at the rate of about two miles in every twenty-four hours, until we reach the open sea."

"But, Doctor," the reporter asked, "suppose you find it impossible to proceed?"

"Then, sir, we shall stay."

Plate 1 The RGS outing during the 'Burton–Speke' meeting of the British Association in Bath, 1864, included David Livingstone (1813–1873), left of center, wearing his famous cap, and Sir Roderick Murchison (1792–1871), in the white suit. (Royal Geographical Society, London)

Plate 2 James Gordon Bennett, Jr (1841–1918): the proprietor of *The New York Herald* for half a century, he not only sponsored many exploring expeditions, but also developed and popularized the now-common technique of creating news. *(The International Herald Tribune)*

Plate 3 Henry Morton Stanley (1841–1904): journalist, explorer, and imperialist, he was both honored and loathed in the United States and Britain. He is shown here with his famous 'Stanley cap.' (Royal Geographical Society)

Plate 4 William Henry Gilder (1838–1900): *The New York Herald's* star Arctic correspondent, he also explored in southeast Asia. (Dartmouth College Library)

Plate 5 Joseph Pulitzer (1847–1911): the proprietor of *The World* (New York) and the *St. Louis Post-Dispatch*, he developed a unique blend of sensationalism and idealism (Portrait by John Singer Sargent; Private Collection)

Plate 6 W. T. Stead (1849–1912): as editor of *The Pall Mall Gazette*, he first showed that American-style sensationalism and crusading could be successful in Britain.

Plate 7 Adolphus W. Greely (1844–1935): the leader and one of the survivors of the infamous Lady Franklin Bay Expedition during the International Polar Year.

Plate 8 Frederick Schwatka (1849–1892): one of the first mercenaries of exploration, his destination included Canada, Alaska, Mexico, and the American southwest.

Plate 9 Fridtjof Nansen (1861–1930): undoubtedly the most creative and respected nineteenth-century explorer, he also was a remarkable scientist, diplomat, and humanitarian.

Plate 10 Alfred Harmsworth, Viscount Northcliffe (1865–1922): perhaps the greatest British press baron, he was the founder of the *Daily Mail* and the *Daily Mirror,* and one-time owner of *The Times, The Observer, The Evening News*, and many other newspapers.

Plate 11 Otto Sverdrup (1854–1930) added more land to the map than any other nineteenth-century explorer, including Axel Heiberg, Amund Ringnes, and Ellef Ringnes islands.

Plate 12 *(left)* Frederick A. Cook (1865–1940): his claims to have climbed Mt. McKinley in 1906 and to have attained the North Pole in 1908 were later widely dismissed as hoaxes.

Plate 13 Roald Amundsen (1872–1928): the most accomplished of modern explorers, including being the first to sail the Northwest Passage, the first to reach the South Pole, the first to fly across the Arctic Basin, and, perhaps, the first to attain the North Pole.

Plate 14 Robert E. Peary (1856–1920): his long and remarkable career in the north culminated in his since-disputed claims to have attained the North Pole in 1909.

7

Exploration: tool and weapon of the press

One of the most significant contributions to the growth of sensationalism in the press of both the United States and England was the success of rapid transit systems in large cities. The adoption of these systems in the late 1870s, the 1880s, and the 1890s meant that people began to read newspapers in commuter trains rather than in the comfort of their own homes (Juergens 1966: 39). Many newspapers responded by developing a smaller format because, as *The Journalist* explained: "We, as a people . . . do not want a paper which requires a whole conveyance in which to turn its pages" (5 November 1887).

Simultaneously, the new transportation encouraged metropolitan newspapers to emphasize shorter, livelier stories with bolder headlines and larger type (although in England this was initially reflected primarily in the evening press). Readers who bought their papers from a newsagent five or six days per week were more likely than subscribers to be attracted to a front page that had exciting, startling, or shocking articles, and editors competed to catch the eyes of these readers in the split second it took to make a decision about which paper to purchase. In fact, the front page would probably never have replaced page one were it not that daily sales to a great extent replaced annual subscriptions (Hughes 1981: 31).

One result of this desire for sensational, and therefore saleable, stories was a proliferation in the three decades after the Civil War of those newspapers traditionally considered sensational. The same period, particularly between the mid-1880s and mid-1890s, also witnessed a stage at which many newspapers before and since considered as part of the quality press – such as *The New-York Times* – began unreservedly to engage in sensational journalism. In fact, many of these supposedly quality papers outdid their competitors in their sensationalism.

During this era, exploration was one of the topics that became most sensationalized. But how did the press make a sensational story of exploration? There were two basic parts of any such story: the headline and the article itself, because illustration or photography did not play a major role in most daily newspapers until the 1890s.

Headlines

Headlines are perhaps the most important part of a newspaper, not only because they have the highest readership (Mårdh 1980: 11), but because, in conjunction with lead paragraphs, they give the reader a large amount of the information contained in most stories.

In actual form, the major American newspapers made few significant departures from established headline typography between 1865 and the mid-1880s. Rather than using streamer or banner heads to report items of special interest – as had been common during the Civil War – papers simply added more decks to a one-column headline. Thus, *The Herald*'s story about the assassination of President Abraham Lincoln was accompanied by a headline with 25 decks (16 April 1865), Stanley's meeting with Livingstone had 20 decks (10 August 1872), Melville finding the bodies of De Long's party had 16 (6 May 1882), and the death of Vice President Henry Wilson had 10 (23 November 1875). During the same period, headlines in England – even those accompanying major stories – generally remained small and sedate.

Throughout most of the 1880s basic American headline typography was just as conservative as in the preceding years. Although *The Herald* continued to use multiple-deck headlines, with each deck being one or at most two lines, the majority of newspapers limited themselves to main – or display – headlines with two subheads, the second of which was three to five lines finishing with hanging indentation. It was not until 1889 that the first double-column headline appeared in *The World* (Juergens 1966: 27), and most of the other newspapers did not adopt the technique until well into the 1890s.

The typograpical look of the English evening press slowly followed that of the US. In 1888 *The Star* adopted an entirely new method (for Britain) of displaying its heads, using upper- and lower-case letters, not engaging in centering, and adopting lengthy subheads with hanging indentations (Morison 1932: 291). In 1892 these Americanizations were brought to the morning press by *The Morning*, which, however, failed because, as Kennedy Jones wrote, "what was wrong with Chester Ives's venture was its appearance. It did not look like a morning paper" (Jones 1919: 124).

The wording of headlines played a considerably larger part in the sensational package. As in other areas, *The New York Herald* introduced many of the techniques of headline writing that later became standard throughout the American newspaper business. One such technique was the emphasis on adventure in far-away places. Decks such as "Voyage upon Victoria Niyanza" (18 October 1875) or "Discovers New Islands Above the Arctic Circle" (2 May 1882) proudly proclaimed the successes of the Bennett-backed ventures.

But *The Herald* did not just concentrate on the expeditions sponsored by its proprietor; it gave special attention to a wide range of foreign news and features. Thus, it was not unusual to see a headline such as RUSSIA IN CENTRAL ASIA, with the accompanying decks "How the Valley of the Oxus is To Be Made Populous" and "A Water Way to Afghanistan" (14 July 1879), or the headline UNKNOWN ICELAND, with decks reading "The Terrible Hrafra Gja" and "The Dreary Desolation of the Lava Lands" (7 September 1874).

The Herald's editors understood that the recalling of historical tragedy could stir emotions, so such events were referred to at every opportunity. Thus, an account about the *Pandora* expedition featured the deck "Remains of the Franklin Expedition" (31 October 1875), even though King William Island was not actually reached. And one of Gilder's features about the Schwatka expedition included the deck "Last Survivors of the Erebus and Terror" (24 September 1880). In its decks *The Herald* also frequently used "buzzwords" such as death, battle, or escape: "The Lesson of his Death" for a feature about De Long (8 May 1882); "Explorers and Eskimaux in Line of Battle" with Gilder's tale of meeting hostile Eskimos (24 September 1880); and "Narrow Escape from an Iceberg which Capsizes in the Night" with MacGahan's account of the return of *Pandora* (31 October 1875).

The Herald also developed techniques to lend color to headlines that might otherwise have been rather dull. One method was to select an aspect of the article that meant nothing by itself – nor indeed did it have to relate a great deal to the main thrust of the story – but was irresistible to the reader. On 2 October 1880, for instance, after more than a week of articles by Gilder about the Schwatka expedition, *The Herald* printed a feature about the expedition members' adoption of the Eskimo life-style. Concerned that the story would not interest the audience because of oversaturation of the subject, the editor gave it the headline THE ARCTIC COW, taking advantage of a colorful and unusual phrase to intrigue the readers, despite being able to relate only one sentence of the article to the headline: "The seal was our beef and the walrus our mutton in this long journey."

Headlines jumped from being virtually unrelated to a feature to emphasizing its most grisly details. Thus, *The Herald* announced: PAYNE'S BRUTALITY, with a subhead "Battering a Fellow Workman to Death to Please His Wife" (12 July 1879), and HER LIFE BLOOD FLOWING, with a subhead "A Woman Afflicted with Melancholia Opens Her Veins in a Bathroom" (2 July 1884).

Other newspapers followed the lead of *The Herald* in the use of sensational headlines. One of the masters of the technique, Joseph Pulitzer, was already refining his skills at the *St. Louis Post-Dispatch*. Pulitzer imitated Bennett's coverage of foreign news, carrying the story of the British bombardment of Alexandria under the headline: IN FLAMES, with decks "The City of Alexandria Given Over to Pillage," "A Night of Horror and a Fight for Life," and "Massacre of Europeans by the Alexandrians" (*St. Louis Post-Dispatch* 13 July 1882).

But Pulitzer's major efforts in sensationalism at the *Post-Dispatch* were more of the kind that Bennett Sr had specialized in. He attracted his audience by pandering to gossip and salacious tastes. Rammelkamp (1967: 167) has pointed out that in the period from 25 June to 4 July 1883 the main headlines on page one of the *Post-Dispatch* included: LOVED THE COOK, A RIOT IN CHURCH, A WILY WIDOW, KISSING IN CHURCH, AN ADVENTURESS, DEACONS DISAGREE, and MY DAUGHTER.

The concept of what was important to the press can perhaps best be determined by comparing a sample of headlines from two papers among the more sensational – *The New York Herald* and the *St. Louis Post-Dispatch* – and two among those reputedly less so – *The New-York Times* and the *New-York Tribune*. The following are what each newspaper ran as the leading daily stories, with its main decks, during the week in July 1879 when *Jeannette* left for the Arctic:

Monday, 7 July

THE NEW YORK HERALD
LIBERIA'S FUTURE
The Fate that Awaits a Colony
  Established by the People of
  This Country
How the British Browbeat the
  Negroes

THE NEW-YORK TIMES
WHAT ONE MAN HAS DONE
The Life and Reminiscences of
  Peter Cooper

ST. LOUIS POST-DISPATCH
HE SHOT TO KILL
Wm. C. Reeves Puts Five Bullets
  Through His Wife,
And Then Tries to Blow Out His
  Own Brains

NEW-YORK TRIBUNE
MR. SEYMOUR BURIED
His Murderer Undiscovered
Theories and Conjectures of the
  Police and Others

Tuesday, 8 July

THE NEW YORK HERALD
A MEXICAN HANGED
How the Honest Farmer Was
  Overhauled and Slain
Texas Rangers Capture the
  Assassins Across the Border

THE NEW-YORK TIMES
DEMOCRATS FOR
  GOVERNOR
Robinson or Dorsheimer to be the
  Candidate

ST. LOUIS POST-DISPATCH
AN INSANE ACT
The Deadly Assault of Reeves on
  His Young Wife
A Rambling Interview With the
  Prisoner

NEW-YORK TRIBUNE
THE SEYMOUR HOMICIDE
The Work of the Police
The Officers Still Undecided as to
  Whether the Shooting Was
  Accidental or with Murderous
  Intent

Wednesday, 9 July

THE NEW YORK HERALD
OFF TO THE POLE
Departure of the Steamer
  Jeannette from San Francisco
Ten Thousand People Cheer the
  Gallant Explorers

THE NEW-YORK TIMES
REJECTING ALL REPORTS
The Aldermen and the Rapid
  Transit Commissioners

ST. LOUIS POST-DISPATCH
THE DEATH DROP
Frank Davidson Hanged at
  Warrensburg, Mo.
Ten Thousand People Witness the
  Execution
The Doomed Man Meets His Fate
  Calmly

NEW-YORK TRIBUNE
VANDERBILT CHECKMATED
Rapid Transit Scheme Defeated

Thursday, 10 July

THE NEW YORK HERALD
THE JEANNETTE'S MISSION
Scientists Deeply Interested in the
  Hazardous Enterprise

THE NEW-YORK TIMES
RACES ON LAKE SARATOGA
The First Day of the Regatta

ST. LOUIS POST-DISPATCH
FLEEING FOR LIFE
The Citizens of Memphis
  Stampeded by Yellow Fever
Trains Crowded With Panic-
  Striken People Trying to Get
  Away

NEW-YORK TRIBUNE
STEAM ON FOURTH AVENUE
Signs of Life in the Scheme

Friday, 11 July

THE NEW YORK HERALD
ACROSS AFRICA
A Story of Dangers and Hair-
  breadth Escapes
African Problems Solved
A Race of White Africans

THE NEW-YORK TIMES
YELLOW FEVER IN MEMPHIS
A Panic Caused by a Few Cases

ST. LOUIS POST-DISPATCH
DASHED TO DEATH
Eight Persons Blown Into Eternity
  at Bodie, Cal.
And Forty Others More or Less
  Seriously Injured

NEW-YORK TRIBUNE
BEACONSFIELD'S EXPLOITS
Defying Parliament Again

Saturday, 12 July

THE NEW YORK HERALD
COLORED CULPRITS
How Williams Murdered the
    Young Telegraph Operator

THE NEW-YORK TIMES
EX-GOVERNOR ALLEN
    DEAD
Dying Suddenly at His Home in
    Chillicothe

ST. LOUIS POST-DISPATCH
A MONK'S DISGRACE
Sentenced to the Penitentiary for
    Five Years for Forgery
He Asks to be Let Loose in Order
    that He May Become a Hermit

NEW-YORK TRIBUNE
THE YELLOW FEVER ALARM
No New Cases in Memphis

The headlines show that the four papers had different concepts of the important news of the day, or at least of what would sell a newspaper. Yet there was a certain amount of agreement. *The Times*, the *Tribune*, and the *Post-Dispatch* each made the outbreak of yellow fever in Memphis the lead story once, and each printed other features about it, as did *The Herald*.

The papers agreed to a similar extent about which foreign stories to publish. Although *The Herald* gave greater emphasis to foreign events than its competitors, on the same day that its major feature was Aleixandre Serpa Pinto's trans-Africa journey that started at Benguela, crossed the mountains to the Zambezi valley, and continued to the east coast in Natal, *The New-York Times* published one and a half columns on page two (picked up directly from *The Standard*) about the same expedition. The headline was similar to that of *The Herald*: ADVENTURES IN AFRICA (*The New-York Times* 11 July 1879).

By the mid-1880s, when Pulitzer's *World* challenged *The Herald* for America's leadership in circulation, the differences between the the the newspapers that were admittedly sensational and those that were considered part of the quality press were at times even less distinct. Throughout the US, editors built on the headline techniques that Bennett had developed in his early years. Words or concepts with distinct emotive power were used as frequently as possible: FROM THE JAWS OF DEATH (*The Chicago Daily Tribune* 18 July 1884); PROOF FROM THE GRAVE (*The New-York Times* 20 August 1884); and FROZEN AND STARVED (*The Chicago Daily News* July 1884).

Another technique was the question headline. After *The New-York Times'* charges of cannibalism on Greely's expedition, *The Herald* asked IS IT TRUE? (13 August 1884) and WERE THEY CANNIBALS? (14 August 1884). The same technique was used in *The World*'s account of the exhumation of Kislingbury: DID HE EAT OF THE DEAD? (16 August 1884); in *The Sun*'s coverage of the Wellman expedition: IS EXPLORER WELLMAN ALIVE?; and by at least two newspapers reporting that the leader of Stanley's "Rear Column" in the Congo, Major Edmund Barttelot, had been killed: WAS BARTTELOT BETRAYED? (*The Boston Daily Globe*) and IS STANLEY DEAD? (*New York Morning Journal*).

A comparison of the supposedly quality press – for example, *The New-York Times*, the *New-York Tribune*, and *The Chicago Daily Tribune* – and the reputedly sensational papers – such as *The New York Herald*, *The World*, and *The Washington Post* – shows the difficulty in differentiating between them. Consider what each ran as its main story during the four days in August 1884 when the charges of cannibalism were first leveled at the Greely party:

Tuesday, 12 August

THE NEW-YORK TIMES
HORRORS OF CAPE SABINE
Terrible Story of Greely's Dreary Camp
Brave Men, Crazed By Starvation and Bitter Cold, Feeding on the Dead Bodies of Their Comrades – How Private Charles Henry Died – The Awful Results of an Official Blunder

NEW-YORK TRIBUNE
THE WALL-ST. BANK CLOSED
A Cashier Who Speculated John P. Dickinson Missing – The Deficiency Perhaps $500,000

THE CHICAGO TRIBUNE
ANOTHER BANK CRASH
Wall Street Bank of New York Closed Its Doors Yesterday
Cashier John Dickinson Charged With Irregularities – Speedy Resumption Probable

THE NEW YORK HERALD
THE EARTHQUAKE
What Made It? – Where Did It Come From? Will It Come Back?
Views of Scientists
Cooling the Earth's Interior Contracts the Earth's Crust

THE WORLD
CASHIER DICKINSON'S TURN
The Wall Street Bank Forced to Suspend on His Account
His Stock Speculations Cause a Deficiency of Between $200,000 and $300,000 –
He Departs From His Summer Residence and "Goes to the Mountains" – Promises that Only the Directors will Suffer

THE WASHINGTON POST
OVER A CENTURY OLD
Chloe Ashby Dies in this City at the Age of 116 years
An Aged Virginian Cook Whose Dinners Were Enjoyed by Gen. Washington – Her Interesting History – All Her Faculties Preserved to Day of Death

Wednesday, 13 August

THE NEW-YORK TIMES
THE SHAME OF THE NATION
Dreadful Sufferings in the Camp at Cape Sabine
Further Facts about the Ghastly Prison in the Arctic Seas – The Seamen of the Relief Party Awestricken by What They Saw and Heard – How Did Dr. Pavy Die? – Talk on the Ship's Decks Yesterday

NEW-YORK TRIBUNE
DICKINSON'S DEFALCATION
The Amount Said to be Under $300,000
Will the Stockholders Save Anything? – Nothing Known of the Fugitive Cashier

THE CHICAGO TRIBUNE
ARCTIC HORRORS
Officers of the Greely Relief Squadron Extremely Guarded in Their Language
Hints from the Seamen As to the Nature of the Horrible Secret

THE NEW YORK HERALD
IS IT TRUE?
Official Utterances on the Latest Greely Story
Secretary Chandler, General Hazen and Others Do Not Deny the Charges

THE WORLD
GREELY'S STARVING BAND
Hunger Said to Have Driven the Men to Cannibalism
The Bodies of the Dead Said to Have Been Mutilated by Men Made Insane by Want – The Tragic Death of Henry – Commander Schley's Denial

THE WASHINGTON POST
THE CANNIBAL CANARD
Something New and Sensational in the Line of Arctic Horrors
A Report that the Greely Survivors Subsisted Upon the Flesh of their Dead Comrades

Thursday, 14 August

THE NEW-YORK TIMES
THE VICTIMS OF A BLUNDER
More Light on the Dreadful Story of Greely's Camp
Henry's Coffin Filled by What is Scarcely More than a Dummy – What Became of the Doctor's Body – The Story of the German Soldier's Crime and Death Told by Lieut. Greely

THE NEW YORK HERALD
WERE THEY CANNIBALS?
Lieutenant Greely's and General Hazen's Statements
An Exaggerated Story
Private Henry Shot for Stealing His Comrades' Provisions

NEW-YORK TRIBUNE
RUINED FOR HIS SON'S SAKE
A Manufacturer's Failure and
  Flight
Henry Hall, Sr., Believed to be
  Insane – The Liabilities Between
  $100,000 and $150,000

THE CHICAGO TRIBUNE
ARCTIC SECRETS
Private Charles B. Henry Shot by
  Order of Lieut. Greely for
  Stealing Food
Seamen of the Relief Fleet
  Anxious to Tell All They Know
  but Dare Not

THE WORLD
CLAMORING FOR HIS BLOOD
Henry Shot in the Arctic for
  Stealing the Last of the Food
Greely Twices Saves His Life from
  the Men Whose Lives He was
  Throwing Away – The Brave
  Commander's Tragic Story of
  the Execution by Two of the
  Imperilled Men – Henry Never
  Seen Again

THE WASHINGTON POST
THE HENRY EXECUTION
Lieut. Greely's Statement of the
  Causes that Necessitated It
A Case Where the Most Rigid
  Military Discipline was
  Necessary – The Manner of the
  Man's Death – All Reports of
  Cannibalism Indignantly Denied

Friday, 15 August

THE NEW-YORK TIMES
CRAZED BY STARVATION
Another Chapter in the Awful
  Story of Cape Sabine
A Ghastly Scene in the Chapel of
  Mount Hope Cemetary in
  Rochester – The Remains Weigh
  "About 50 Pounds" – The Skin
  and Most of the Flesh Removed
  From the Gallant Officer's
  Frame – His Friends Agitated
  and Angry with the Authorities
  Who Tried to Conceal the Truth

NEW-YORK TRIBUNE
GEN. LOGAN TO SOLDIERS
Addressing Grand Army Posts
An Enthusiastic Gathering at
  Watertown – Recollections of
  the War

THE NEW-YORK HERALD
DISTRESSING REVELATIONS
Lieutenant Kislingbury's Body
  Found to Have Been Mutilated
Testimony From the Tomb
Official Report of the Execution of
  Private Henry

THE WORLD
EATING DEAD COMRADES
The Flesh of Lieut. Kislingbury's
  Body Hacked Off With Knives
Ghastly Story Told by the Naked
  Bones – The Body Taken From
  Its Grave and Examined by
  Physicians – The Terrible Sight
  Revealed to the Dead Soldier's
  Brothers – Were the Weak
  Starved and Slain by the Strong?

THE CHICAGO TRIBUNE
MR BLAINE'S REPLY
To the Abominable Slanders
Circulated by the Bourbons
Regarding Him
A Suit for Heavy Damages
Brought Against the
Indianapolis "Sentinel"

THE WASHINGTON POST
GREELY'S WELCOME HOME
An Ovation Extended to Him by
His Fellow-Citizens at
Newburyport
Further Revelations from the Dead
– An Examination that Discloses
a Ghastly Proof of the Charges
of Cannibalism

With the exception of those from the *New-York Tribune*, one cannot determine from these headlines which newspapers were supposedly sensational and which not. The headlines in *The New-York Times* testify to an exploitation of the sensational aspects of the story far more than do those of *The Herald* or *The Washington Post*, both of which initially presented the report as unsubstantiated. It is also apparent that *The World* printed the most sensational headlines, proving that even Pulitzer concentrated on events in remote places if they promised sales.

During these same decades, the content of most English headlines, including those about exploration, remained uninspired. Those in the evening papers such as CAPTAIN LUGARD'S JOURNEY (*The Echo* 4 November 1892), ACROSS GREENLAND ON SNOW SHOES (*The Pall Mall Gazette* 10 November 1892), and NORTHWARD HO! (*The Evening News and Post* 4 July 1894) were thrilling only by comparison to their morning counterparts: THE GREELY EXPEDITION (*The Manchester Guardian* 14 August 1884), DR. FRIDTJOF NANSEN'S JOURNEY (*The Times* 25 May 1889), and THE WELLMAN EXPEDITION (*The Standard* 6 August 1894).

Article content

A comparison of article content likewise indicates that there was not necessarily a well-defined distinction between the sensational and quality press. *The New-York Times* not only challenged *The Herald* in sponsorship of expeditions, it also did so in its desire for exciting writing. *The New-York Times* correspondent with Schley's expedition wrote:

> The wind had increased to well-nigh a hurricane. It tore over the hills in furious blasts, driving the water in sheets before it, and heeling the ship. . . . Some one was seen on the ice signalling with flags . . . "Send doctor with stretchers and Harlow with photograph machine; seven alive." When it came to the last two words I made him repeat them. With what careful interest I watched them no one can recognize. It might be D-E-A-D, but no; A-L-I-V-E waved plainly through the air. . . . Passing a small fire on which pots of milk were warming we came to the tent, under which lay four of the poor fellows. Two lay outside, one with his face so swollen that he could barely show by his eyes the wild excitement that filled his being. . . . Pushing aside the flags of the tent we saw a sight the like of which we trust never to see again. Crowded together in the little of

the tent that was left standing lay Greely and three of his men in their sleeping bags, their faces black with dirt. Their hollow cheeks and their gleeming eyes made a picture that we will never forget and that told a story that has but few rivals in the histories of miserable sufferings. The short glance revealed four men with the hand of death laid upon them. . . . (19 July 1884)

Conversely, the correspondent for *The Herald* simply stated, "The scene at the camp beggars description. It is sufficient to say that they were starving, and but for the timely relief afforded, some of them would have died during the night" (18 July 1884).

A similar overlap existed between the supposedly sensational and quality English papers. In the lurid aftermath of Greely's expedition, *The Weekly Times* simply commented, "The charges of cannibalism against the expedition seem to have been confirmed by an exhumation of the body of Lieutenant Kislingbury, which has just been buried at Rochester, New York. However, further evidence will be needed to make the findings indisputable" (17 August 1884). Meanwhile, *The Daily Telegraph* and *The Manchester Guardian* each ran short and skeptical articles obtained from Reuter's, and *The Daily News* only added "Despite the lack of evidence and the certain inaccuracies of the testimony, such charges fill the public mind with unspeakable sorrow" (14 August 1884). Conversely, *The Times* shifted from its normally austere position to a bold and sensational commentary:

The cannibalism was more frightful than it is possible to describe. . . . The body of Lieutenant Kislingbury has been exhumed, and it was found that the flesh had been cleanly stripped off the bones, the remains weighing only 50 pounds. How many members of the party engaged in such behaviour has not been determined, but the practice must have been known about by all because the amount of flesh missing would have taken a considerable period of time to consume. (16 August 1884)

Although this passage was far more sedate than many in the American press, by comparison to the normal English style it was enthralling. Moreover, in it can be seen the beginning of a style not unlike that from across the Atlantic. As an impartial observer from Auckland, New Zealand, commented: "The example of the *New York Herald* is now being largely followed by the chief London journals, and the great strides of modern journalism is one of the astonishing progressive features of a progressive age" (*The Daily Southern Cross* 10 June 1875).

The press against the press

Just as *The Herald* was the object of frequent attacks as it grew larger and more powerful, the emphasis on the growth of circulation in the last decades of the nineteenth century led more newspapers than ever before to launch assaults on their rivals. Although these were often simply weapons in continuing circulation wars, they more and more became cloaked in anti-sensational garb.

As the most successful papers in the United States, *The World* and *The Herald* received large shares of this abuse. One aspect of Pulitzer's newspaper that was easy to criticize was its clumsy prose (Juergens 1966: 36). Dana, a self-admitted purist in grammatical usage, was particularly fond of taunting his former employee's less-than-perfect literary style. Pulitzer responded defiantly: "*The World* does not attribute a particle of its great success to its knowledge of grammar. Its syntax is entirely satisfactory to itself and a large number of American citizens who manage to get along tolerably well without pedantry, hyper-criticism or snobbish affectation of grammatical knowledge" (*The World* 4 December 1884).

Pulitzer also emphasized to his staff that they needed to appeal to an audience with little education, rather than to one more able to appreciate the nuances of language (Juergens 1966: 58). To do this, he said, their writing had to be clear and simple:

> The first object of any word in any article at any time must be perfect clarity. I hate all rare, unusual, non-understandable words. Avoid the vanity of foreign words or phrases or unfamiliar terms. . . . What is the use of writing over the heads of the readers? Go over that testimony, analyze it, summarize it, condense it, so that a child can understand it. (Dilliard 1947: 9)

A more common – and vicious – method of attack was one that had been used in the 1870s against Stanley and *The Herald* – sniping at a paper by attacking its correspondents' accuracy, effectiveness, or personal lives. Throughout the 1880s, Bennett's paper remained a prime target for such assaults. One of the most scathing came from *The New-York Times* and focused on Gilder's North Pole attempt.

The day after Gilder had been scheduled to leave New York for Cumberland Sound, *The Times* gleefully announced that he had missed his ship because he had been arrested. Dollie Adams, a professional swimmer, had claimed that Gilder had stolen a $1,000 bond that she had entrusted to him in 1883. The explorer had been taken to the city jail the day he was due to depart, and he had been unable to post bail until several hours after the ship sailed (*The New-York Times* 14 July 1886). The case actually never went to court, and it has since been suggested that Adams was romantically involved with Gilder and that her intent was to keep him from a perilous journey (Barr 1988: 35). But *The Times* still continued to mistreat the unfortunate Gilder. On 3 March 1887 under the headline HE DID NOT REACH THE NORTH POLE, it ridiculed his decision to return south. Then, upon his arrival in New York, it derided him in its most sarcastic and biting tones:

> W.H. Gilder, who started in a white flannel suit on a ramble to the north pole in August last, returned to this city day before yesterday, having changed his ramble into a mere stroll of a thousand-mile dash and repeat. Mr. Gilder's stay is only for a day or so, as he is busily occupied with preparations for an immediate return. He has traveled some 2,000 miles, but as the pole is still there and is yet without the Gilder monogram carved upon its pedestal, the adventurous explorer looks upon his present achievement as nothing. The absence of grocery stores beyond the arctic circle, and the inability of the polar bears to

speak English as she is spoke, was partly the cause of his return, the other part being certain business arrangements, a hitch in which demanded his presence here.

The walking in Greenland is not all that it might be at present, the cracks in the sidewalk sometimes expanding to the distance of several miles. The ice is also reported as quite cold and the water unusually wet. Later on, however, the adventurous gentleman may confidently be expected to sit astride of an iceberg fishing for gamy walrus in Symme's Hole, with a fishing pole consisting of the centre of things in general, rigged with a silk line and fly hooks. (28 April 1887)

The New-York Times also received such attacks. Two days after proudly announcing Schwatka's Alaskan discoveries – including the Jones River – *The Times* was shaken by *The Sun*'s comment that the same river had been shown on W.H. Dall's map of 1870 (22 September 1886). The next day *The Times* printed a rebuttal:

It is clear that Jones River had never been explored by white men previous to the visit of Lieut. SCHWATKA and his party. And the great point is that, whatever guesses may have been made about Jones River, Lieut. SCHWATKA was the first to describe it and give it a name. This honor cannot be stolen from him by any such method as the *Sun* has adopted. For it cannot be said that a man who merely guessed at a river and inserted it upon his map was its discoverer . . . . (23 September 1886)

The same day *The Sun* printed two small maps with the intention of showing that Lake Castina had not been discovered by Schwatka. It also declared that *The Times* had purposely falsified its map. A response brought yet another charge, in which *The Sun* claimed that the charts of the expeditions led by Jean-François Galaup, Comte de la Pérouse (1785–88) and George Vancouver (1791–95) proved *The Times* was wrong (25 September 1886). Another rejoinder from *The Times* commented that *The Sun*

ransacks the libraries of the geographical and historical societies, scrutinizes every guesswork map of Alaska that can be made to serve its purpose, willfully distorts geography, and . . . gives free play to the talents of all its most skillful falsifiers. . . . And all this expenditure of malevolent energy is prompted by the *Sun*'s jealousy of enterprise on the part of THE TIMES. (26 September 1886).

As the debate continued, both the *Tribune* and *The World* found the temptation to poke fun at the name "Jones River" irresistible. *The World* was particularly light-hearted about it, rewording the lyrics for the southern tune "Swanee River" (5 October 1886):

> Way up upon de Geojones Ribber
> Far, far away,
> Dere's where de mud am running ebber,
> Into de Icy Bay.
>
> All de mouth am wide and muddy,
> Eb'rywhere am stones;
> Oh darkies how we smile at Schwatka,
> An dat funny ribber Jones.

The issue fizzled out three weeks later, long after *The Times* had demanded: "Will the editor of the *Sun* retract his misstatements concerning Lieut. SCHWATKA'S work and apologize to him and to THE TIMES, or does he prefer . . . to have these lies crammed down his throat by THE TIMES?" (3 October 1886).

The press against explorers

The strongest and broadest salvo on an explorer was aimed at the long-time whipping boy of so many newspapers – Stanley. When Stanley returned to England in April 1890, having "saved" a reluctant Emin Pasha, he became the toast of London, attending reception after reception, including again meeting Queen Victoria and other members of the Royal Family. His hastily completed book about the expedition, *In Darkest Africa*, became the most commercially successful expedition account yet produced, selling more than 150,000 copies. But Stanley's role in the already controversial expedition soon came under critical examination, and by late in the year he had become a more popular target than at any other time of his tumultuous career.

It quickly became apparent to many observers that the real reason for the expedition had not been to save Emin Pasha from the Mahdists, but to establish a British commercial empire in the region of Lake Victoria and the headwaters of the Nile; this would have stopped both the expansion of Germany from the east and of Leopold's personal empire from the west (Fox Bourne 1891; Smith 1972). Stanley was taken to task for his role in this economic imperialism, as well as for his dealings with the Arab slaver Tippu Tip, the large numbers killed on the expedition, and his self-serving, at times highly inaccurate, portrayal of the events of the expedition. But the most controversial subject was the disaster of the "Rear Column," which Stanley had left behind on the Congo while he dashed ahead to Lake Albert and Emin Pasha. Burdened with the sick and injured members of the expedition, confused by Stanley's conflicting orders, and depending on the hoped-for but non-existent good will of Tippu Tip to continue its progress, the Rear Column under Major Edmund Barttelot degenerated into a disaster that included the killing of Barttelot and the deaths of many of its members.

In October 1890 the family of Barttelot released his memoirs, which charged Stanley with a lengthy list of wicked behaviors, including negligence, intentional desertion, and misrepresentation (Barttelot 1890). This was quickly followed by the account of one of the other members of the Rear Column, J. Rose Troup, indicting Stanley in equally bitter terms (Troup 1890). The press jumped in with glee, sensing a kill of its age-old enemy. *The Pall Mall Gazette* and *The St. James's Gazette* both demanded a public accounting to determine the true facts of the Rear Column (11 November 1890). Dana's *Sun* tracked down Herbert Ward, an expedition member who voiced criticisms not only of Stanley's handling of the Rear Column but of his personal interactions with Emin Pasha (28, 29, 31

October 1890). Pulitzer's *World* indicated that Stanley had abandoned the Rear Column for simple political expediency: in order to get Emin Pasha out of Equatoria before the Germans reached him (2 November 1890). And a large number of papers in both Britain and the US roundly condemned Stanley and his actions.

But this was no novice with whom the press was dealing. After the newspapers' initial attacks, Stanley unleashed his counter-offensive in the form of the disclosures of William Bonny, a member of the Rear Column, who produced a picture of Barttelot as a jealous, tyrannical, sadistical, raving brute whose inhumanity after the departure of Stanley brought about his well-deserved death (*The Times* 8, 10 November 1890). Bonny's account was quickly supported by other individuals who had been associated with Barttelot through the years (*The Times* 12, 14, 15 November 1890; *Sunday Times* 9 November 1890). Stanley also cleverly side-stepped issues of responsibility by seeing that the press was reminded of the attendance at and sketching of a cannibal feast by one of the expedition's English members. As Stanley had undoubtedly planned, the ensuing scandal ultimately helped the issues of the management of the Rear Column slip from public view, something astutely noted by the journal that knew him best (*The New York Herald* 16 November 1890).

The Herald and its owner had not escaped totally unscathed themselves. Although the aftermath of the Emin Pasha Relief Expedition was not nearly so vicious in the United States as in Britain, when Stanley was vilified in the American press, so frequently was Bennett, despite the fact that he had not actually contributed any money to the effort. During the worst of the Rear Column sensations, *The Sun*, *The New-York Times*, and *The World* all took free shots at the owner of *The Herald*, based on his supposed sponsorship of the explorer.

The English did not need Stanley as an excuse to demean *The Herald* or any other American newspaper. Many felt that the reasons for doing so were self-evident. Matthew Arnold was a spokesman for a remarkably wide range of English individuals when he stated:

> I should say that if one were searching for the best means to efface and kill in a nation the discipline of respect, the feeling for what is elevated, one could not do better than take the American newspapers. The absence of truth and soberness in them, the poverty in serious interest, the personality and sensation-mongering are beyond belief. (Arnold 1888: 490)

There must therefore have been some trepidation among those of this frame of mind when rumors surfaced that Pulitzer himself was considering entering the daily market in England:

> Speculation as to the proprietorship and editorship of the *Pall Mall Gazette* continues rife. Mr. Stead's former organ is said to have become the property of Mr. Joseph Pulitzer of the *New York World*. Mr. Pulitzer's success in American journalism has been unparalleled. . . . Unlike Mr. James Gordon Bennett . . . Mr. Pulitzer keeps in close personal touch with his organ, and at one time devoted himself so assiduously to supervision of contributed matter as to become almost blind. Since the collapse of the London edition of the *New York*

Herald he has been quietly prospecting for a newspaper property here. (*The Evening News & Post* 15 November 1892)

Although there was no truth to the rumor, *The Pall Mall Gazette* might have been appropriate for Pulitzer; under Stead, it had been among the first papers in England regularly to mock or lecture its rivals. But Pulitzer was more concerned with defending American newspapers against charges such as those by Arnold than with entering English journalism:

> The criticisms you hear about the American press are founded on a dislike for our headlines and for the prominence we give to crime, to corruption in office, and to sensational topics generally; the charge of inaccuracy is just thrown in to make it look worse. I do not believe that one person in a thousand who attacks the American press for being inaccurate has ever taken the trouble to investigate the facts. (quoted in Ireland 1938: 96)

Accuracy and honesty

The facts – and their accuracy – were all-important to Pulitzer. The novelist Theodore Dreiser touched on Pulitzer's consuming passion for accuracy when he wrote of how he first secured a job at *The World*. While waiting to talk to the city editor, Dreiser looked around the huge office of the city desk. The only wall decorations were placards proclaiming: "Accuracy, Accuracy, Accuracy!" "Who? What? Where? When? How?" and "The Facts – The Color – The Facts!" (Dreiser 1922: 465–7).

Pulitzer also assumed that the American press as a whole believed in accuracy:

> I think that almost every paper in America tries to be accurate. I will go further than that. There is not a paper of any importance published in French, German or English, whether it is printed in Europe or in America, which I have not studied . . . and I will tell you . . . that the press of America as a whole has a higher standard of accuracy than the European press as a whole. I will go further than that. I will say that line for line the American newspapers actually *attain* a higher standard of news accuracy than the European newspapers. (Ireland 1938: 94–5; emphasis Pulitzer's)

However, Pulitzer's assessment was not without its flaws; much of the American press, both editors and correspondents, at times shamelessly deviated from the obvious truth. In the case of the editors, *The Herald* constantly claimed credit for Sir Henry Bartle Frere's mission to Zanzibar to negotiate a treaty with the sultan for the suppression of the slave trade – an expedition actually sent by the British Foreign Office (*The New York Herald* 13 August, 5 November 1872, 2 January, 18 June 1873). Bennett also changed datelines (for example, from Aden to Zanzibar; *The New York Herald* 2 July 1872) and held back the release of news in order for a story to have a bigger impact. This was not just a problem afflicting *The Herald*, however; upon the return of Peary's North Greenland expedition (1891–92), *The New-York Times* printed the story under the subhead "Our Flag Planted Nearer Than Any Other to the North Pole" (13 September

1892). In reality Peary's mark was well short of Lockwood's farthest north, and although this point was clarified in the story, the headline was still misleading.

The reporters also made their share of mistakes, intentional or otherwise. Stanley once filed a story detailing how he had landed on the coast of Crete, joined a guerrilla force struggling for independence, and fought in a battle against a Turkish column (*The New York Herald* 8 November 1868). It has recently been shown that the entire story was fiction, because Stanley was in Athens on the days he claimed to be in Crete (McLynn 1989: 77–8).

There were numerous other discrepancies in the accuracy of newspaper accounts that were not as flagrant. Many explorers were simply guilty of embellishment or understatement. For example, Schwatka described the vicinity of Mount Saint Elias in perhaps overly generous terms when he wrote: "Here . . . is a group of Alpine peaks that will rival all of those of Switzerland put together over and over and over again" (*The New-York Times* 14 September 1886). And his Jones River, which today is known as the Yahtse River, was later proven to be of little significance (Sherwood 1965: 77–9).

Some explorers might well have just made honest mistakes. According to the calculations of a couple who later followed Stanley's route to find Livingstone, he reported the village of Simbamwenni some miles north of where it apparently was (Stanley 1872; Jackson 1962: 62–72). This was not necessarily surprising considering that Stanley had difficulty accurately recording his direction when his view was obscured by trees, that clouds frequently blotted out the sun, and that the magnetic variation was uncommonly high in that region of Africa.

Thus, it is hard to fault some of Stanley's reporting. Yet, did there have to be mistakes? Other than his statements favorably comparing the accomplishments of Schwatka's expedition with those of others, Gilder was virtually never guilty of inaccuracies. Later explorations confirmed almost to the word what Gilder said about the lands he passed through in 1879. But then, Gilder was more the exception than the rule. The quantity of exaggeration in the reporting about the Arctic thoroughly repelled Lieutenant G.C. Doane, who had sailed on *Gulnare* as the military commander of Henry Howgate's luckless expedition to establish a permanent post at Lady Franklin Bay in 1880. In response, Doane wrote a taunting report on his return, which was printed in *The Chicago Times*:

> We did but little, but left a great many things undone requiring some moral courage to refrain from doing. We did not change the names of all the localities visited, as is customary, nor give them new latitudes. . . . We did not hunt up nameless islands and promontories to tag them with the surnames of plethoric merchants and wildly enthusiastic females who had given up plug tobacco and button-hole bouquets. We did not even erect cenotaphs. . . . We received no flags, converted no natives, killed no one. . . .
>
> The primary geographical iceberg, which in perspective towers above first-class ships in the foreground, and has a contemplative bear gazing seaward from the loftiest pinnacle, oblivious of the herd of fat seals on its beach, is not produced any more. . . . The present ones are not so high by several hundred

feet, and instead of being in a freezing condition were rapidly thawing whenever afloat. The rocks and bluffs of the Arctic are not at all clouded with water-fowl, as pictured, nor is it dangerous to run a whale-boat lest it should be ground on a sleeping whale, be pierced through by the horn of a narwhal, or captured by an angry herd of walrus. (6 April 1881)

So where was the line drawn between unfortunate inaccuracy and actual dishonesty? It is difficult to say, because one not only has to try to judge what the explorers saw, but what they thought they saw. Despite the problems that such perceptual differences cause, there are notable examples of reports that under no circumstances could be anything but, politely put, "expedient exaggerations." Among the most obvious of these was the claim of Hugh Lowther, the Fifth Earl of Lonsdale, who, in February 1888, left England for the Canadian Arctic. Fifteen months later he returned to London, but it was uncertain what exactly he had done.

Lonsdale's most-frequently stated motive for going to the Arctic was that he had been sent to obtain specimens for the Scottish Naturalist Society. Yet not only has no evidence of such an organization been found, Lonsdale regularly gave other, conflicting reasons. *The Daily News* stated that he was traveling "as far north as possible for the purpose of shooting white bears and other wild animals" (24 February 1888); *The St. James's Gazette* said he had left in search of the North Pole (7 September 1888); and Lonsdale later claimed that he had gone at the invitation of Bennett and with the financial assistance of *The Herald* (Dawson 1946: 60–61).

The stories about his Arctic travels were just as varied. He claimed to have headed toward the North Pole with "a realistic chance of arriving there" (*The Pall Mall Gazette* 1, 4 January 1889); to have made a "long and tedious journey of four thousand miles overland from Banks Land, in latitude 75 degrees north" (*The New York Herald* 6 April 1889); and to have found a race of giant Eskimos in the Mackenzie Delta (*San Francisco Daily Reporter* 23 April 1889). He also later claimed the first definite confirmation of gold in the Klondike (Dawson 1946: 82) and wrote about an Arctic journey that matched any for its difficulties and triumphs:

> It was one of the worst parts of the journey, the temperature being sixty-four degrees below zero. I started at six that morning, and crossed over the highest point, which was 5,200 feet. . . . When I got across I had only seven dogs left out of sixty-nine, and there were seven Indians and five sleds missing. I set off back to find the missing men. Eventually I brought them down safe and sound, they being frozen only about the hands and feet. (quoted in Sutherland 1965: 86)

It may be that Lonsdale eventually realized that the different stories he had reported would, collectively, prove his dishonesty. Perhaps that is why he did not long pursue his role as media hero, and why, despite at one point contemplating writing an expedition account with the assistance of Gilder, he never did (Krech 1989: 92). Lonsdale's success – based almost totally on carefully misleading hints, innuendo, and inaccurate represen-tations – was diametrically opposed to the concepts espoused by Pulitzer:

> It is not enough to refrain from publishing fake news, it is not enough to take ordinary care to avoid the mistakes which arise from the ignorance, the careless-

ness, the stupidity of one or more of the many men who handle the news before it gets into print; you have got to do much more than that; you have got to make everyone connected with your paper – your editors, your reporters, your correspondents, your re-write men, your proof-readers – believe that accuracy is to a newspaper what virtue is to a woman. (quoted in Ireland 1938: 94)

In one small expedition, one insignificant footnote to the history of the north, Lonsdale had shown that for all of Pulitzer's concern and for all of the efforts of honest journalists, the press was helpless in the hands of unscrupulous story-tellers. In the long run, Lonsdale undoubtedly encouraged later explorers to exaggerate their claims. And these men – such as Frederick Cook and Robert E. Peary – would not simply be footnotes in history. The basic problem, according to Stanley, was that being an accurate journalist and setting down the facts was a mistake. The public wanted action and adventure; what it did not want, Stanley claimed, was the truth.

8

The unknown and commercial journalism

The Norwegian ascendancy: Fridtjof Nansen

In the history of Arctic exploration, one man remains supreme in creativity, daring, intellect, and international stature: Fridtjof Nansen. A better example of a Renaissance man is difficult to imagine: Nansen excelled at virtually everything he undertook, whether it was the study of zoology or oceanography; the improvement of travel technology; the art of political statesmanship; or aiding individuals affected by war or famine. Nansen's mind was always moving ahead, wandering to another challenge. In the tundra and ice of the far north he was methodical, painstaking, and logical, just as in his academic research. He was, as it were, an intellectual of exploration, a pedagogue of the wilderness, a man who would put up with any hardship to satisfy his curiosity.

When Nansen's intellectual restlessness led him to propose his polar drift, he continued his innovations on a new front – the development of the most famous polar ship ever. Under the direction of the noted shipbuilder Colin Archer, the small, rounded *Fram* was designed and constructed to withstand the pressure of the ice. *Fram*'s sides sloped sufficiently to prevent the ice, when it pressed together, from getting a firm hold on the hull; thus, rather than nipping her, the ice simply raised her out of the water. In addition, *Fram* not only was equipped with but the third marine diesel engine ever installed in a ship, she was also furnished with electric lights, the dynamo for which could be driven by the engine, wind-, or hand-power. In June 1893 Nansen and the 12 other members of the expedition set out, disappearing into the mysterious regions north of central Siberia.

In February 1895, acknowledging that *Fram* was not going to drift directly over the top of the world, Nansen made a dash for the North Pole with a single companion – Hjalmar Johansen – sledges, dogs, and skis. They reached 86° 14', 170 miles farther north than anyone had ever been before, then made a dramatic retreat over the drifting pack ice. The two men wintered in a makeshift hut on a forlorn island in Franz Joseph Land before, the next spring, having a Stanley-and-Livingstone encounter with Frederick George Jackson, the leader of the Jackson-Harmsworth expedition. *Windward*, the expedition's relief ship, brought them back to civilization, and, one week after they returned, *Fram* landed in Norway. As Nansen had predicted, she had continued to drift across the Arctic basin, leisurely making her way through the ice. Once again, Nansen had triumphed over the armchair explorers, the self-proclaimed experts. He had come back, not only with yet another classic story of Arctic adventure, but with a tale for the times, one of danger and difficulty without despair, trial without tragedy or the loss of a single man, and the victory of man over nature.

To most of the world, Nansen's reappearance was like that of a man returning from the dead. The impact far exceeded that of his crossing of Greenland, not only because the achievement was greater, but because the audience was broader. Before, Nansen had been a European figure. Now he became the darling of the international popular press, the embodiment of man's conquest of the world to the publics of both Europe and America, and, as Livingstone had been, that most unusual of mythic heroes, the living icon. *The Pall Mall Gazette* described Nansen as "the most eminent explorer ever known" (24 August 1896), and *The Washington Post* described in detail not only his plans, voyage, and adventures, but his early life, studies, even his wife (14 August 1896).

Nansen was ideal for his role as media hero: tall, fair-haired, and photogenic, with a long Nordic face that was at once intense, melancholy, and almost fierce. He gave the press and public everything they could want: a man of unequalled accomplishments but with the right combination of modesty and vanity; an individual of unsurpassed dignity and reserve, but one still comprehensible to the average man; a scientist but at the same time a writer and artist; an exemplar of the forces of nationalism – a patriot ever bringing honor to his country; and a gambling adventurer willing to risk everything on one throw of the dice.

Some of these views of Nansen were entirely accurate. His scientific, writing, and artistic skills were outstanding. His reserve was legendary: he shared a sleeping bag with Johansen on Franz Joseph Land, yet maintained the formal mode of address, including the use of surnames – no one dared call Nansen "Fridtjof" (Huntford 1980: 74–5). And he was a partisan of Norway's separation from Sweden. His desire to champion his country's independence by proving the success and abilities of her people was echoed in the words of the Australian explorer of the Antarctic, Sir Douglas Mawson: "It seemed to me that here was an opportunity to prove that the young men of a young country could rise to those traditions that have made the history of British Polar Exploration one of triumphant endeavor" (Mawson 1915: xiv).

Yet the presentation of Nansen as a man who willingly took unnecessary risks reveals that the Anglo-American press understood neither him nor the Norwegian approach to exploration. It has been suggested that

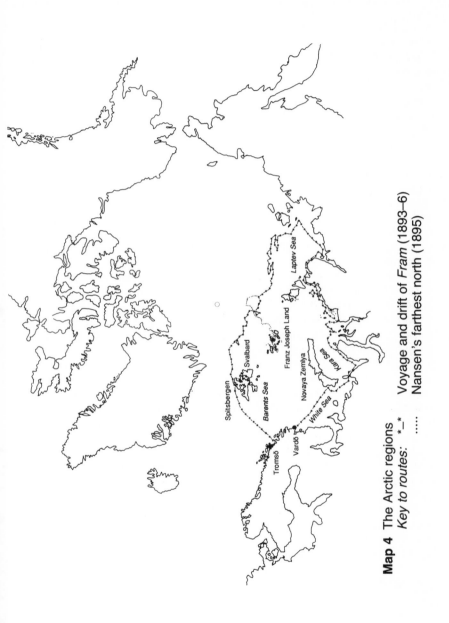

Map 4 The Arctic regions
Key to routes: *–*   Voyage and drift of *Fram* (1893–6)
    ......   Nansen's farthest north (1895)

Spitsbergen

Svalbard

Franz Joseph Land

Laptev Sea

Novaya Zemlya

Kara Sea

Barents Sea

White Sea

Tromsö

Vardö

Norwegians, like other Scandinavians, believe that an individual life is of the utmost value and that nothing – even reaching the most inaccessible point on the globe – is so important as to place that life at risk (Castberg 1954). This belief found expression in Nordenskiöld's careful management during the voyage of *Vega*. It also had an effect on Nansen, whose startling new concepts – deliberately cutting off his line of retreat by beginning his crossing of Greenland on the desolate east coast, and intentionally entering the pack ice in *Fram* – were not symptomatic of madness or bravado, as they appeared to be in England and the United States, but were meticulously calculated to improve his chances of success.

One reason that Nansen's plans might have been misunderstood by the Anglo-American press and public was that they were viewed as similar to those of the Emin Pasha Relief Expedition. Stanley had stated that if he marched directly to Lake Albert from Zanzibar, he would have to go through the territory of the warlike Masai, which would lead his porters to desert. However, if he landed them on the west coast they would realize their only hope of survival was to remain with him until he reached the Indian Ocean, and, at the same time, they would quicken their pace in order to get home (Stanley 1890: I, 34–5). Many of the disasters of the expedition were in part attributable to this route, which might have made the public question Nansen's judgment.

Nansen actually was very similar to Stanley in some respects: he was daring, but not reckless or impetuous. He was coldly professional, and, although he admired the Anglo-American explorers for their determination, he did not relish their notion of heroism, which "in the corrupt sense of the age almost by definition, meant wanton self-sacrifice and bungling" (Huntford 1980: 71). Rather he trusted in careful preparation, and believed that the narrow escapes, often perceived as an unavoidable part of exploration, were simply signs of poor planning or judgment.

Of course, even Nansen was not totally infallible, and he was carried beyond logic by the thought of reaching the North Pole. He took an ill-advised gamble when he and Johansen left *Fram* on skis. As A.H. Markham later commented, "They could not expect to reach the *Fram* again. She would probably have drifted a good deal in their absence, so that it was a case of 'burning their boats,' as Nansen did before when he crossed Greenland" (*The Daily Telegraph* 15 August 1896). Nansen was fortunate that the move was not disastrous. When he met Jackson, the equipment he used to determine his latitude and longitude was no longer functional, so he was not sure if he were on Franz Joseph Land or the eastern islands of Svalbard. He was faced with braving a long journey from a point he could not definitely identify (and therefore could not use to plan exactly in which direction to head) in a leaking kayak, with no assurance that he would meet anyone at the end of his next journey. But, as was the case most of Nansen's life, when a rare occasion arose in which his skill did not suffice, his luck did. Possessing both skill and luck, Nansen was supremely confident, something he stressed when he wrote in his diary on 13 June 1894:

But the *Fram* will not be crushed, and nobody believes in the possibility of such an event. We are like the kayak-rower, who knows well enough that one faulty stroke of his paddle is enough to capsize him and send him into eternity; but none the less he goes on his way serenely, for he knows that he will not make a faulty stroke. This is absolutely the most comfortable way of undertaking a polar expedition; what possible journey, indeed, could be more comfortable? Not even a railway journey, for then you have the bother of changing carriages. (quoted in Nansen 1897: I, 400)

The passage also illucidates a common Scandinavian belief that nothing is worth doing unless it is enjoyable. Unlike most British and American explorers, who had fought against the Arctic, Nansen was convinced that it was not necessary to subdue nature to survive in the north. Rather, he enjoyed the Arctic for what it was, a thing unlike his home only in degree; in fact, he perceived the crossing of Greenland simply as an extended ski tour.

Despite Nansen's mythic status, his very efficiency, like that of Nordenskiöld, did not allow him to fulfill all of the Anglo-American public's desires for excitement. The expeditions of less competent men – such as Evelyn B. Baldwin and Anthony Fiala – were in some senses more thrilling reading than Nansen's exploits, because they involved constant struggle, disaster, and uncertainty of outcome. These were also more appealing stories for the press because the participants were American and therefore fit the nationalist preferences of the Anglo-American readership.

The era of yellow journalism

The mid-1890s saw a fundamental change in journalism in both the US and Britain. For the first time there was a virtually complete concentration on the commercial aspects of what had previously been considered a method of political expression, an agency to enlighten the public, or a form of public service. Certainly earlier proprietors such as Bennett Sr had intended to make money, but they also cared about informing their publics, and men such as Pulitzer and Stead believed the primary purpose of the press was to enlighten and crusade for the people. But with the arrival of William Randolph Hearst and Alfred Harmsworth, the editor and champion gave way to the businessman. As the American journalist Will Irwin noted: "We are here to supply a commodity – news . . . we will give the public exactly what it wants, without bothering to elevate the commonwealth. If we find that people prefer murders, then murders they shall have" (Irwin 1911b: 18).

One frequent result of the press' worship of commercialism was an even greater emphasis on sensationalism, a decision reflected in many areas of coverage, including exploration. In fact, Nansen's return from the polar drift coincided with the most blatant and sensational circulation war in the history of the American press.

This struggle for circulation began with the invasion of New York by the western impresario William Randolph Hearst, who, in September 1895,

143

purchased the *New York Morning Journal*, which, coincidentally, had been established by Albert Pulitzer in November 1882, six months before his older brother Joseph came to New York. As a penny daily, it enjoyed considerable popularity, with guidelines altogether different than those of *The World*. Albert Pulitzer defined what he wanted his paper to be when he visited England in 1884:

> I think that what mankind most desires is to laugh, to cheer the life of the average man, to lighten by a pleasant smile the sombre round of his daily toil, to cast a gleam of sunlight, however transient it may be, into the darkness and dullness of a careworn existence. The rules that I laid down for myself with my new journal were, that it must be personal, local, good-tempered, gay, but first of all scrupulously pure and inoffensive. To the last I attached the very greatest importance. It is a common superstition among many journals that success . . . can only be attained by trenching upon doubtful ground; indulging in dubious innuendoes; and, in short, wrapping up in tolerably decent English intolerable suggestions. That I believe is an utter delusion. (*The Illustrated London News* 19 July 1884)

This strategy was successful until Pulitzer raised the price of the *Morning Journal* to 2¢ in 1894. A sharp decline in circulation followed – from 135,000 to 30,000 within a year (Older 1936: 30) – and Pulitzer sold the paper to John R. McLean, the ambitious owner of *The Cincinnati Enquirer* (and eventual proprietor of *The Washington Post*), for $1 million. Even McLean's sensationalism could not revive the *Morning Journal*, however, and in 1895 Hearst bought it for $180,000.

For more than a month Hearst quietly developed a new approach for his paper, while not publicly acknowledging his ownership. On 7 November 1895 the first issue in Hearst's new style was printed. It was everything that one could have expected from the proprietor of *The Examiner*, engaging in the same kind of sensations, self-promotions, stunts, crusades, scandals, and fakes. It proved beyond doubt that Hearst was serious when he wrote: "The modern editor . . . does not care for facts. The editor wants novelty. The editor has no objection to facts if they are also novel. But he would prefer a novelty that is not a fact to a fact that is not a novelty" (quoted in Brendon 1982: 134). Indeed, in a single issue of the *Journal* there were garishly illustrated stories about travels among headhunters, the wife of a French criminal successfully encouraging her husband's suicide, the downfall and illicit career of a young woman following her answer to a personal advertisement in Bennett's *Herald*, the torture of Siberian prisoners, an operation to remove Queen Victoria's cataracts (with an illustration of a scalpel slicing through one of her eyes), and the murder of a black rapist in Georgia by one of his intended white victims (Brendon 1982: 136).

Hearst quickly shortened the name of his scandal sheet to *The Journal* (which he changed eight months later to the *New York Journal*), cut the price to 1¢, increased the size from 8 to 12 pages, and started an evening edition called the *New York Evening Journal*. Within a year, Hearst's virtually unlimited funds had allowed him to hire a staff equalled by none, including Julian Ralph, who had been with *The Sun* since 1875 and was later called "the greatest newspaper reporter who ever lived" (Barry 1924);

the renowned foreign correspondent James Creelman, who Hearst stole from *The World*; Richard Harding Davis, America's greatest war correspondent; S.S. Carvalho, the publisher of *The World*; and Morrill Goddard, who had built the Sunday edition of *The World* into the largest single edition in the nation.

By February 1896 *The Journal*'s sales had rocketed from 77,000 to 150,000. That month, in an effort to cripple his new competitor, Pulitzer cut the price of *The World* to a penny. Although it immediately increased the circulation of *The World*, it had little effect on the *Journal*; it was *The Herald* that lost the greatest circulation, while smaller papers such as the *Morning Advertiser*, the *New York Mercury*, *The New York Press*, and *The Recorder* were virtually destroyed (Hughes 1981: 219). At the same time, the move conceded the new power of the *Journal*, just as similar cuts in 1883 by *The Herald*, *The Times*, and the *Tribune* had acknowledged Pulitzer's powers. Like Pulitzer before him, Hearst was too effective a businessman not to make the competition pay for such a move, regularly pointing out that *The World* was now challenging him, not vice-versa. Pulitzer later recognized his error: "When I came to New York Mr. Bennett reduced the price of his paper and raised the advertising rates – all to my advantage. When Mr. Hearst came to New York I did the same. I wonder why, in view of my experience" (quoted in Seitz 1924b).

The hiring of Goddard by Hearst ultimately led to the term "yellow journalism." As editor of the Sunday edition of *The World*, Goddard had started the country's first regular comic section in 1889; it had become the first comic section to be printed in color on 18 November 1894. Goddard had also hired the artist Richard F. Outcault, whose "Shantytown" and "Hogan's Alley" comics depicted life in the tenements. Hogan's Alley had as one of its main characters the "Yellow Kid," a hairless street urchin dressed in yellow flowing robes and with one tooth sticking out of a constantly grinning mouth. The popular Yellow Kid soon outgrew Hogan's Alley and became a comic strip in his own right. When Goddard became the editor of the *Sunday Journal* in 1896, he brought Outcault and his comics with him (Lundberg 1936).

Pulitzer responded by giving complete control of the Sunday edition of *The World* to Arthur Brisbane, who had been the paper's managing editor. Brisbane first equalled, then surpassed Hearst's sensationalism, clearly going well beyond anything in which Pulitzer had yet engaged. In 1895 Goddard had used the first banner headline in *The World*, but in the next several years Brisbane used them regularly, justifying them by stating: "Perhaps headlines do take up too much space. The display windows of the big stores take up too much space also. But in a busy nation the first necessity is to attract attention. The big store window, wasting space, and the big type, apparently wasting space, are necessary features of quick development" (quoted in Winkler 1928: 119).

Within a year, Brisbane's program of sensationalism led to an increase in circulation of the Sunday edition of *The World* from 450,000 to more than 600,000. Meanwhile, Brisbane used George B. Luks to continue Outcault's original cartoon, and soon both newspapers were featuring the Yellow Kid in their advertising. To many journalists and readers, the cartoons seemed symbolic of the negative aspects of the use of sensationalism; the phrase "yellow journalism" soon began to be applied to any sensational publication.

Throughout 1896 *The World* and the *Journal* fought an ever-increasing battle with astounding results. *The World* soared to a daily circulation of 370,000. But between February and October the *Journal*'s circulation jumped from 150,000 to 322,000. In November it surpassed *The World* when it jumped more than 100,000 to 438,000. At the same time, *The Herald*'s circulation dropped to under 150,000 before rising again. Within a year the *Sunday Journal* had caught the Sunday edition of *The World* at 600,000 (Tebbel 1952).

In 1897 Hearst lured Brisbane to the editorship of the *Evening Journal* by offering a raise of $100 a month for every thousand added to the circulation figures (Irwin 1911a: 16). Brisbane expanded all of the techniques he had begun to use at *The World* and soon became the highest-paid employee in the history of journalism. He invented the job-type head – half the front page devoted to two or three sensational words. And he developed trick headlines in which the first and third lines, in immense type, proclaimed a sensation, while the middle line, in very small type, reduced the head to a commonplace meaning: for example, WAR Will Probably be DECLARED (Irwin 1911a: 17).

The *Evening Journal* was also the first large-circulation newspaper to regularly publish photographic halftones. In 1897 the *New-York Tribune* printed the first halftone from a photograph in a mass-circulation newspaper (Taft 1938: 446). It did not take long for Brisbane to follow this success with many sensational halftones.

In the midst of this craze for sensation, on 14 February 1898, the United States Navy ship *Maine* was blown up in Havana Harbor. There followed six months of rumors of war, preparation for war, and, finally, the four-month Spanish-American War. Hearst and Brisbane made the most of it, with Pulitzer not far behind. With deliberate falsifications presented as important facts, violent scareheads, raving editorials on the front page, and huge photographs and illustrations, the era marked the height of sensationalism in the history of the American press. The situation prompted the famed journalist E.L. Godkin to write:

> Nothing so disgraceful as the behavior of two of these newspapers in the past week has ever been known in the history of American journalism. Gross misrepresentation of the facts, deliberate invention of tales calculated to excite the public, and unwanton recklessness in the construction of headlines which outdid even these inventions. . . . It is a crying shame that men should work such mischief simply in order to sell more papers. (*The Nation* 24 February 1898: 139)

The result of this sensationalism was that during the Spanish-American War, Hearst's morning paper (which had purchased the *Morning Advertiser* and become the *New York Journal and Advertiser*) achieved an almost-unbelievable daily circulation of 1,320,000, while *The World* also had more than one million readers. After the war, Pulitzer and Hearst took distinctly different routes. By 1899, Pulitzer had dropped yellow journalism, the product of a brief period that he later regretted. He did not want a stodgy newspaper, but he was no longer willing to play games with the truth, and his sensations reverted to their forms of the 1880s.

Conversely, the *Journal and Advertiser*, which had proclaimed in its front-page ears, "How do you like the *Journal*'s war?" (*New York Journal and Advertiser* 9, 10 May 1898), engaged in even more furious yellow journalism. Ultimately about one-third of the nation's metropolitan dailies followed Hearst's lead, the wave of sensationalism not subsiding until World War I (Emery and Emery 1988: 241).

At the same time that Hearst began to rebuild the *Journal*, another New York daily was on the verge of disappearing. George Jones had died in 1891, and without his guiding influence *The New-York Times* had faltered badly. By 1896 it had, at 9,000, the smallest circulation of any of the New York dailies (Berger 1951: 569). In August of that year, however, control of *The Times* passed to 38-year-old Adolph Ochs, the owner of the *Chattanooga Times*. Ochs did not have the capital to buy *The New-York Times* outright, but an arrangement was made whereby he would gain ownership of the paper if he succeeded in revitalizing it within four years (Johnson 1946).

Despite the commercial emphasis of this agreement, Ochs' plan was as concerned with quality as with making money. Just as Raymond decided to publish a quality paper despite the trends set by Bennett Sr and Day, Ochs ignored the methods of Hearst and Pulitzer and determined to make a high-standard newspaper, clean, dignified, and trustworthy. In the first issue after he took control, Ochs outlined plans that would have made Raymond and Jones proud:

> It will be my earnest aim that THE NEW-YORK TIMES give the news, all the news, in concise and attractive form, in language that is parliamentary in good society, and give it as early, if not earlier, than it can be learned through any other reliable medium; to give the news impartially, without fear or favor, regardless of any party, sect, or interests involved; to make the columns of THE NEW-YORK TIMES a forum for the consideration of all questions of public importance. . . . (19 August 1896)

Ochs hired a fine staff of writers and editors, and in the next two years *The Times* (which dropped the hyphen from "New-York" on 1 December 1896) established a reputation based on hard work and factual reporting. However, it still did not have a large readership, numbering only 25,726 in September 1898. That month Ochs dropped the price from 3¢ to a penny. The results were almost immediate: in 1899 circulation increased to 76,260, and by 1901 it had reached 102,472 (Berger 1951: 569).

In 1904 Ochs hired a new managing editor, Carr Van Anda. In the next 25 years Van Anda established himself as one of the top American editors of the twentieth century, simultaneously building *The Times* into the foremost news agency in the US. Among Van Anda's most notable editorial achievements were his handling of the Battle of the Sea of Japan in the Russo-Japanese War (29 May–3 June 1905) and *The Times*' unsurpassed information on the sinking of *Titanic* (15–18 April 1912). But Van Anda also pushed *The Times* towards expanded coverage of one of his personal interests – exploration. In so doing, he helped involve what was becoming America's foremost quality newspaper in its most sensational episode.

George Newnes and commercial journalism in Britain

As in America, late in the nineteenth century there was a rapid commercialization of the press in Britain. Between 1885 and 1910, the number of individuals purchasing newspapers on a daily basis almost quadrupled (Williams 1961: 204). Concurrently, a shift occurred from newspapers owned as small, family or personal businesses to those owned by large companies (Wiener 1988: 56–7); in the late 1890s, the *Daily Mail* became the first British newspaper to become a public company. Proprietorship in Britain had traditionally been viewed as a type of public service and the journalist as a kind of public philosopher. In the 1890s proprietors became businessmen and journalism a trade (Lee 1978: 118). As Kennedy Jones of *The Evening News* put it, he and Alfred Harmsworth had "found journalism a profession and left it a branch of commerce" (Jones 1919: 202).

Despite the emphasis on the business of journalism, sales of newspapers could not cover production costs. For substantial profits, the owners also needed advertising incomes. Previously, advertising revenue had been a valuable prop to newspaper sales, but in the 1890s it became the keystone to the business. The rapidly developing mass market for consumer goods meant that the greatest profits were to be made selling space to large commercial businesses that would place advertisements day after day, year after year. To the new proprietors, the newspaper's importance was not as a vehicle for ideas, but in its ability to put advertisers in touch with the mass of consumers.

The man who first recognized this new mass market of working-class millions – the reading skills of which had been assured by the Forster Education Act of 1870 – did not start as a journalist, but as the Manchester representative of a mercantile firm's fancy-goods department. George Newnes had a taste for snippets of information and odd facts about people, and decided there was a market for a publication full of such items. In order to gain the capital for his venture, he exploited another craze of the time, opening a vegetarian restaurant (Friederichs 1911: 61–4).

On 22 October 1881 Newnes published the first issue of *Tit-Bits From All the Most Interesting Books Periodicals and Newspapers in the World*, a halfpenny weekly that had 16 pages, paid absolutely no attention to politics, and consisted of articles culled from dailies, weeklies, and any other sources Newnes could find. Its formula was simple: short words, short sentences, short paragraphs, and short articles. *Tit-Bits* (as it was known) was an immediate success, and within three months Newnes had moved the operation to London. Not only did Newnes give his readers fast, easily assimilated information, he brought his new publication to wide notice by a series of exciting promotions, such as giving a life-insurance policy to anyone killed in a train accident while carrying a copy of *Tit-Bits*; holding a contest for the best short story, with the prize being a seven-room house; and burying tubes of gold sovereigns worth £500 for discovery by those clever enough to spot the clues hidden in a serial story (Friederichs 1911: 84–97). The sales and advertising soared, and within a brief time the circulation of *Tit-Bits* reached 900,000, three times that of *The Daily Telegraph*.

Newnes amassed a fortune, with which he launched a number of different publishing enterprises. In 1890 he started *Review of Reviews*, first hiring Stead as editor, and then, within three months, selling it to him. The next year, Newnes founded the most successful of his new ventures, *The Strand Magazine*, a serious illustrated monthly directed towards middle-class households. He next entered daily journalism. In September 1892 *The Pall Mall Gazette* was sold to William Astor, who changed his new paper to a Conservative Party journal. E.T. Cook and his staff resigned, but the following January they were reunited when Newnes financed *The Westminster Gazette*. Printed on green paper for the better preservation of the readers' sight (according to the commonly held belief of the time), *The Westminster Gazette* continued the journalistic traditions of Cook at *The Pall Mall Gazette*. Although it cost Newnes £40,000 in its first two years, it gained him a knighthood for services to the Liberal Party.

It was through *The Strand Magazine* that Newnes became one of the first British publishers directly involved in the world of polar exploration. After the conflagration surrounding the Emin Pasha Relief Expedition, the English press began to decrease its coverage of African exploration, in agreement, coincidentally, with the assessment of Stanley's work both during and after the expedition by *The New York Herald*: "Whatever else these terrible charges and countercharges may have done or left undone, they have killed African exploration as a profession" (16 November 1890). Despite an increasing British political presence in Africa, the English newspapers shifted the venue of most of their exploration and adventure coverage to the polar regions. This coincided with a similar change in the interests of the geographical community, which, under the guidance of Clements R. Markham, President of the RGS 1893–1905, began particularly to focus on the Antarctic.

In 1898, against the wishes of Markham who was trying to obtain funds for an RGS-sponsored expedition, Newnes spent £40,000 to finance his own Antarctic expedition in the ship *Southern Cross*. Sailing under the British flag but led by Carsten E. Borchgrevink, a Norwegian, this expedition became, in 1899, the first to winter on the Antarctic Continent (Borchgrevink 1901).

Harmsworth conquers English journalism

Perhaps the single most important contribution made by Newnes was his influence on the greatest English press baron, Alfred Harmsworth (later

Lord Northcliffe). As a young man Harmsworth contributed articles to *Tit-Bits*, was a staff writer for *Wheel Life*, a cycling paper, and then became the editor of *Bicycling News*.

On 2 June 1888 the 22-year-old Harmsworth launched *Answers to Correspondents on Every Subject Under the Sun* (shortened on 28 December 1889 to *Answers*), a halfpenny weekly that followed Newnes' formula of jokes, puzzles, curiosities, and odd facts, while adding to it an invitation to the readers to ask their own questions. This gave *Answers* a constant supply of editorial material, with questions such as "Can Fish Speak?" "Why Don't Jews Ride Bicycles?" "Do Dogs Commit Murder?" and "Can a Clergyman Marry Himself?" (quoted in Brendon 1982: 112). Nevertheless, the success of *Answers* was not assured until it ran a competition offering £1 per week for life to the person who made the nearest guess to the amount of cash in the banking department of the Bank of England on a specific day. There were 718,000 responses, and the magazine's circulation rose to more than 200,000 (Clarke 1950: 66).

Harmsworth had long disliked "penny dreadfuls," periodicals that appealed to youths, with lurid tales of violence, crime, sex, and mystery. He felt that boys would not leave these magazines for solemn and pretentious weeklies, but that they might be attracted to comic papers containing clean humor and plenty of drawings (Clarke 1950: 70). The product of this belief was *Comic Cuts*, a halfpenny magazine for boys, the slogan of which was "Amusing Without Being Vulgar." Its first issue on 17 May 1890 sold 118,000 copies, and it continued with such success that 10 weeks later Harmsworth started a similar journal, *Illustrated Chips*, soon shortened to *Chips*.

By 1893 Harmsworth and his brother Harold owned six journals, with a total circulation of 1,473,000. In the next two years, they started seven more, and by mid-1894 the Harmsworth empire included at least seven weeklies with circulations of more than 100,000 – *Comic Cuts*, *Answers*, *Chips*, *The Marvel*, *Forget-Me-Not*, *Union Jack*, and *Home Chat* (Pound and Harmsworth 1959: 171). The staples of these magazines were sensational adventure and imperial military campaigns in distant lands (Springhall 1989). This juvenile literature was but one place, along with Sunday School tracts and children's theatre, where the major images of Africa and the Arctic were initially affirmed to the youthful public. Once these images had become set in the minds of the young, they usually persisted when those youths became the new generations of explorers, newspapermen, or administrators. Thus, when they went to new lands, they went with a fixed idea of what they would find (as had their predecessors who had expected to discover the sublime or the picturesque). Invariably they found what they expected, and their reports reflected and confirmed these sensational images.

Harmsworth's next step in becoming a central figure in the transfer of knowledge and images was to follow Newnes into the evening newspaper market. But whereas Newnes had established a quality, politically aware journal, Harmsworth chose the sensational route. In 1894, with help from Kennedy Jones (who first obtained the option to buy), he purchased the foundering halfpenny *Evening News and Post*. Within a brief period of time, Harmsworth shortened the name to *The Evening News*; changed its typography and make-up; cut down on the length of the leaders and the amount of political coverage; added a daily short story; and established a column for women, which soon was expanded to the "Women's World" page. Within a year, the circulation had doubled to 160,000.

Two years later Harmsworth entered the morning market, and, after some 80 unpublished test issues, printed the first edition of the halfpenny *Daily Mail* on 4 May 1896. From that day on, the *Daily Mail* was the vanguard of the New Journalism; but without screaming of sensationalism like some of the American newspapers. The *Daily Mail* looked very much like the quality morning journals: it was eight standard-size pages, with advertisements on page one; the Royal Arms were featured in the middle of the title; its headlines were in the dignified morning-daily style and were of modest size; and the make-up was extremely traditional (Morison 1932: 296).

The differences of the *Daily Mail* were in its content and news selection. The leaders were short and lively, as were the news stories. Although it carried political, foreign, and financial news, it also had reports on fashion, travel, sport, and society. Like *The Evening News*, it carried an installment of a serial story and a number of features for women. And interspersed with its leading articles were ones about notable people, adventure, and aviation – the last a development in which Harmsworth was particularly interested.

The *Daily Mail* had another major difference from the other morning dailies: it was aimed not at the upper or middle class, but at the white-collar, lower-middle class. It was Harmsworth's understanding of this class that made the *Daily Mail* so successful. As Philip Gibbs, who later earned an international reputation for his investigations about the initial claims of Frederick A. Cook to have reached the North Pole, recalled:

> He had only one test of what was good to print, "Does this interest Me?" As he was interested with all the passionate curiosity of a small boy who asks continually "How?" and "Why?" in all the elementary aspects of life, in its romances and discoveries, its new toys and new fads, its tragedies and comedies of the more obvious kind, its melodrama and amusements and personalities, that test was not narrow or one-eyed. It was not what the public wanted that was his guiding rule. It was what he wanted. His luck and genius lay in the combination of qualities which made him typical, in a supreme degree, of the average man. (Gibbs 1923: 84)

Harmsworth's success in his new field was immediate. The first number of the *Daily Mail* sold 397,215 copies, more than had ever been sold by any English daily before (Pound and Harmsworth 1959: 199). Within two years its circulation reached about 500,000 copies, and, after rising to just short of a million during the Boer War, it settled at about 800,000. In 1900 it became the first paper able to achieve early morning distribution throughout England when it started printing in Manchester as well as London.

Northcliffe did not relax after the success of the *Daily Mail*. On 2

November 1903 the first edition of the *Daily Mirror*, promoted as a "newspaper written by gentlewomen for gentlewomen," was published. When, after several weeks of enormous losses, Harmsworth decided "that women can't write and don't want to read" (quoted in Fyfe 1949: 115), he changed it to the first illustrated morning daily in Britain, a tabloid with, according to Harmsworth, "pictures stuck in anyhow and hardly any words at all" (quoted in Gardiner 1926: 290). The *Daily Mirror* became the first major daily aimed at the lower class, and in 1911 it became the first British daily to reach and maintain a circulation of more than one million (something *Lloyd's Weekly Newspaper* had achieved in 1896).

Northcliffe's last great purchase (although he continued to build his empire with weeklies and provincial papers) occurred in 1908, when he took over *The Times*, the circulation of which had dropped to only 38,000. Northcliffe never truly made *The Times* a paper in his own image, both because of opposition from virtually the entire staff and because he was forced to admit that to change the character of *The Times* would have eliminated its prestige and ended its position as Britain's most influential paper. However, by dropping the price from 3*d*. to a penny and by making it more of a middle-class organ, he raised its circulation to 318,000 within a decade.

Despite his excursions into "quality" newspapers, Northcliffe remained primarily a force in the popular press. In fact, he helped establish guidelines for a successful tabloid newspaper. Harmsworth did not invent the tabloid – the *New York Daily Graphic* had been a tabloid, as had Frank A. Munsey's short-lived *Daily Continent* in 1891 and Newnes' *Daily Courier* in 1896 – but he popularized it in Britain with the *Daily Mirror*. Hearst later credited him with being the originator of tabloid journalism, although he reserved for Dana the title of originator of "the intelligently condensed newspaper," and noted that Northcliffe had admitted that he had modeled the *Daily Mail* on Dana's ideas (Hearst 1948: 308).

But Harmsworth's approach to journalism affected more than just the look of periodicals. It also influenced the perceptions of events, places, and individuals. One of the places particularly affected was the Arctic, which had begun to intrigue Harmsworth, as it did many of his publishing contemporaries (Montefiore 1895: 504).

The goals of the Pole: circulation and fame

The origin of Harmsworth's interest in the Arctic was not particularly different from that of most other publishing proprietors of the time. In fact, the motives of the press had not changed since Bennett first became involved in the Arctic: exciting stories still sold newspapers and magazines. They also sold books, and the publishers of expedition accounts followed the press in demanding melodrama. "Don't blame me for being great, seeing that 'greatness' had been 'thrust upon me' in my absence, behind my back, as it were," Vilhjalmur Stefansson wrote to a friend. It was to the financial advantage of his publishers if "they can hoodwink the public. You and I know it is rot – we both know the great explorer too intimately – but you and I will both profit if Macmillan's can get away with it" (quoted in Hunt 1986: 111).

But Harmsworth was too much a man of action to be content with just "getting away with" the advantages that exciting stories about Arctic expeditions would bring his publications. He decided to follow the American lead and send his own expedition north, hoping to accrue the same kind of profits that *The Herald*, *The New-York Times*, and *Frank Leslie's Illustrated Newspaper* had made.

In 1894, familiar with Wellman's plans for reaching the North Pole from Svalbard and believing that a similar British effort should be made, Harmsworth agreed to finance the Jackson-Harmsworth Expedition, which was to explore Franz Joseph Land and, it was hoped, find a route to the Pole. The leader of the expedition was Frederick George Jackson, who the previous winter (1893–94) had sledged through the Russian Arctic to test his clothing, equipment, and food and to draw attention to – and hopefully gain financing for – his proposed trip to the far north.

Harmsworth maintained that his sponsorship was not a ploy to gain readers, writing: "The expedition is in no way connected with *Answers*. So far as I am concerned, it is a personal hobby" (quoted in Pound and Harmsworth 1959: 162). However, his publications took full advantage of his connection with the expedition. On the voyage from England to Franz Joseph Land, the expedition members were accompanied by two men who had been commissioned to write articles for the Harmsworth magazines. These were Cutcliffe Hyne and Herbert Ward, the latter having initially come to the public's attention as a member of the Emin Pasha Relief Expedition. But it was *The Evening News and Post*, purchased the same year that the expedition began, that benefited most, running prominently placed accounts whenever they became available.

Before Jackson left England, Harmsworth's new evening paper regularly promoted the expedition, as well as its leader and sponsor:

> Mr. Frederick G. Jackson is the plucky not-so-young man who is determined to hang up his hat on the North Pole. . . . Mr. Alfred C. Harmsworth, whom the world best knows as the editor of *Answers*, is the equally enterprising young man who has lent his aid and countenance, to say nothing of his counting-house, to the scheme. . . . Mr. Jackson feels as sanguine as one can feel about a Polar trip . . . [although] in the Arctic regions nothing is so likely to happen as the unforeseen. (*The Evening News and Post* 5 July 1894)

The other English papers also followed the preparations of the expedition with interest. As the departure date approached, more and more aspects of the expedition were featured, including the supply ship *Windward*, to which *The Standard* devoted an entire story (10 July 1894); the use of aluminum boats, condensed food, Siberian ponies, and brandy (the last as an anti-scorbutic), upon which *The Daily News* focused (7 July 1894); and the abilities of the leader, "a modern Ulysses, to whom scarcely any region of the earth is unfamiliar" (*The Times* 10 July 1894). Several of the papers also published a letter from Clements Markham, stating:

I cannot let you leave England without wishing you all possible success in the glorious, but most arduous enterprise which you have undertaken. . . . In your hands, for the time, is the Arctic fame. Your country and I feel sure that you will rise to the high level of your great undertaking and worthily uphold British credit and renown. (*The Times, The Daily Telegraph, The Evening News and Post* 11 July 1894)

Despite such high hopes for the attainment of the North Pole, Jackson and his party did not come close to it. They spent three years meticulously exploring and mapping Franz Joseph Land, proving in the process that it was an archipelago rather than a larger land mass, as some Arctic experts had supposed (Jackson 1899). But the most memorable moment of the expedition came on 17 June 1896, when Jackson unexpectedly met Nansen. Six weeks later, *Windward* delivered supplies and then sailed to Norway with Nansen on board (Nansen 1897: II, 456–99; Jackson 1899: II, 61–104).

Suddenly, the Jackson-Harmsworth Expedition repaid its sponsor handsomely. On 15 August 1896, the day after Nansen's return was announced, newspapers around the world carried the story about the meeting of Jackson and Nansen, and paid glowing tributes to both Jackson and Harmsworth. More importantly, the subsequent publication of letters from Jackson and Nansen to Harmsworth helped increase the circulations of *The Evening News* and the new *Daily Mail* (*Daily Mail* 12 September 1896).

The burst of enthusiasm accompanying Nansen's return eventually proved deleterious to Jackson, however, because in England enormous hopes were raised for his attainment of a new farthest north. An interview with Harmsworth was typical:

Mr. Jackson . . . has the field to himself, and I know him well enough to be convinced that he will strain every nerve to push forward . . . the opportunity of reaching the highest known latitude ever attained will obviously not be allowed to pass. . . . I do not care to talk about so problematical a matter as the future of any Arctic expedition, but I may say that every effort will be made to recover for England the record previously held by Admiral Markham. (*Daily Mail* 18 August 1896)

When Jackson returned to England in September 1897 without having sledged beyond the northern limits of Franz Joseph Land, the bitter disappointment among both the British polar community and press was demonstrated by the lack of attention he received. Even when he was mentioned in the press, it was with a focus on his failure to reach the North Pole rather than on any accomplishments. The kindest thing any major paper said was that if he had stayed another year, he might have made a more successful attempt on the Pole (*The Times* 4 September 1897).

The North Pole: although some sponsors continued to cover adventurous expeditions with a scientific veneer, the goal, both actual and stated, was more and more frequently the attainment of the Pole. Harmsworth himself could not make up his mind whether to claim that the goal of this expedition was to reach the Pole or to advance the cause of science. He once stated: "If Mr Jackson plants the Union Jack nearer the Pole than the

Stars and Stripes, I shall be glad, but if he came back, having found the Pole but minus the work of the scientists, of which our expedition consists, I should regard the venture as a failure" (quoted in Jackson 1935: 97). On the other hand, Harmsworth also wrote:

> We may rest assured that just as the records of Lockwood and Markham have been lowered by Nansen, so will Nansen's farthest north be beaten. . . . The fact that Mr. Jackson and his party are remaining in that strange home of theirs, in what is, in fact, probably the most desolate country in the world, points to the conclusion that he is alive to the splendid possibilities of his position. May we wish him good luck in reaching the Pole. (*Daily Mail* 15 August 1896)

The Pole: what *Harper's Weekly* called the "symbol of man's final physical conquest of the globe" (26 April 1904). Nansen addressed this desire for the conquest of the world – not only by the explorers, but by the press and the readers – in the introduction to Amundsen's book about the other end of the world, *The South Pole*:

> People stop again and look up. *High above them shines a deed, a man.* A wave of joy runs through the souls of men; their eyes are bright as the flags that wave about them.
> Why? On account of the great geographical discoveries, the important scientific results? Oh no; *that* will come later for the few specialists. This is something *all* can understand. A victory of human mind and human strength over the dominion and powers of Nature. (Amundsen 1912: I, xxix; emphasis Nansen's)

At the turn of the century, the increasing number of expeditions with the sole goal of attaining the North Pole was indicative of this desire for a victory over nature. It was also a sign of a personal lust for fame, fame that it was assumed would accompany such a conquest. Few showed this obsession more clearly than Robert E. Peary, whose mother told him: "If fame is dearer to you than anything else, what am I to say. I think if you should look at the matter calmly and dispassionately you would be less enthusiastic – such fame is dearly bought" (quoted in Herbert 1989: 65).

Jackson was another revealing example of the private goals of Arctic exploration. Despite Harmsworth's statements to the contrary, Jackson was not a scientist, and the expedition did not produce a wealth of scientific results. Jackson's greatest pleasure was hunting, and he devoted an entire chapter of his book to a list of game bagged (Jackson 1899: I, 399–429). But his strongest motivation for traveling to the Arctic was that he wanted fame, which he thought he had secured when he assisted Nansen. Initially, he was enormously pleased about the meeting, writing:

> You will understand how greatly this meeting affected me. My interest in Nansen dates so far back, and what I saw of him before he left had made me think continually of him as a colleague and a friend. I am all the more pleased, therefore, that this extraordinary chance has thrown it in my way to render him this service, and restore him to his friends in Norway. (*Daily Mail* 15 August 1896)

But in subsequent years, Jackson became embittered about the adulation given to Nansen, because at the same time he, Nansen's savior, received only fleeting publicity (Jackson 1935: 170–72).

Jackson was proof that, regardless of the press' backing, men did not achieve lasting recognition simply by venturing into unknown regions. The fate of two of his contemporaries illustrated this even more clearly. Evelyn B. Baldwin became prominent only as a result of the furor over the munificent funding provided by William Ziegler for Baldwin's attempt on the North Pole (1901–02). Ziegler had made millions as the founder and owner of the Royal Chemical Company, which specialized in producing baking powder. With his generous support, Baldwin left for Franz Joseph Land proclaiming: "I . . . emphasize the fact that the Baldwin-Ziegler Expedition was organized *to reach the Pole*. Neither scientific research, nor even a record of 'Farthest North,' will suffice; only the attainment of that much-sought-for spot where one can point only to the south can satisfy our purpose" (Baldwin 1901: 422; emphasis Baldwin's). Baldwin returned to the US the next year having achieved nothing. According to Joseph Knowles Hare, the artist of the expedition, the foremost accomplishment of the expedition was cruising around the south of Franz Joseph Land looking for a passage north that did not exist, while at the same time using up the coal supply. "After we landed," Hare reported, "Baldwin started a sledging expedition, and succeeded in losing more than 300 dogs and 30,000 pounds of pemmican" (*The New York Times* 16 September 1902). Ziegler removed Baldwin from command of the expedition, and the explorer faded into an obscurity relieved only by being occasionally asked to assess someone else's achievements.

Anthony Fiala, the photographer under Baldwin, similarly flirted with fame when he commanded Ziegler's second North Polar expedition (1903–05). Despite spending two years on Franz Joseph Land, Fiala and his party failed miserably in their three attempts on the Pole (Fiala 1907). William C. Champ, the secretary to Ziegler, and the man who commanded the relief expedition for Fiala in *Terra Nova*, made a succinct assessment of the contributions of Baldwin and Fiala when he commented: "The scientific results of Mr. Ziegler's lavish outlay of money in the past four years have been practically next to nothing. The expeditions could not even start on the 'dash for the pole.' They found nothing new, made no collections, and added not a mile of coast line to the maps" (*The New York Times* 27 August 1905). And fame certainly eluded Fiala; he returned to a job in a New York sporting goods store.

Even if a man could receive continuing sponsorship from newspapers or magazines, neither his success nor his long-term fame were assured. Walter Wellman's second expedition (1898–99), sponsored by the National Geographic Society, aimed to reach the Pole via Franz Joseph Land. However, it was a catastrophe, as *The New York Times* indicated in an article headlined WELLMAN BACK, A CRIPPLE:

> By the middle of March all hands were confident of reaching latitude 87 or 88, if not the pole itself. Then began a series of disasters. Mr. Wellman . . . fell into a snow-covered crevasse, seriously injuring one of his legs and compelling a retreat. . . . Two days later the party was roused at midnight by an icequake

under them, due to pressure. In a few moments many dogs were crushed and sledges destroyed. The members of the expedition narrowly escaped with their lives. . . . Mr. Wellman still can not walk, and it is not certain if he will ever regain complete use of his legs. (18 August 1899)

But Wellman made the most of his experience, and built a reputation by writing articles not only for his newspaper, but for a host of geographical journals and popular magazines. In the long run, his injuries healed well enough to allow him to make three more attempts on the North Pole – in 1906, 1907, and 1909 – all by dirigible. The first two were sponsored by *The Chicago Record-Herald* and its editor, Frank B. Noyes, who told Wellman: "Build an airship, go find the north pole, and report by wireless telegraphy and submarine cable the progress of your efforts" (*The Chicago Record-Herald* 31 December 1905). Each of the attempts was a ridiculous failure, once never getting the dirigible unpacked and twice crashing a short distance from where he started.

It was not only the explorers who hoped to achieve fame through their association with new lands. Men whose finances were greater than their courage, drive, or physical prowess attempted to gain a reputation by sponsoring expeditions. They hoped both to bask in the glow of the press attention and to be immortalized by having geographical features named after them. One of these was Ziegler, whose motives were captured by William C. Champ in the preface to Fiala's account of the second Ziegler expedition:

> The crowning desire of the late Mr. William Ziegler was to link his name with some scientific achievement which would be considered great when compared with others of the 20th Century, and he thought there was no mystery, the solution of which would be so heartily welcomed by the world at large as the exact location of the North Pole and accurate information as to the conditions existing there. (Fiala 1907: ix)

If wealthy individuals such as Ziegler did not seek out explorers to whom to donate money, they were actively recruited, not only by the explorers themselves, but by newspapers. Whitelaw Reid, the owner of the *New-York Tribune*, appealed to many potential contributors on behalf of Peary. Not only did Reid describe in glowing terms Peary's personality, ability, and goals, he suggested that the financing of such expeditions not only had tremendous public relations value professionally, but, if Peary reached the Pole, meant an instant and worldwide fame that would outlast that of Carnegie and Rockefeller.

The Scandinavian successors to Nansen

One reason the Norwegian school of polar exploration was so successful was that the Norwegians, unlike many British and American explorers, did not view the Arctic simply as an effective path to fame and fortune.

To a certain extent, the Scandinavian motives for exploration were anachronistic in the Anglo-American experience. Some explorers, such as

A.G. Nathorst, reflected the interests of Nansen in the entire Arctic, its answers to the questions of science, its unexplored regions, and its unusual peoples. Some, like Otto Sverdrup, were primarily drawn by the lure of the north, showing a mentality by then passé in the United States. And some, like Roald Amundsen, quested for a fame that would result from accomplishing a personal goal, rather than setting out to accomplish something – anything – in order to gain fame.

But none of them dealt with the Anglo-American public and press in a way specifically designed to make them popular. They presented the Arctic as they saw it, not as the readership in England and the United States had come to perceive it, and certainly not as the press wanted to continue interpreting it. Thus, many Scandinavian explorers were unable to equal the reputations of their British or American contemporaries who had sold themselves to the press. Among those rarely receiving international note was Nathorst, who led several Swedish expeditions, one of which, in 1898, explored the northeastern part of Svalbard, including Kvitøya, which had never been visited or mapped. The financing of Nathorst's expedition was the last contribution to Swedish Arctic study by Oscar Dickson, who died the year before the expedition left (Nathorst 1897). Another who did not receive great recognition in England or the US was Ludvig Mylius-Erichsen, the commander of a Danish exploring and scientific expedition (1906–08). He explored an unknown stretch of coast in northeast Greenland but died before the expedition returned to Denmark with a wealth of data (Amdrup 1913).

The first Scandinavian other than Nansen to receive the press coverage regularly given to American and British explorers was Salomon August Andrée, a social reformer who saw in technology the method whereby science could properly be applied for the betterment and ease of mankind. Andrée's interest in technology led him to propose the use of a hydrogen-filled balloon for the exploration of the Arctic Ocean north of Svalbard and the attainment of the North Pole. His novel method of travel, combined with his charm, good looks, and ease with the English language and people, made Andrée almost the equal of Nansen as a favorite of the English press. From the standpoint of publicity, his visit to London following his initial proposal was a huge success: "The young explorer, with his engaging manners and designs, at once plucky and novel, is the lion of the season's fag end, and has far more invitations than he knows what to do with. . . . He looked decidedly well groomed, and might have passed current anywhere as a typical varsity man" (*The Westminster Gazette* 26 August 1895).

Yet Andrée was no equal to Nansen in his groundwork or his anticipation of what might occur. And simple confidence was no substitute for the preparations that he ignored:

> I don't see that there will be any dangers at all. I have every confidence in the success of my enterprise, and am sure that before long I shall find any amount of imitators. I do not care a snap of the fingers what my critics say, for I have got the money, and nothing can prevent me from starting. . . . As for food, I am not yet sure what we shall take. . . . Mr. Ekholm, my companion, will calculate just

what we should have. Then I will say to him, "Well, my friend, you know what we want. I leave it to you to decide." I will not trouble about matters which others perfectly know. (*The New-York Times* 1 September 1895)

In 1896, partially funded by Dickson, Andrée traveled to Svalbard, but his plans were foiled by contrary winds. The experience did not deter either Andrée or his admirers. As A.H. Markham commented, "I think he may get to the Pole. He is an enthusiast, like Nansen, with a great belief in himself and the courage of his convictions . . . he knows too much about navigating the balloon to drop himself into the Atlantic" (*The Daily Telegraph* 15 August 1896).

Unfortunately, Markham's confidence was misplaced. The next year, despite conflicting opinions about the winds, Andrée and two companions departed in the balloon *Örnen*, never to be seen alive again. The expedition did not get near the Pole; the balloon, which was virtually uncontrollable because of an accident on take-off, was abandoned on the ice 200 miles northeast of Svalbard; and the three men died on White Island (Kvitøya), where their remains and diaries were found 33 years later (Andrée *et al.* 1931). Despite his negligble achievements, Andrée's pre-expedition publicity, combined with his disappearance, gave him posthumous celebrity status in England and the US. Accounts speculating about his fate or reporting the discovery of parts of his equipment appeared regularly in newspapers and magazines during the next several years. The *Daily Mail* even published an interview with a man who predicted where Andrée was, based on the explorer's horoscope (3 September 1897).

In contrast, Sverdrup accomplished much as Nansen's successor – arguably more than all of his contemporaries combined – but received little credit from the English or American press. Sverdrup was with Nansen on the first crossing of Greenland, and then was the ship's captain on the drift of *Fram*. Following his return to Norway, he was given command of *Fram* for an expedition to explore the north coast of Greenland. Sverdrup and his party could not pass the ice of Smith Sound, so they spent four years (1898–1902) charting the west coast of Ellesmere Island and the Sverdrup Islands, adding approximately 130,000 square miles to the map, including discovering Axel Heiberg Island, Amund Ringnes Island, and Ellef Ringnes Island (Sverdrup 1904).

Sverdrup also made significant contributions to polar travel. Like Nansen, he constantly worked to improve both his equipment and his techniques:

> There was hardly a thing in connection with the equipment of the sledge expeditions that I did not find could be made just a little better than it was before; and yet my sledge equipment, when we left home, was considered to be on par with that of any previous expedition. One learns as long as one lives, it is said, and certainly it is a saying which cannot be used with greater truth than with reference to sledging expeditions. (Sverdrup 1904: I, 291–2)

Sverdrup's greatest contribution was demonstrating that skis could be used on most kinds of snow and sea ice. He initiated the creative interplay between skis and dogs, proving that skis could be used to keep up with dogs, and that dogs could be driven by men skiing instead of riding on sledges, so that bigger loads could be carried. He also showed that Europeans could drive dogs as effectively as Eskimos, while indicating that Eskimo dogs from Greenland were more able to stand the constant rigors of long Arctic field trips than the Siberian breeds. Sverdrup was perhaps the first European explorer to understand dogs. He showed that "the Eskimo dog only reacted to a sympathetic mind. The relation between dog and driver had to be that between equals: a dog was not a horse, he was a partner, not a beast of burden" (Huntford 1980: 81). Sverdrup also understood men; he was a natural leader, admired by those who served under him. This was a quality that neither Nordenskiöld nor Nansen possessed to nearly the same degree.

So why, despite his achievements, did Sverdrup not become a heroic, or even popular, figure with the English and American readership? The answer is threefold. First, he received negative publicity from Peary's supporters, who believed that, by going near Smith Sound, Sverdrup had poached an area that Peary had the exclusive right to explore.

This attitude was widely accepted by the American newspapers. In fact, the only major articles in the American press about Sverdrup's expedition – stories widely published on 10 November 1900, after an Associated Press interview with the scientist Leopold Kann – emphasized Sverdrup's "trespass." Under headlines such as FELL OUT WITH PEARY, Kann, who had gone to Ellesmere with Peary, recalled the unexpected meeting with Sverdrup's party: "From conversations I elicited that some feelings had been engendered between Lieut. Peary and Sverdrup, the former rather resenting what he considered the latter's intrusion into ground which, for exploring purposes, the American was inclined to regard as his own."

The English were not disturbed by Peary's ludicrous notions of exclusivity. The Times published a three-column account by Sverdrup describing the adventures and accomplishments of his expedition (22 September 1902). And a widely printed letter by Clements Markham declared Sverdrup's expedition the most successful ever undertaken in the Arctic for the exploration of land, and the most productive since the time of John Franklin (for example, The Daily Telegraph 25 September 1902).

Despite the momentary praise for Sverdrup, the British press and public soon forgot about him for a simple reason: he was a foreigner and, even worse, not a native English speaker. The British and Americans had their own heroes, and although they would accept those of each other, there still was a tendency to ignore European explorers regardless of their accomplishments. (Southern Europeans received even fewer accolades than the Norwegians. The expedition of Luigi Amedeo di Savoia, the Duke of Abruzzi, was hardly mentioned in the English and American press despite attaining a farthest north of 86° 34' on 24 April 1900).

The third reason Sverdrup did not become a media hero was that, although he had the same vision as Nansen, he lacked his mentor's appeal. They both were enamored of the Arctic and viewed it as an enjoyable habitat rather than as a frighteningly dangerous environment, but Nansen had attained age-old goals, the thrill of which was obvious. Sverdrup discovered and charted almost as much new Arctic land as had been mapped in the whole of the previous half century (Huntford 1980: 81), but, unlike Nansen, he seemed to have had no adventures. His account made his four years seem too easy, and gave visions of men in comfortable settings, well-fed, and able to enjoy their leisure time reading, smoking, or conversing. That was neither what the public expected to hear nor what the press wanted to publish. So he was ignored by both.

Neither the press nor the public could totally ignore Amundsen, the man who succeeded Sverdrup as the dominant Norwegian polar explorer: his accomplishments were too overwhelming. Amundsen was the second mate on *Belgica* when she became the first ship to winter south of the Antarctic Circle. He led the expedition that was the first to complete the Northwest Passage by sea. And he was the first man to reach the South Pole.

But a simple list of achievements does not do justice to Amundsen. He was a new kind of man in the Arctic, a modern man who at the same time had many attributes of the *condottiere* in Renaissance Italy. He was not impelled by a belief in empire, in trade, or in bringing enlightenment to native peoples. He had no overwhelming interest in anthropology, botany, or geology. He was rather out to accomplish personal goals and desires, and to make a name for himself while doing it. He was in some ways a businessman-explorer, not in the sense of his wanting to go to the Arctic for commercial reasons, but in the extremely logical, sensible, and efficient way in which he set up expeditions and got them to their destination. Like Stanley, he was ruthless, but remarkably successful.

Part of this success was brought about because Amundsen fused and perfected the three major elements of the Norwegian school: the technical advances, the interplay of dogs and skis, and the feeling of oneness with the environment. Like Sverdrup, he constantly strived to improve both his equipment and his technique. For his expedition to the South Pole (1910–12), he constructed a non-magnetic sledge in order not to affect the compass; he had cans for paraffin made on board *Fram* (which Nansen allowed him to take to the Antarctic) and used silver solder because the commercially made products allowed loss of paraffin through "creeping"; and for his land navigation, which was based on dead reckoning, he developed snow-proof sledge meters (Huntford 1980: 306–7).

Amundsen also was a dedicated student of travel who, more than even his fellow Norwegians, was willing to learn from anyone: his immediate predecessors, such as Nansen and Sverdrup; his earlier forerunners, such as Rae and Hall; and those with the greatest experience, the northern peoples. These reasons behind Amundsen's amazing achievements were summed up by Nansen in the introduction to *The South Pole*:

> For the victory is not due to the great inventions of the present day and the many new appliances of every kind. The means used are of immense antiquity, the same as were known to the nomad thousands of years ago. . . . But everything, great and small, was thoroughly thought out, and the plan was splendidly executed. . . . Like everything great, it all looks so plain and simple. . . . Apart from the discoveries and experiences of earlier explorers – which, of course, were a necessary condition of success – both the plan and its execution are the

161

ripe fruit of Norwegian life and experience in ancient and modern times. The Norwegians' daily winter life in snow and frost, our peasants' constant use of ski and ski-sledge in forest and mountain, our sailors' yearly whaling and sealing life in the Polar Sea, our explorers' journeys in the Arctic regions – it was all this, with the dog as a draught animal borrowed from the primitive races, that formed the foundation of the plan and rendered its execution possible – when the man appeared. (Amundsen 1912: xxx)

Amundsen's willingness to learn extended beyond polar travel, and into relations with the press. Before his Northwest Passage expedition (1903–06), Amundsen had avoided members of the press. But Fritz Zapffe, an energetic freelance newspaper correspondent, hunted down the elusive young explorer, who stated, "I don't want to say anything before I have accomplished something. I wish to leave with the least possible attention. I want to have done something before letting anything appear in the press" (quoted in Huntford 1980: 79). However, Amundsen was not having great success at gaining financial backing, so Zapffe suggested ways publicity might persuade various philanthropists to support him. Although the thought had not occurred to him, Amundsen needed no further prompting; he allowed Zapffe to interview him, and he ultimately became a master of fund-raising. In fact, he became, according to Stefansson, "the most unblushed advertiser of the lot" with "deliberately laid plans that out-Herod Herod" (quoted in Diubaldo 1978: 45). And yet Amundsen never attempted to focus attention upon himself in the same way as Peary or even Nansen. Amundsen had an artist's attitude: he said, in his fashion, "look not at me, but at my achievements." But in doing so, he misread the English and American press and reading public, who wanted not just great deeds, but heroes to accomplish them.

Strangely, the coverage of Amundsen's deeds was never as lustrous as the deeds themselves; there was always something that seemed to obscure his triumphs. From 1903 to 1906, Amundsen's expedition in *Gjøa* not only brought to an end the 300-year-old quest for the Northwest Passage, it discovered the exact location of the Magnetic North Pole, proving that it indeed migrated (Amundsen 1908). This was a combination of adventure and scientific discovery that had rarely been equalled.

Yet the way the story was released stole considerably from Amundsen's glory. Nansen had negotiated on Amundsen's behalf for a lucrative international syndication of his Northwest Passage story and late in 1905, while *Gjøa* was wintering at King Point on the Yukon Coast, Amundsen telegraphed his story to Nansen. But the message was first held up, and then leaked to the press in Seattle. The story made its way around the world not by Amundsen's telegraph message, but from paper to paper. Amundsen lost a significant payment, but even more important, he lost much of the credit for the completion of the Northwest Passage. Because he had not yet sailed through the Bering Strait when he sent his message, many papers did not credit him with completing the Passage (although the difficult part was behind him, and all that remained was a voyage in open ocean once the ice broke). Rather, the majority of coverage attributed to him success only at locating the Magnetic North Pole, an achievement of

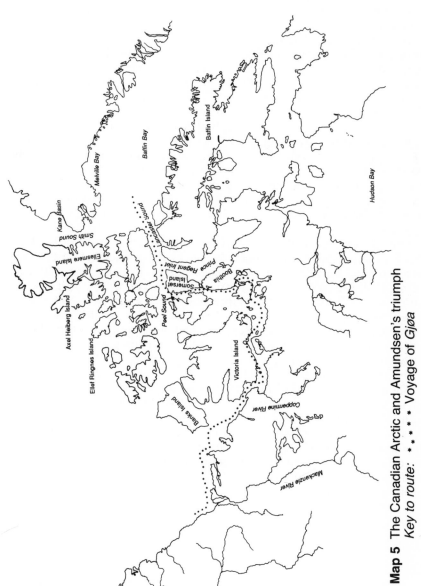

Map 5 The Canadian Arctic and Amundsen's triumph
Key to route: * * * * * *Voyage of Gjøa*

much less interest to the public. Yet by the time Amundsen arrived in San Francisco on 19 October 1906, the completion of the Northwest Passage was yesterday's news, and the press did not want to rehash the story.

Similarly, Amundsen's greatest achievement, the attainment of the South Pole, was not only overshadowed by the death of the British explorer Robert Falcon Scott, it was resented by much of the Anglo-American press and public, which believed that Amundsen had stolen the South Pole from Scott as surely as Sverdrup had interfered with Peary's exploration.

But it was not just fate that conspired to keep Amundsen from being the same kind of international hero as Nansen; his own inadequacies played a part. Like Sverdrup, Amundsen was neither a compelling speaker nor an outstanding writer. In fact, William Heinemann, the London publisher, wrote to Nansen about Amundsen's *The South Pole*: "I am . . . disappointed with the want of imagination he displays . . . in even so thrilling a thing as his achievement. . . . I cannot help feeling that however great Amundsen's feat is, he is not likely to write a good book" (Huntford 1980: 552). Ultimately, despite understanding the advantages of good publicity, Amundsen never gave the British and American readers what they wanted. Not only did he not create exciting images in his books, when he wrote for newspapers or was interviewed for them, he was possibly the one polar explorer who actually toned down what he had recorded in his journals.

Thus, Amundsen made the same error of judgment as had Nordenskiöld and Sverdrup. None learned that it was not achievements that were the key to journalistic hero-creation, but struggle and excitement. This difference of emphasis was noted by the Christiania newspaper *Morgenbladet*, which observed that Scott gave "the impression that terrain and weather were much worse [than] Amundsen's. This can hardly be the case. From Amundsen's account, one can see, for example, that he was forced to lie still for four days in a snow storm. But he considers it as something that belongs to such a journey – it's 'all in the day's work,' and he doesn't make a fuss about it" (quoted in Huntford 1980: 549).

There is a great deal of truth to the assessment that making a fuss was what the English and American press wanted. And the biggest fuss in the history of exploration occurred at the end of the first decade of the twentieth century. This dispute drew from the members of both the reputedly sensational and quality press more sensational coverage than had ever previously been given to geographical discovery. It also marked the zenith of the press in determining the public's images of and beliefs about explorers and exploration.

9

Peary, Cook, and the war of the New York press

Robert E. Peary, American hero

There is little doubt that today the most revered of all American explorers is Robert E. Peary. His is the one name related to the polar regions that schoolchildren in the US will almost certainly learn, and he is widely considered by the American public to be the man who first reached the North Pole. He is also remembered as a great patriot: a man who explored for the glory of the United States, who named his ship after President Theodore Roosevelt, and who proclaimed the attainment of 90° north with the message, "Stars and Stripes nailed to North Pole" (*The New York Times* 7 September 1909).

But there was another side of Peary, the comprehension of which is necessary to understand his role in the events of late 1909, when he was thrust with his arch-adversary, Frederick A. Cook, before the eyes of the western world. This side of Peary was considerably less pleasant than that presented in school books: he was perhaps the most self-serving, paranoid, arrogant, and mean-spirited of all nineteenth-century explorers. He was suspicious of and hateful to those he considered rivals either in actual geographical discovery or as heroic figures. He was condescending and insensitive to his subordinates, and he was ingratiating and servile to those he felt could help his quest for personal glory.

These aspects of Peary found their origin in his burning obsession for fame, which he himself acknowledged as early as 1887 in a letter to his mother: "I *must* have fame, and I cannot reconcile myself to years of commonplace drudgery and a name late in life when I see an opportunity to gain it now and sip the delicious draughts while yet I have youth and strength and capacity to enjoy it to the utmost. . . . I want my fame *now*" (quoted in Herbert 1989: 65; emphases Peary's).

Yet these very qualities, which can so easily be perceived in a negative light, might well have been important factors in Peary's success. He was energized by his insatiable hunger for fame and fortune. When others might have turned back, Peary's ambition drove him relentlessly until he had traveled more miles through the Arctic than any other explorer of his era.

Not that Peary had a deep emotional attachment to the Arctic; it was simply a setting in which fame and fortune could be gained. The marginal notations in his diary in the final weeks before his supposed attainment of the North Pole in 1909 are exceptionally revealing of Peary's goals, giving ample proof that he was concentrating on neither scientific observations nor geographical discovery, but that he was carefully weighing the benefits that reaching the Pole would bring him: fame, social standing, and wealth. His jottings indicate his intention to patent and sell a wide variety of objects, including "Peary North Pole sledges"; "Peary North Pole snow-shoes"; and North Pole coats, suits, tents, and cookers. He noted that Kane had received $75,000 in book royalties and Nansen $50,000, so that he should be able to obtain $100,000 from Harper's for his books, maga-zine articles, pictures, and stories. He figured that he should be promoted, because the US had made Melville and Schley admirals and Greely a general due in large part to their Arctic work. And he planned the picture of himself that he wanted distributed, writing: "Have Borup take a 5″ x 7″ 3 ½ to 4 ft. focus portrait of me in deer or sheep coat (face unshaven) with bear roll, & keep on till satisfactory one obtained. Have Foster color a special print of this to bring out the gray eyes, the red sun-burned skin, the bleached eyebrows and beard, frosted eyebrows, eyelashes, beard" (quoted in Herbert 1989: 239).

Peary had long believed that the north could be the setting for the attainment of these self-centered goals. In 1884, his first sight of San Salvador prompted him to write:

> Birthplace of the New World, land which first gladdened the eyes of Columbus, purple against the yellow sunset as it was nearly four hundred years ago when it smiled a welcome to the man whose fame can be equaled only by him who shall one day stand with 360 degrees of longitude beneath his motionless foot, and for whom East and West shall have vanished; the discoverer of the North Pole. (quoted in Weems 1967: 65)

Peary's own path turned to the far north in 1886, when he first went to Greenland. In the next decade, his two major expeditions to northern Greenland (1891–92 and 1893–95, the latter partially sponsored by *The Herald* and *The Sun*) earned him an international reputation. By 1898, when he abandoned Greenland for the lure of the North Pole, he was widely recognized as America's greatest explorer, and was even inaccura-tely portrayed as a sort of father of Arctic exploration: "He was the pioneer who inspired the present wide interest in polar research, his first expedition on the then untrodden ice-cap of Greenland, made more than fifteen years ago (in 1886), having encouraged Nansen to embark on polar work" (Rand 1902: 355).

By the same time, Peary had gained many wealthy and influential friends. He received extensive backing from the National Geographic Society, the Explorers' Club, and the newly formed Peary Arctic Club, an exclusive band of nationalistic millionaires led by Morris K. Jesup – one of the founders of the American Museum of Natural History and the president of the American Geographical Society – with the intention of assuring that Peary placed the flag of the United States at the North Pole before anyone else reached it. Peary's patrons included Jesup; George Crocker, a director of the Southern Pacific Railroad; Henry W. Cannon, the president of the Chase National Bank; James J. Hill, who built the Great Northern Railroad; and Herbert L. Bridgman, the publisher of the *Brooklyn Standard-Union*. Before leaving for the north in 1898, Peary was even given the whaler *Windward* by Alfred Harmsworth after Frederick Jackson's return from Franz Joseph Land (Peary 1899: 425; 1907: 296).

Peary's reaction to his encounter with Sverdrup on Ellesmere Island on 6 October 1898 was indicative of both the American's obsessive drive and his powerful paranoia. Despite the fact that Sverdrup made it clear before and after his expedition that he had no intention of trying to reach the North Pole (*Geographical Journal* 1898; Sverdrup 1904: I, 1), when Peary found that the Norwegian was in the north, he became frantic to reach Fort Conger, Greely's old headquarters on Lady Franklin Bay, which Peary intended to use as a base for his route to the Pole. He left for Fort Conger in late December, traveling in only the light of the winter moon, with temperatures below –50° Celsius. Peary, his black assistant Matt Henson, Dr Thomas Dedrick, and four Eskimos reached Fort Conger on 7 January 1899. Shortly after arriving, Peary's feet began to bother him:

[Henson] ripped the boots from both feet and gently removed the rabbitskin undershoes. Both legs were a bloodless white up to the knee, and as Matt ripped off the undershoes two or three toes from each foot clung to the hide and snapped off at the first joint.

"My god, Lieutenant! Why didn't you tell me your feet were frozen?" Matt cried.

"There's no time to pamper sick men on the trail," Peary replied tersely. . . . "Besides, a few toes aren't much to give to achieve the Pole." (Robinson 1947: 135–6)

Peary went no closer to the Pole for the time being. Dedrick was forced to amputate all but two of the explorer's remaining toes, and, after being immobile for a month, Peary was taken back to *Windward* on a sledge.

Nevertheless, after a year of relative inaction in northern Greenland, Peary was back on the ice. In May 1900, hobbling on his mangled feet or riding in a sledge (and accompanied by Henson and one Eskimo), he surpassed the American farthest north set by Lockwood and Brainard 18 years before. He also reached the top of Greenland – which he immediately assumed was the most northerly point of land in the world (Peary and Bridgman 1901) – and which he named Cape Morris Jesup. Two years later, on 21 April 1902, Peary and Henson bested their own mark, reaching 84° 17' (Henson 1912: 11).

Despite his achievements at such a high personal cost, Peary did not receive the acclaim he so desired. The expectations in the United States for his success had been incredibly high – in part because he had helped make them so himself – and they were equaled by the subsequent disappointment. Peary's accomplishments especially paled when compared to those of Sverdrup, who arrived in Norway eight days before Peary's return from the north, or to those of the Duke of Abruzzi, whose expedition surpassed Nansen's farthest north. *The New York Times* summed up the general feeling with the headline of its first story about Peary's expedition: PEARY FAILED TO REACH THE POLE (19 September 1902). To save face, in an interview with *The World*, Peary declared:

> The gain to the scientific world by the results of my work in the Arctic regions are of far more actual value than if I had discovered the North Pole. The discovery of the North Pole is merely a more or less spectacular fact. . . . The departments of science which will be benefited by my sojourn in the north are geology, meteorology, anthropology, and natural history. The full result of my labors cannot be fully ascertained or even imagined until the observations I have taken have been worked out by scientists. . . . the work I have done, I am vain enough to think, is great. (20 September 1902)

That a man who never learned the Eskimo languages or did any ethnographic or archaeological studies claimed important anthropological success was absurd. And Peary's stated emphasis on science was hypocritical; it came from a man who several months later wrote to a prospective sponsor: "You and I are no longer chickens, and we both know that no man would give a few facts of so-called scientific information the slightest weight, if balanced against the Pole" (quoted in Green 1926: 239).

Although many people considered Peary to have failed, he still had several important backers. In September 1903, at the order of President Roosevelt, Peary was granted another three years paid leave from active naval duty to pursue his goal. With the support of Jesup and another backer, Captain Charles Dix, he managed to raise enough money to build his ship *Roosevelt*, which borrowed some design principles from *Fram*, and would, it was hoped, be able to force its way through the narrow, ice-locked channels between Greenland and Ellesmere Island and deposit Peary and his party on the very edge of the frozen Arctic Ocean.

Peary also changed his strategy for what he assumed to be his last polar push. He introduced what he called the "Peary System," a method of reaching the Pole consisting of 14 parts (Peary 1910a: 201–12). Essentially, his system called for three platoons: a pioneer party to break the trail and build igloos for overnighting; support groups to shuttle caches of supplies forward; and the polar party, which would bring up the rear so that, rested and lightly equipped, it could make the final dash to the Pole (Peary 1910a: 204–8). Actually, it is questionable if any of the 14 parts of the Peary System were really his own. Much of what he claimed credit for was universally known and practiced among Arctic explorers, and the specifics of the progressive parties had first been introduced by Fedor Vrangel' (Ferdinand von Wrangel) in the 1820s (Vrangel' 1844). Peary later went so far as to write a book almost entirely devoted to an expansion of the system he claimed to have developed (Peary 1917). He also frequently claimed credit for the initial adoption of Eskimo clothing, methods of travel, and living techniques. These were no more his developments than the Peary System, having been used by Rae, Hall, Schwakta, Gilder, and others before Peary ever considered going north.

One result of Peary's "new" plans and improved ship was that he was able to claim that on 21 April 1906 he, Henson, and several Eskimos achieved a farthest north of 87° 6'. Yet the announcement of this feat created little elation in the press and ultimately received only slightly more attention than had his previous journeys. In New York City, the story was lost in the efforts to defeat William Randolph Hearst's campaign for governor. Even *The New York Herald*, which had helped sponsor Peary, gave the initial story only two columns and five decks. Certainly, it was proud that, "By an American route, in an American vessel, an American, Robert E. Peary, has beaten all records and, in what he announced on his departure as his 'last' dash for the North Pole, has reached . . . about thirty-five miles nearer the long coveted prize than his nearest rival, the Duke of Abruzzi" (3 November 1906). But the expectations for success were higher than ever – again due in part to Peary's promises – and the resulting disappointment was equally strong. The words of Jesup upon hearing the news must have placed devastating pressure upon Peary: "It would be useless to deny that I am disappointed that Commander Peary failed to reach the Pole" (*The Washington Post* 3 November 1906).

To Jesup, to the Arctic Club, and – most of all – to Peary, the farthest north was still a failure. With all the funding and time invested, nothing short of the North Pole could be considered a success. Thus Peary decided to make yet one more effort. And, despite the death of Jesup in 1908, he managed to obtain the funds for his ultimate "final attempt" on the Pole. By now there was virtually unremitting pressure on Peary: would he have a magnificent triumph or a last, humiliating defeat? Not only those intent on the Pole, but everyone seeking fame of any kind had become a competitor to Peary, as was shown by a comment that his departure for the north in July 1908:

will mark the beginning of an international race between the American explorer and Lieut. Ernest H. Shackleton, R.N., [*sic*] who is trying to accomplish in the south pole regions what Peary is in the north. Despite the fact that Lieut. Shackleton has a year's start, Peary, nevertheless, expects to get further north than the British explorer does south, and to let the world know the results of his expedition before Shackleton reports his results. (*The New York Times* 14 July 1908)

However, it was not the departure of Shackleton in 1907 that should have concerned Peary, but that of another polar explorer the same year, a man who actually was a rival to Peary: Dr Frederick A. Cook.

In the shadow of the giant

Dr Cook was nine years younger than Peary and altogether a different type of man. Rather than being hard-driven, obsessed, and intolerant, he was courteous, charming, and remarkably impulsive. Cook had settled into an unproductive medical practice in Brooklyn when he saw an advertisement in the *Brooklyn Standard-Union* asking for volunteers to join Peary's 1891 North Greenland expedition. He responded to it and was accepted as expedition physician. Cook was immediately captivated by the Arctic. And Peary was quite pleased with Cook, as he related in *Northward over the great ice*:

> To Dr. Cook's care may be attributed the almost complete exemption of the party from even the mildest indispositions, and personally I owe much to his professional skill, and unruffled patience and coolness in an emergency. In addition to his work in his special ethnological field, in which he has obtained a large mass of most valuable material concerning a practically unstudied tribe, he was always helpful and an indefatigable worker. (Peary 1898: I, 423–4)

Upon their return, Cook agreed to accompany Peary north again as his second-in-command in 1893. But before they left, the two men had a disagreement. Cook asked that he be allowed to publish an article on the medical and ethnological studies he had made in the north, but Peary refused. Peary always required that everyone who accompanied him sign a contract stating that they would refrain from publishing or lecturing on the subject of the expedition, which was a safeguard preventing competition to Peary's own money-making efforts. Cook felt that because his article would appear in a medical journal and could not possibly affect the sales of any book Peary might write, he should be released from this agreement. When Peary refused to budge, Cook resigned from the expedition.

In the following years, Cook slowly built a polar reputation for himself. In 1893 he led a small expedition to West Greenland, which was financed by the Yale University professor James H. Hoppin to enable his son Benjamin to spend a summer in the Arctic (Freeman 1961: 36–7). The next year, he organized another expedition to West Greenland, one that was to feature a combination of sports-hunting and science. Or, in the assessment of *The New-York Times*: "There is no specific object in the trip, each member of the party being allowed to pursue his own inclinations regarding arctic investigations" (23 April 1894). The expedition was a fiasco, however, as the ship, *Miranda*, first struck an iceberg, and then, after repairs had been made, ran into a submerged rock and had to be abandoned.

In 1898–99, Cook served as the physician on *Belgica*, participating in the first Antarctic wintering and contributing mightily to holding the crew together. He forced upon his shipmates, over their objections, a regime of fresh meat – seal and penguin – thereby avoiding massive scurvy. Later, *Belgica*'s escape from the ice was, according to Amundsen, the second mate of the expedition, "due first and foremost to the skill, energy, and persistence of Dr. Cook" (*New York American* 19 September 1909). The *Belgica* expedition made Cook an internationally known traveler. He was knighted in Belgium, and his articles appeared in a host of popular magazines.

Cook again became involved with Peary in 1901, when Herbert L. Bridgman, the secretary of the Peary Arctic Club, requested he go north on the relief ship *Erik* in case Peary needed a doctor other than Dedrick. Cook examined Peary in Greenland and found him to be exhibiting the early symptoms of pernicious anemia. He told the older man to eat raw meat and liver, to which Peary responded, "I would rather die" (Eames 1973: 25). "You are through as a traveler on snow on foot," Cook said, "for without toes and a painful stub you can never wear snowshoes or ski" (Eames 1973: 25). Peary ignored Cook and, if he had not already, turned against the doctor.

Five years later, when Peary returned from his farthest north, he was confronted by Cook again. Cook had just claimed the first ascent of North America's highest mountain, Mount McKinley, and the triumphant honors that Peary had expected to receive were shared with the younger man (*The New York Herald* 16 December 1906). Then, to Peary's further dismay, Cook's book about the ascent (1908), became a bestseller, while Peary's account of his farthest north was a dismal failure, selling only 2,230 copies its first year.

But these exasperations were only a prelude for what was to come. In July 1907 Cook sailed north with the wealthy sportsman John R. Bradley. The trip was reputedly planned as a big-game hunt, but Cook took along the supplies he said he would need for an assault on the North Pole. Although he attempted to do this quietly, rumors reached Peary and other members of the Arctic community that Cook might try for the Pole. Despite Cook's obvious abilities and achievements, virtually no one with serious knowledge of the Arctic considered him the equal of Peary or able to accomplish such a task. So the rumors were generally ignored.

However, finding what he described as "auspicious weather" (Cook 1911a: 68), Cook decided to remain in northwest Greenland. From Etah, he wrote a letter to Bridgman, which he sent back south with Bradley. When received, it sent shockwaves through the exploration community: "I have hit upon a new route to the north pole and will stay to try it. By way of Buchanan Bay and Ellesmere and northward through Nansen Strait over the Polar Sea seems to me to be a very good route. There will be game to the 82d degree, and here are natives and dogs for the task. So here is for the pole" (quoted in *The Washington Post* 2 September 1909).

Peary was outraged. He felt Cook was not only stealing the territory he had pioneered, but *his* Eskimos and *his* dogs. Cook was also stating that he would try to succeed by using the methods with which Peary had so long failed and a route that Peary had not found in all his years in the north. As far as Peary was concerned, Cook was unethical, insulting, and a fool.

The older explorer was still incensed when, on 6 July 1908, *Roosevelt* left New York for his last attempt on the Pole. He did not depart without a crescendo of attacks on Cook, however, including stating that the doctor should have to show "proper proofs" if on his return he claimed to have reached the Pole. Peary also insisted that his rival should be shunned by all reputable geographical societies, because "Dr. Cook's action in going north . . . for the admitted purpose of forestalling me [is] one of which no man possessing a sense of honor would be guilty" (*The New York Times* 28 May 1908).

171

The Pole attained or only claimed?

On 2 September 1909, while Peary was still in the far north, his nightmare came true. That morning, papers around the world featured Cook's sensational announcement that he had reached the North Pole.

The story originated in Lerwick, Shetland Islands, from where Cook – a passenger on the steamship *Hans Egede*, traveling between Upernavik and Copenhagen (København) – had sent messages to his wife and to the Brussels Observatory announcing his attainment of the Pole. He also sent a cable about his success to James Gordon Bennett, stating, "Message left in care of Danish consul, 2,000 words. For it $3,000 expected. If you want it, send for it" (Cook 1911a: 465). Bennett pounced on such an opportunity, and the next day *The Herald*, both in New York and Paris, published five full pages about Cook's expedition, including more than an entire page in the explorer's own words (2 September 1909).

According to his story, Cook had left Annoatok (Anoritoq) on 19 February 1908, accompanied by Rudolph Francke – the former steward on Bradley's yacht, who had remained in Greenland – and nine Eskimos. The party crossed Smith Sound to Cape Sabine on Ellesmere Island. Fighting record-low temperatures of –86° Celsius, they then crossed Ellesmere to Cape Stallworthy, the northernmost point of Axel Heiberg Island. From there, Cook and four Eskimos headed northward. Three days later, two of them turned back, leaving Cook with two young Eskimos to accompany him to the Pole.

Cook's article told of the usual trials encountered by those attempting to reach the North Pole: back-breaking efforts to hack through enormous pressure ridges; desperate advances despite Arctic storms that would have stopped most travelers for days; gaping leads a mile or more across; and crucial shortages of food and fuel. Nevertheless, he claimed that on 21 April 1908 he and his companions reached the Pole. The return was even more dramatic, as the three missed their depot on Axel Heiberg Island and continued south to Devon Island, where they wintered at Cape Sparbo in an underground den, living on musk-oxen killed with lances made from the sledges (Cook 1951). The next spring, they returned to Annoatok, from where Cook sledged south to catch *Hans Egede*.

Although Cook's story went directly to Bennett, it did not end up being an exclusive for *The Herald*. It received unprecedented coverage (for a story of exploration) throughout Europe and the United States. In the latter, many large papers published Cook's personal account on 2 September, the same day it appeared copyrighted in *The Herald*, some having paid for permission, and some (such as *The New York Times*) having stolen the copy from the Paris edition (with its nine-hour-earlier release time). All the major New York papers ran Cook's story no later than the next day. Throughout the American press, Cook's claim was sensationally presented, with banner headlines, two or more full pages of coverage, comments from noted polar explorers, and eulogistic editorials, such as the one in the *New York American* (the name given to the morning edition of Hearst's *New York Journal* in March 1903, when the evening

Figure 4 The front page of *The New York Herald* on 2 September 1909, featuring a banner headline about Frederick A. Cook's claimed attainment of the North Pole.

173

edition received the former name) that called 1909 a "year of wonders" and Cook's attainment of the Pole "an epoch of marvels."

Although most of the English morning dailies did not break with the standard single-column headline typography, they did use more than four decks, the maximum common at the time (Hutt 1973: 82). They also gave the story considerable space, particularly the *Daily Mail*, which published six columns about Cook on 3 September despite a recent decision by Northcliffe that "adventure" stories were not to receive the kind of prominent play that he felt should be reserved for important national topics (Startt 1988: 279).

The coverage actually increased in the following days, as more information was obtained and more individuals were interviewed for their reactions. But although the newspapers realized that Cook's story was too important to ignore, they did not all immediately accept his claims. From the beginning, *The New York Times* was skeptical, and Carr Van Anda wrote an editorial under the headline HAS MAN REACHED THE POLE? (2 September 1909). Likewise, the *New-York Tribune* (the owner of which, Whitelaw Reid, was an admirer of Peary) did not proclaim Cook's discovery a fact, but headlined its initial story NORTH POLE REPORTED FOUND BY DR. COOK (2 September 1909).

This skepticism was also initially shown by the public at large, according to *The Daily Telegraph*, which stated:

> Keen business men on their way to their offices, who paused to read the announcement, usually smiled incredulously, and passed along without comment. It is not denied that Dr. Cook may have reached the North Pole, and there is no patriotic American who does not wish most fervently that the New York physician may have achieved this dream of ages, the goal for which so many heroes of all nations have vainly struggled and died, but, to speak frankly, the average American has become so entirely accustomed to the announcement of wonderful discoveries in the American newspaper Press, which subsequent events have failed to justify, that he pauses by instinct, and, before accepting the announcement literally, he naturally demands abundant proof. (3 September 1909)

There certainly were doubters in the polar community. George W. Melville of the *Jeannette* expedition immediately stated, "Without backing, money, outfit or equipment, I don't see how Dr. Cook could have reached the pole, let alone lived through the return journey. . . . I can't conceive that Mr. Cook has done it on 'his nerve,' so to speak" (*The New York Herald* 2 September 1909). Evelyn Baldwin thought the claim even more dubious, proclaiming, "This cannot be substantiated. . . . It is perfectly easy for a man to go to a certain point and then to say that he has reached the Pole. . . . I cannot accept this statement . . . unless far better evidence is offered" (*New York American* 2 September 1909). The day after these statements, Melville made a stronger condemnation: "After reading the dispatches to-day I am more convinced than ever that the reported discovery of the north pole is a fake" (*The New York Times* 3 September 1909). Even some members of the Explorers' Club, of which Cook was one of the founders and had succeeded Greely as President, were quoted as expressing concern with the original story, and not understanding why, if Cook had reached the Pole in only 35 days, it had taken him more than 16 months to return to civilization (*The World* 2 September 1909).

Meanwhile, scientific doubts were expressed by the noted British geographer Hugh Robert Mill (*The World* 4 September 1909); Louis C. Bernacchi, a physicist who had been a member of two Antarctic expeditions (*The Daily News* 3 September 1909); and the Harvard astronomer Percival Lowell, who added, "scientifically the discovery of the North Pole is of just the same significance as a new record in the 100 yard dash" (*The Boston Daily Globe* 3 September 1909).

Despite the doubters, however, most newspaper reports were overwhelmingly favorable to Cook. On 2 September *The Herald* announced that Cook had received the congratulations of Amos Bonsall, the last living member of Kane's expedition; Adolphus W. Greely, who called Cook's journey "the most extraordinary feat in polar exploration" (and who had been antagonistic toward Peary ever since 1902, when the latter had decried "Greely's folly" for abandoning Fort Conger to head south); Anthony Fiala, who for many years had been a close friend of Cook's and had even recommended him for the position Fiala received as leader of the second Ziegler North Polar expedition; Robert Falcon Scott, who had obtained a farthest south in 1902 as the leader of the British National Antarctic Expedition (1901–04); Ernest Shackleton, the Anglo-Irish explorer who had broken Scott's farthest south by reaching only 97 miles from the South Pole in January 1909; and Roald Amundsen, who was quoted as saying that it must have been "the most brilliant sledge trip in the history of polar exploration."

The belief in Cook's veracity took a quantum leap on 4 September, when he arrived in Copenhagen, where he was met by the Danish crown prince, the United States minister to Denmark, and tens of thousands of cheering well-wishers (Egan 1910). He was immediately swept away in a current of impassioned hero-worship and feted almost continuously. Few things show the heights to which his reputation soared more clearly than the immediate popularity of the Dr Cook hat and Dr Cook toys. By the day after Cook's arrival in Copenhagen, the hat was the rage of women's fashion in both London and New York:

> The Dr. Cook hat is suggestive of the polar region. It seems as high as the cartoonist's picture of the pole, although in reality it is only two feet tall. It is constructed of brown fur, fuzzy and expensive. It . . . looks massive and solid enough to supply a good soup stock in case of Arctic exigency. Further heightening its chilly effect is a snowlike spray of aigrette high up on the left side. (*New-York Tribune* 5 September 1909)

Dr Cook toys were huge sellers for several months, and included both large dolls that looked like Cook and were dressed in white furs, and small, fur-clad Cook figures on sledges.

Meanwhile, Cook was also deluged with so many reporters, that it seemed "Fleet Street had moved to Copenhagen" (Cook 1911a: 465). In a triumphant press conference attended by more than 80 journalists, Cook disarmed his critics by stating that he had proofs of his exploit and that he would soon produce them for the proper scientific organizations. His incredible story, along with his apparent *naïveté*, honesty, and sincerity, kept the reporters spellbound and won them to his cause (Gibbs 1923: 45). W.T. Stead, as doyen of the press, asked most of the questions, and, at the end of the session, spoke for the assembly when he paid a tribute of admiration and homage to Cook.

Literally overnight, Cook became the media darling of the Western world. Stead's assessment of the explorer was typical of those of the next several days: "Everything a clever rogue would do instinctively if he wished to hoax the public Dr. Cook did not do" (Stead 1909: 328). Stead's initial trust of Cook meant a great deal to the reading public, because Stead was not enough a believer in the innate goodness of man to be easily fooled by a simple fraud. He also had earned a reputation as one of the most insightful interviewers in all of journalism. After additional contact, he was even more positive about the explorer: "Dr. Cook leaves the impression on those whom he met at Copenhagen that he is the furthest possible remove from the type of man who would set out to befool the public on a matter of such universal interest. He seemed to us all an honest man at first acquaintance, and those who saw most of him believed in him most" (Stead 1909: 329).

Yet one reporter continued to hold out against the beliefs of the majority. Philip Gibbs, who was later knighted for his outstanding correspondence from the front during World War I, was the first English journalist to contact Cook, managing an interview while the explorer was still on board *Hans Egede*. When Gibbs asked to see Cook's diaries, journal, or observations, the American exploded at him, "I bring the same proofs as every other explorer. I bring my story. Do you doubt that? When Shackleton and Peary came home you believed what they told you. Why, then, should you disbelieve me?" (*The Daily Chronicle* 7 September 1909). However, the comment served only to make Gibbs suspicious: "I had believed him. But at that strange, excited protest and some uneasy, almost guilty look about the man, I thought, 'Hullo! What's wrong? This man protests too much.' From that moment I had grave doubts about him" (Gibbs 1923: 43).

Disturbed not only by Cook's aggressive behavior and evasiveness, but by the inaccuracies and lack of cohesion in his story, Gibbs reported his suspicions in *The Daily Chronicle*, beginning with a front-page feature with the two-column headline DOUBTS ABOUT DR. COOK'S STORY (6 September 1909). For the next week, Gibbs continued to attack Cook's claim. He pointed out that Cook had already changed his claim of temperatures from Celsius to Fahrenheit, that his average of 15 miles a day was greater than any expert thought probable, and that his measurements of longitude and latitude were too accurate to be realistic:

> All Arctic explorers . . . are agreed that at the time of the year when Dr. Cook claims to have reached the Pole, it would have been impossible to fix its position within minutes to say nothing of seconds. It is not necessary to dispute Dr. Cook's contention that he got an observation of 89deg. 59min. 46sec. – that is quite possible, but no trained observer would have drawn the conclusion that he

must necessarily be within 14sec. of the Pole. (*The Daily Chronicle* 7 September 1909)

Gibbs also expressed disbelief that a man who had no white companions accompany him to the Pole would have been willing to part with his proofs that he had accomplished the deed. Yet, he pointed out, Cook had done exactly that. Or had he? In fact, Gibbs said, Cook had changed his story about his proofs a number of times, telling the *Daily Mail* that they were with Harry Whitney in Etah; telling *The Evening News* that his observations and notebooks were with him in Copenhagen, telling *The Daily News* that part of his original observations had been sent to America and part kept in hand; and telling Gibbs that all of his material had gone on to the United States (*The Daily Chronicle* 8 September 1909). "This explorer," Gibbs wrote, "is a man who says one thing to one man and a different thing to another man, and how to build a bridge over these contradictions is beyond my imagination" (*The Daily Chronicle* 7 September 1909).

But Gibbs' reports generally fell on deaf ears. Cook was the man of the hour, admired the world over and in Denmark caught in a whirl of banquets, presentations, royal congratulations, and honorary degrees. So even when Gibbs and the Danish explorer Peter Freuchen analyzed Cook's statements about distances traveled, sledge weights, the amount of food drawn by the dogs, and the timetables, and showed they were not only contradictory but downright absurd, the public was on Cook's side (Gibbs 1923: 46; Freuchen 1953: 90–93). Gibbs found himself vilified in the Danish and English press and even challenged to a duel (Gibbs 1923: 51). And Freuchen's editor refused to publish his stories about Cook, commenting: "We cannot wine and dine a man one day and call him a fraud the next" (Freuchen 1953: 92).

It was at just one of these occasions – in fact, a farewell banquet in Copenhagen for the journalists who had been covering Cook's return – that the entire complexion of the North Pole story changed. The Danish host received a message that so surprised him he handed it to Stead to read out. The man who had done more than anyone else to bring the New Journalism to England made the most sensational announcement of his career: "In a wire from Indian Harbor, Labrador, dated September 6, 1909, Peary says, 'Stars and Stripes nailed to the Pole'" (*New York Evening Journal* 6 September 1909).

"The Pole at last!"

On 7 September 1909 Peary's claim to have reached the North Pole was splashed throughout the papers of the United States and Europe. And no paper gave the story more coverage than *The New York Times*, which had first become involved with Peary the previous spring, shortly before he left for the north. For a number of years, Peary had sold his exclusive accounts to *The New York Herald*, but in 1908 Bennett's executives did not express much interest in what they viewed as likely yet another fruitless expedition toward the Pole. Peary's accounts had made less and less of an impact on the paper's sales, and its executives assumed that another such story would not bring with it anything more than had Peary's farthest north of 1906.

However, one editor who did believe in Peary was William Reick, who in 1908 moved from *The Herald* to *The Times*. Reick persuaded his superiors to pay Peary $4,000 for his story of the attainment of the North Pole, with a clause in the contract stating that Peary would repay the money if he did not reach 90° north. Thus, when Peary returned, his messages went directly to *The Times* (Bartlett 1931: 218–20).

Actually, Peary's full story, which ran to some 7,300 words, came in only slowly, due first to weather problems slowing the progress of *Roosevelt* and then to the fact that it was being transmitted from Indian Harbor, a small station on the coast of Labrador. The story was not published until 10 and 11 September, and then appeared again in one piece in the Sunday supplement of 12 September. It told how throughout March 1909 the forward parties had methodically moved supplies closer and closer to the North Pole. One by one the supporting parties had turned back, until only Peary, Henson, Bob Bartlett (the captain of *Roosevelt*), and a number of Eskimos remained. On 31 March, the expedition had reached a latitude of 87° 47', the farthest north ever recorded. The next day, Peary selected Henson and four Eskimos to accompany him to the Pole and sent Bartlett and the remaining Eskimos back, despite the fact that Bartlett had agreed to skipper *Roosevelt* on Peary's final two expeditions only if Peary promised that he might accompany the explorer all the way to the Pole.

Peary and his party had been averaging fewer than 12 miles per day before Bartlett's return, but suddenly their speed increased dramatically – Peary claimed the interfering leads and pressure ridges disappeared – and the 150-mile final dash took them only five days. On 6 April 1909, almost one year after the date Cook claimed to have been at the Pole, Peary also reportedly reached it, marking his achievement, according to his book *The North Pole*, with the entry into his diary: "The Pole at last! The prize of three centuries. My dream and ambition for twenty years. Mine at last. I cannot bring myself to realize it. It all seems so simple and commonplace" (Peary 1910a: 288).

Peary's trip back to his last camp was even more impressive than his outward journey, taking only three days. He then returned directly to his main base at Cape Columbia, reaching it only five days after Bartlett.

Peary's announcement received greater attention than had even Cook's. *The New York Times* and *The Chicago Daily Tribune*, the latter to which *The Times* had sold the rights to Peary's story – as it also had done to *The Times* of London – had enormous coverage, with the New York paper giving the news five full pages and the Chicago journal four pages. Both papers also published numerous photographs of Peary and the members of his expedition. But the other major newspapers were not outdone. *The New York Herald* gave the story five pages; the *New-York Tribune* gave it four and one-third; and *The World*, *The Sun*, and *The Washington Post* four; all printed photographs of Peary and his company. As they had with

Cook, *The Herald* and the *American* both ran their initial stories under three-line banner heads, and within two days, even the headlines of *The New York Times* had expanded from their normal two columns to four: COMMANDER PEARY'S PRELIMINARY ACCOUNT OF HIS SUCCESSFUL VOYAGE TO THE NORTH POLE.

As usual the English newspapers gave the story neither the total space nor the headline size of the American papers. But the amount was staggering compared to normal articles. For example, *The Daily Telegraph* proclaimed Peary's feat with six decks and eight columns of copy running onto two pages.

The literary world also immediately became involved. On the day Peary's attainment of the Pole was announced, Cassell's publishing house telegraphed the adventure author Frank Shaw, asking if he could produce within a month a 70,000-word children's book about polar exploration, embodying the growing Peary myth. Shaw wrote the book in a week, and it was on sale by 1 November (Shaw 1958: 143).

But it was not just Peary's claimed achievement that received the attention. Even more dramatic were his attacks on Cook. Before Peary's full story had even been received, he had denounced Cook as a liar, had stated that no trace of him had been found at the Pole, and had claimed to "have him nailed" (*The New York Times* 8 September 1909). When Peary's story of his journey to the Pole was run in *The New York Times*, beside it ran a statement from Peary that said:

> Do not trouble about Cook's story or attempt to explain any discrepancies in his statements. The affair will settle itself. He has not been at the Pole on April 21st, 1908, or at any other time. He has simply handed the public a gold brick. These statements are made advisedly, and I have proof of them. When he makes a full statement of his journey over his signature to some geographical society or other reputable body, if that statement contains the claim that he has reached the pole, I shall be in a position to furnish material that may prove distinctly interesting reading for the public. (11 September 1909)

Peary's vicious attack was directly contrary to Cook's flowery tributes to his rival. Upon the announcement at the banquet in Copenhagen that Peary had reached the Pole, Cook had graciously stated: "I am proud that a fellow American has reached the pole. As Rear Admiral Schley said at Santiago, 'There is glory enough for us all.' He is a brave man, and I am confident that if the reports are true his observations will confirm mine and set at rest all doubts" (*The New York Herald* 8 September 1909).

Nevertheless, with the influx of Peary's messages, *The New York Times* quickly perceived a sensation that could increase its circulation like that of *The World* or the *New York Journal* a decade earlier. Even better, it hoped that its gains could be made at the expense of *The Herald*, which not only was a more reasonable target than the papers of Pulitzer or Hearst, but was the strongest supporter of Cook. So Peary and *The Times*, which staked its entire reputation on the older explorer and his claims, began an aggressive, unrelenting campaign against Cook in the hope that the acknowledgement of Peary's success and Cook's attempt at perpetrating a fraud would increase the sales and reputation of *The Times* while concurrently damaging those of *The Herald*.

Peary was not, of course, the first person to attack Cook. In the days immediately following Cook's announcement, Peary's followers had condemned him for using the senior explorer's route (even though Cook was many miles to the west of Peary) and his Eskimos and dogs (even though Peary did not, of course, own these people or their animals). The biased coverage by *The Times* led the *Tribune*, which was partial to Peary but still open-minded, to comment about the real reason for the reportive zeal of *The Times* on these issues: "The controversy between Commander Peary's backers and Dr. Cook respecting the employment of Eskimaus and the use of dogs is not likely to make an impression in England, although Sir George Nares has prematurely discussed the matter. Jealousy of *The Herald*'s journalistic enterprise is not felt in London, as it is in New York" (5 September 1909).

The reports of Philip Gibbs also continued after Peary's announcements, and, after speaking to Cook following a lecture in Copenhagen, Gibbs reported that the doctor "flushed and perspired under the stabbing queries," and that his answers "prove conclusively that his claims to have reached the North Pole belong to the realm of fairy tales" (*The Daily Chronicle* 10 September 1909). At that stage, *The New York Times* began to reproduce *The Daily Chronicle*'s articles at great length.

Van Anda also began to emphasize *The Times*' success in other ways. Next to Peary's first account was a front-page box giving notice to other publishers that Peary's story had been copyrighted and that any reproduction of it, without permission, was illegal and would be prosecuted. It was a typical Van Anda action. He shrewdly predicted that it would serve to drive home to the reading public the fact that *The Times* was first with great stories (Berger 1951: 176).

A number of competing newspapers – including *The World* and *The Sun* and, in Chicago, *The Daily Inter Ocean*, *The Record-Herald*, and Hearst's *Chicago American* – tried to surmount the copyright problem by having their London correspondents cable the story to them as run in *The Times* of that city. *The New York Times* quickly obtained an injunction against these papers. Van Anda later admitted that the point of the exercise was not to protect Peary's financial position, as had been stated, but to make the public believe *The Times* had to protect its own hard work from the grasping and unscrupulous efforts of its competitors (Fine 1933).

Meanwhile, Bennett had paid Cook $25,000 for the rights to four exclusive installments to be used in *The Herald*'s Sunday supplements, accounts that Bennett serialized in September and October and then sold to a number of other papers for a profit. These papers, and particularly *The Herald*, felt compelled in their own interests to advocate Cook's claims for as long as practical and either to believe the doctor's story or at least to pretend to believe it. Although this was later perceived by some as an unfortunate lapse from impartiality (Davis 1921: 293; Berger 1951: 176–7), it was no more so than that of *The Times*, and was natural since Cook still had more supporters than Peary.

Thus, while most of the press saw the Cook-Peary controversy as an exciting event that would help sell newspapers, to *The Times* and *The Herald* it became a war, and the two immediately lined up behind their respective candidates. *The Times* became more aggressive and negative about Cook, while *The Herald*, which had initially been profoundly positive towards Peary – running the headline ROBERT E. PEARY, AFTER 23 YEARS SIEGE, REACHES NORTH POLE: ADDS "THE BIG NAIL" TO NEW YORK YACHT CLUB'S TROPHIES (7 September 1909) – and had carried Cook's congratulatory comments, was put in a defensive position and slowly began to try to protect Cook and itself.

During this period, *The Herald*'s campaign was not nearly as negative as that of *The Times*. Rather than attack its opponent, it concentrated mainly on positives about Cook, under such headlines as MEDAL PRESENTED TO DR. COOK AS THE DISCOVERER OF THE POLE (8 September 1909), THRONGS CHEER DR. COOK AS HE LEAVES COPENHAGEN ON HOMEWARD VOYAGE (11 September 1909), and GERMAN PRESS LEANS TOWARD DR. COOK (13 September 1909). At the same time, it tried to offset some of the accusations about Cook using Peary's territory and men by discussing the seizure of Cook's supplies at Etah by Peary (13 September 1909) and telling how Peary had been willing to leave white men behind in the Arctic if they did not do as he bid (14 September 1909). However, perhaps the most subtle dig at Peary was that *The Herald* constantly avoided calling him "Commander," rather using the term "Mr." (Throughout his naval career, Peary maintained the rank of Civil Engineer. Although he called himself "Lieutenant," then "Commander," and, finally, "Rear Admiral," he never actually received one of these line ranks. Throughout his life he remained sensitive about his rank, so *The Herald* did not let him forget what that rank actually was.)

The Herald received some help in its fight from an unexpected source – Peary himself. His announcement of reaching the Pole had been welcomed by many who had doubted Cook. Melville stated, "Good for Peary. I am not surprised that a message has been received from him announcing his success" (*The New York Herald* 7 September 1909). And Nares, who had been one of Cook's most vocal English skeptics, sent the message: "Owing to your well-known veracity, all will accept your statement that you have reached the north pole" (*The New York Times* 8 September 1909).

But Peary's personal and brutal accusations quickly had a far different effect than he had intended. Between 11 and 13 September, a large number of statements from the press throughout both the US and England showed that Peary's aggressiveness was losing him more support than it was gaining. "Our correspondent adds that quite a number of new supporters of Dr. Cook have come out in the last twenty-four hours, some of them bluntly stating that they do so because Commander Peary has been over-hasty in denouncing his rival" (*The Daily News* 11 September 1909). "It is not putting it too strongly to say that Washington, which was predisposed to be friendly to Robert E. Peary, this being his home, has become disgusted with his savage attacks on Dr. Cook's claim to discovery of the great prize of exploration" (*The New York Herald* 12 September

1909). "The Germans tend to believe that both Peary's friends as well as himself have shown too bitter a feeling toward Dr. Cook, a feeling which, they say, is neither sportsmanlike, scientific nor ethical" (*New-York Tribune* 12 September 1909).

Many members of the polar community also began publicly to back Cook over Peary. Explorers had traditionally kept their bickerings and bad feelings out of the public eye because, as Amundsen once put it, "It is a pleasant and proper trait . . . to try to forget these things when success has crowned one's efforts, and to bury them in the agreeable oblivion of mutual felicitation" (Amundsen 1927: 130). Peary's attacks had violated this dictum, with a result that Evelyn Baldwin, one of Cook's most severe critics, now came to the doctor's defense, while Sverdrup, never a fan of Peary, stated: "Dr. Cook is amply prepared to demolish Commander Peary at the proper time. He has scientific ammunition with which he can riddle every accusation that Peary, in his disappointment at not being the first to reach the Pole, may make" (*The World* 9 September 1909).

Suddenly Peary's negativity and hostility, with his demands for Cook to produce proofs, began to be deflected back at himself: "A change has set in. Feeling in favor of Dr. Cook is on the increase. If Peary is to prevent further damage to his reputation, he must prove his assertions at once. If he has any evidence the world is entitled to hear it without further delay" (*The Boston Daily Globe* 14 September 1909).

Indeed, the proofs demanded by Peary from Cook were just as danger-ous to his own claim as to that of his rival, as was shown in the days while Cook was at sea between Copenhagen and New York (12 to 20 September). There had been considerable eyebrow-raising by both the scientific community and Peary's supporters when they heard that Cook had averaged 14 to 15 miles per day, and even Shackleton, who was kindly disposed to Cook, had stated that "no other expedition has been able to do anything near this" (*Daily Mail* 3 September 1909). But when Peary's pace of 30 miles per day to the pole and closer to 50 on the way back was announced, the carping ended. Moreover, even Peary's supporters "ex-press keen disappointment that their hero was not accompanied to the Pole by anyone except a negro and four Eskimos. On all sides it is now conceded that the controversy is one of one white man's word against another's, and the witnesses for Dr. Cook are as good as those for Commander Peary" (*The Daily News* 11 September 1909).

Despite, or possibly because of, Peary's attacks, Cook remained the man of the hour. A series of newspaper polls showed that Cook was the heavy favorite of the reading public as the one who had reached the North Pole. In a poll in the *Toledo Blade*, 550 readers responded that they believed Cook, while only 10 believed Peary. Out of more than 76,000 votes cast in a similar poll taken by *The Pittsburgh Press*, an amazing 96 per cent responded that Cook had reached the North Pole first, while more than 76 per cent did not believe that Peary had attained it at all. Remarkably, not one voter challenged the claims of both men.

As both men approached the US, Cook due to arrive in New York on 21 September on the Danish steamer *Oscar II*, and Peary due a few days later from the north, the New York papers were thick with charges and counter-charges. The next few weeks, if not months, promised to be unpleasant for the two explorers, but blissful for the press. As Anthony Fiala summed up for *The Daily Telegraph*: "All things considered, the controversy has now become more mystifying than ever; and the signal has been given for a mud-slinging contest, which promises to furnish ample scope for fanatics on either side" (16 September 1909).

A triumph for Peary and *The Times*

By 21 September, when Cook arrived in New York, the polar controversy was no longer the top story for most newspapers in either the United States or Britain. Certainly it received attention, but it was only those papers that had sold their souls to either Cook or Peary, that continued to make it the lead story of the day. The two most notable of these – *The New York Herald* and *The New York Times* – seemed to have settled down into a long-term war; on the part of *The Herald* it was a war of sniping and attrition, while to *The Times* the strategy was one of carpet bombing.

Cook was met by a huge cheering crowd probably numbering somewhere between the 50,000 claimed by *The Times* and the "hundreds of thousands" mentioned by *The Herald*. But before he even disembarked, Cook lashed out for the first time at his antagonist, raising a point that would ultimately help lead to an inquiry as unwelcome to Peary as the current one was to Cook:

> Commander Peary has yet given to the world no proof of his own case. My claim has been fully recognized by Denmark and the King of Sweden; the President of the United States has wired me his confidence. . . . Why should Peary be allowed to make himself a self-appointed dictator of my affairs? In justice to himself, in justice to the world and to guard the honor of national prestige, he should be compelled to prove his own case. (*The New York Times* 20 September 1909)

But in addition to making this one valid point, Cook almost immediately made several rash statements, answering the demands of Peary's followers by claiming that he had "brought irrefutable proof of my right to the title of discoverer of the North Pole" (*The World* 21 September 1909), stating that he had originals or duplicates of all of his records with him (*The New York Times* 21 September 1909), and insisting that "the Danish Government and the University of Copenhagen as well as the Danish Geographical Society, have . . . taken over the virtual guarantee for the sincerity and authenticity of my records. They have stood up for them, so to speak, before the world" (*The New York Herald* 21 September 1909).

Actually, the Danes had not "stood up" for Cook, but had simply accepted his word, in the long tradition of polar exploration. And after his assertions, Cook produced no proofs whatsoever. Instead, he stated that all of his proofs would have to go back to the University of Copenhagen to be examined. Then, on 24 September, he launched a national lecture tour.

Shortly afterwards, he announced that it would be at least three months before his proofs were ready to be submitted. This drew a severe reproach from the most high-minded of all New York papers, *The Evening Post* of E.L. Godkin:

> Now this might be allowed, perhaps, to pass without comment, were it not for the fact that Dr. Cook has been utilizing this period of suspended judgment on the part of competent critics to transmute into very handsome profits the uncritical enthusiasm of the multitude, and that there is no indication that he means to do otherwise with any additional time that may be gained by further postponement of a decisive test . . . Dr. Cook has finished the publication of his serial newspaper story; he has given a number of lectures in various parts of the country, at high admission price, to great audiences; now let him address himself to the task of establishing his case to the satisfaction of competent and impartial inquirers. (9 October 1909)

Meanwhile, the attacks on and evidence against Cook were mounting. Bridgman's paper, the *Brooklyn Standard-Union*, revealed that two of the photographs published with Cook's story in *The Herald* were actually seven years old. Upon Peary's return (which *The Times* called "triumphal" and *The Herald* "cheerless"), the older explorer, despite efforts from the members of the Peary Arctic Club to get him to stop, continued his attacks on his rival. And George Kennan, the respected Siberian traveler, took a lead from Gibbs and Freuchen and published three articles analyzing Cook's food consumption on his Arctic journey (Kennan 1909a, b, c). "No man and no dog has ever lived and worked for twelve weeks, under polar conditions, on eight ounces of pemmican, or its equivalent, per day," Kennan wrote, commenting that if he had been restricted to the same diet in Siberia, "I should have expected to perish on the ice in less than thirty days" (Kennan 1909b: 341).

But the most devastating blow came from an unexpected place – Alaska. Before Cook had ever left on his North Pole journey, rumors had surfaced that his ascent of Mount McKinley in 1906 had been faked. After the initial expedition had broken up, Cook had suddenly returned inland with one horsepacker, Ed Barrille. They reappeared several weeks later, with Cook claiming to have conquered the mountain. Belmore Browne, the artist on the expedition, later described the aftermath:

> At this time we heard the rumor that Dr. Cook and Barrille had reached the top of Mount McKinley. We knew the character of the country that guarded the southern face of the big mountain, we had traveled in that country, and we knew the time that Dr. Cook had been absent was too short to allow of his even reaching the mountain. We therefore denied the rumor. At last the Doctor and Barrille joined us and to my surprise Dr. Cook confirmed the rumor. . . . As soon as we were alone I turned to him [Barrille] and asked him what he knew about Mount McKinley, and after a moment's hesitation he answered: "I can tell you all about the big peaks just south of the mountain, but if you want to know about Mount McKinley go and ask Cook." I had felt all along that Barrille would tell me the truth, and after his statement I kept the knowledge to myself.
>
> I now found myself in an embarrassing position. I knew that Dr. Cook had not climbed Mount McKinley. Barrille had told me so and in addition I knew it in

the same way that any New Yorker would know that no man could walk from the Brooklyn Bridge to Grant's tomb in ten minutes.

This knowledge, however, did not constitute proof, and I knew that before I could make the public believe the truth I should have to collect some facts. I wrote immediately on my return to Professor [Herschel] Parker telling him my opinions and knowledge concerning the climb, and I received a reply from him saying that he believed me implicitly and that the climb, under the existing conditions, was impossible. (Browne 1913: 70–71)

In 1907 Browne and Parker stated to the members of the American Geographical Society and the Explorers' Club that they were convinced Cook had faked his climb of Mount McKinley. But such talk was stopped by Cook's threat of a libel suit and then by his sudden disappearance to the Arctic.

The topic resurfaced shortly after Cook's arrival in Denmark. On 5 September *The Sun* commented: "A previous achievement of Dr. Cook, the ascent of Mount McKinley, in Alaska, was effected under conditions which were not dis-similar to those incidental to his latest feat, that is to say, he ascended the mountain unaccompanied by geographers and men of science had been disinclined to credit him with the performance." There followed a statement by Fred Printz, one of the guides who had accompanied the initial expedition before returning with Browne and Parker: "I am just as sure as I am living that Cook never saw the North Pole. Any man who made the representations he did of his alleged ascent of Mount McKinley is capable of making the statements credited to him in the press today."

Although the subject was initially ignored by the hero-worshipping public, it did not go away entirely. On 9 September, Parker's doubts about Cook appeared in *The Washington Post*, the *New-York Tribune*, *The Examiner*, and dozens of other papers across the US. Three weeks later, with Cook at the height of his lecture tour, Bridgman leaked to *The New York Times* a letter from the Cornell University professor of geography and geology Ralph Stockman Tarr, who had just returned from Alaska, where he found that it was "the almost unanimous verdict of Alaskans knowing that country that the feat was impossible" (*The New York Times* 29 September 1909). Tarr also stated:

I . . . shall gladly do what little I can to further the inquiry regarding Cook's claim to have climbed Mt. McKinley. . . . I was informed by a number of people that the prospector, Ed Burrill [Barrille], now living in Hamilton, Mont., admitted to his friends that they never got up above 5,000 feet and that he jokes about the way in which the public has been fooled. (*The New York Times* 29 September 1909)

Cook denied all of the charges, but the National Geographic Society (making it unequivocally clear that it was not the impartial observer that it claimed to be) hired the Pinkerton Detective Agency to delve into the Mount McKinley affair. The crushing blow came on 14 October, when the *New York Globe*, owned by General Thomas H. Hubbard, the new president of the Peary Arctic Club, published Barrille's signed affidavit, which stated that at no time had he and Cook been nearer than 14 miles in an air line from the top of Mount McKinley, that the photograph of the summit published in *To the top of the continent* was a peak no more than 8,000 feet high and at least 20 miles in an air line from the top of McKinley, and that Barrille had kept a diary in which Cook had forced him to fill in certain false entries about the days in question.

This report set off a full-fledged controversy of its own, and affidavits and counter-affidavits appeared in the press in rapid succession. *The Herald* sent its reporter Roscoe C. Mitchell to Missoula, Montana, where he obtained an affidavit from Barrille stating that he had been offered $5,000 for his previous affidavit (*The New York Herald* 20 October 1909). *The Herald* also noted that, prior to his denunciation of Cook, Printz had written to the explorer offering his support in return for an all-expenses-paid trip to New York (20 October 1909). When Cook did not reply, Printz made the statement that had appeared in *The Sun*. Bennett's paper then published an account of the activities of Barrille, showing that he had come to New York at the request and expense of the Peary Arctic Club and that he had maintained frequent contact with Hubbard and Bridgman. The same story also hinted that Barrille's testimony was totally false and had simply been bought by Peary's backers, including *The Times* (*The New York Herald* 22 October 1909). *The Herald* restated its case after Cook and Barrille confronted each other in Hamilton, Montana, quoting Cook's statement that his former traveling companion had lied for "more than thirty pieces of silver" (29 October 1909).

Despite the efforts of *The Herald* in Cook's behalf, Barrille's initial statement and the ensuing field day that *The New York Times* had with the destruction of Cook's Mount McKinley claim turned public opinion from the side of Cook to that of Peary. The public now made the disjointed and curious inversion of logic that if Cook had not reached the top of Mount McKinley, he had not reached the North Pole, and that if he had not reached the North Pole, then Peary must have.

But the change in public opinion did not dampen the vigor with which *The Times* continued to attack Cook, seeing in his demise both the triumph of Peary and the discrediting of *The Herald*. One of *The Times'* most sensational denunciations of Cook was that he had hired two men, George Dunkle and August Loose, to compile a fake set of observations that could be used to support his claim with the commission at the University of Copenhagen. The story, which ran on 9 and 10 December 1909, filled fully 17 columns, and the subsequent allusions to it ignored the fact that Cook's secretary, Walter Lonsdale, had explained to the *New York American* that the two men had been employed, "for the purpose, not of fabricating records, but merely checking observations by the doctor. . . . Loose, however, did not inspire confidence and was told by Dr. Cook that he did not want his services or figures" (10 December 1909). Despite such indications that Cook had not used these men to help him defraud the public, *The Times* continued to emphasize these charges, particularly when Cook actually sent his materials to the University of Copenhagen.

The Dunkle and Loose scandal, on top of all the other charges, was enough for *The Herald* and the other papers that had supported Cook. He was all but abandoned, as the stories about him grew slimmer and less frequent; he was not forgotten, however, as *The Times* continued its vicious attacks whenever possible.

Any slender hopes that Cook might have had for a return to public favor were further injured in December when the committee in Copenhagen to which he had sent his reports utterly rejected them. Under the headline COOK'S CLAIM TO DISCOVERY OF THE NORTH POLE REJECTED; OUTRAGED DENMARK CALLS HIM A DELIB-ERATE SWINDLER, *The New York Times* quoted the commission's conclusion:

> The data in the documents submitted to us are of such an unsatisfactory character that it is not possible to declare with certainty that the astronomical observations referred to were actually made; there is likewise lacking details in practical matters – such as sledge journeys – which could furnish some control. The Commission is therefore of the opinion that the material transmitted for examination contains no proof whatsoever that Dr. Cook reached the North Pole. (21 December 1909)

An even stronger statement was made the next day by the Danish explorer Knud Rasmussen, who initially had been a strong supporter of Cook: "The papers Cook sent . . . are almost impudent. No schoolboy could make such calculations. It is a most childish attempt at cheating. Cook has killed himself by his own foolish acts" (*The New York Times* 22 December 1909).

He had indeed, despite a plea from *The Sun* for considered thought before any more action was taken: "Cook was too hastily acclaimed as the discoverer of the North Pole. Let us not be too hasty in acclaiming him the prince of imposters" (22 December 1909). Two days later, however, even the man who had been perhaps Cook's strongest supporter, Anthony Fiala, had had enough. On Christmas Eve 1909 Fiala signed his name to the decision that Cook should be dropped from the Explorers' Club.

As Cook's reputation tumbled, Peary's soared. With the accusations about Mount McKinley and Dunkle and Loose, Peary again became a national favorite. His popularity increased even more after his meeting on 1 November with the committee selected by the National Geographic Society to examine his proofs. Not that the results of this meeting were ever in doubt. The three members of the committee – Henry Gannett, the Society's vice president; Rear Admiral Colby M. Chester; and O.H. Tittmann, the Superintendent of the US Coast and Geodetic Survey – were all long-time admirers of Peary, and the first two were his close friends. All three had voted in favor of awarding Peary the Society's Gold Medal in 1906, had supported giving a grant to the very expedition they were now investigating, and had stated in advance that they were confident Peary had attained the Pole (Herbert 1989: 299–300). Their "examination," which was cursory at best, took but several hours, during which time, as Gannett later testified to the House Naval Affairs Committee, "We simply sat down with him and read his journal from his original records" (quoted in Hall

1917: 221). Yet what – and how much – they read was uncertain, especially since Tittman later admitted he hardly looked at the material because he "was very much occupied with other matters" (quoted in Hall 1917: 219). Gannett, meanwhile, was so badly informed about what he was reviewing that he later had to be prompted in an interview by the Society's editor Gilbert Grosvenor. And when Peary's instruments were examined, it was after dusk, at a time that even Peary later admitted, "I should imagine that it would not be possible to make tests" (quoted in Wright 1970: 263).

Despite such flawed investigations, the National Geographic Society immediately acknowledged Peary's claims. However, growing pressure to have them more stringently validated came in the form of a call by Schley for Peary to "submit his proofs that he had reached the North Pole to some scientific body other than the National Geographic Society. . . . The University of Copenhagen should . . . examine the Peary proofs, for in that way they would be submitted to the same test that was applied to those of Cook" (*New York American* 22 December 1909). But Peary withstood all pressure to release his observations and notes to any other American organizations, including the US Navy, which had paid his salary, or even the House Naval Affairs Committee. The only official organization that received any of his documents was the Royal Geographical Society, which was sent a copy of his journal and a limited number of observations. When his submission was considered for approval (*after* he had received the Society's gold medal), only 17 of the 35 committee members appointed to study his claims were present. Eight voted for Peary, seven against, and two abstained, thus passing his proofs with less than 23 per cent of the committee in favor (Rawlins 1973: 237).

Peary was even more successful with the general public. Cook, who seemed friendly and agreeable, had been more easily able to please an audience as a speaker than the cold, superior Peary. But Peary was the winner, and people flocked to hear him. He soon was charging a minimum of $1,000 per lecture, and occasionally receiving as much as $7,500. In addition, more people could be influenced by newspapers and magazines than by personal appearances, and, perhaps more than any other explorer of his day, Peary understood the way the print medium generated images, its ability to assure fame and support, and how to use it. So he exploited the press and publishers as they usually exploited explorers. He demanded huge fees for the rights to different, although hardly exclusive, articles about the same adventures. He wrote editorials that said virtually the same thing as his accounts and sold them to different newspapers. And he frequently employed ghost-writers, with the dramatist A.E. Thomas writing 80 per cent of his book *The North Pole* (Herbert 1989: 238)

For this book, Peary received an advance of $15,000, but he made even more from *Hampton's Magazine* and *Nash's Magazine*. The former paid him $40,000 for a nine-part series of articles that appeared between January and September 1910, a series actually written by Elsa Barker, a poet and romance novelist (Peary 1910b). The latter, which had initially offered Cook $100,000 to write his account, then paid Peary $50,000 for an eight-part series that it billed as "the last of the great earth-stories for which the world has waited nearly four hundred years – and it will go down to all ages" (Peary 1910c). Although it is virtually certain that this story was also scripted for Peary, the identity of the author is unknown.

With the support of *The New York Times* and other members of the print medium, the National Geographic Society, a number of influential politicians, and a professional lobbyist, Peary began a powerful push for the official recognition he felt he deserved. In February 1910 the United States Senate passed without opposition and referred to the House of Representatives a bill to retire Peary with the honors and pension of a rear admiral. Things were not so easy in the House, however. The hearings of the House Naval Affairs Committee began in March 1910, then were adjourned until January 1911 because Peary refused to produce his original records – the same kind of proofs that he had required of Cook. However, by the time the hearings were resumed, the polar controversy seemed a thing of the distant past: Peary had published a best-selling book, had been credited with two lengthy and successful magazine series, and had – with the help of numerous mediators, including *The New York Times* and the National Geographic Society – become established as an American heroic myth.

Cook, meanwhile, had continued to be disparaged by *The New York Times*, and his reputation had further suffered despite these attacks having nothing to do with the North Pole. One of the most savage assaults was the charge that Cook had plagiarized material from the Reverend Thomas Bridges, who had spent some 30 years among the Yahgan Indians of Tierra del Fuego. Cook had once written a short article based on observations made during the weeks that *Belgica* was in port in Punta Arenas. Under the headline COOK TRIED TO STEAL PARSON'S LIFE WORK (20 May 1910), *The Times* implied that Cook had attempted to pass off as his work the grammar and vocabulary of these Patagonian natives that Bridges had compiled. Although the incident had no intrinsic importance to the polar controversy – and occurred seven months after Peary's proofs had been accepted by the National Geographic Society – it showed the determination of *The Times* to hound Cook and *The Herald*.

Ultimately, despite several members of the House Committee who were prepared to require actual proofs and straightforward answers from Peary, and who, disbelieving his testimony and data, steadfastly opposed him, the explorer received the approval of the Committee and, subsequently, the entire House. He was retired with the pension of a rear admiral, a title he proudly, and inaccurately, used the rest of his life.

Meanwhile, the press had one last major role to play in the Cook-Peary controversy. In October 1910, a month after *Hampton's* had concluded its series of articles by Peary, one of its editors, T. Everett Harré, invited Cook to give an exposé of how he actually had not reached the North Pole. Cook declined to write such an article, but *Hampton's* still purchased his four-part story in which he defended himself. It also received his signature on a contract that stated, in the small print, that the magazine was making "no editorial guarantees whatsoever." With this legal safeguard, Cook's story was then rewritten – reputedly by associate editor O.O. McIntyre –

and published as if it were his confession both of not reaching the Pole and of being so mentally confused that he did not know if he *could* have reached the Pole or not (Cook 1911b).

As if that were not bad enough, shortly before the release of the first issue, *Hampton*'s held a press conference in which it emphasized Cook's mental confusion. The following day, *The New York Times* feasted on its enemy, commenting that: "in these articles Dr. Cook will admit frankly that he doesn't know whether he reached the north pole. He now says that his privations during his travels toward the pole put him in a 'mental condition,' which the American public has not been able to understand" (2 December 1910).

Regardless of what fraud he had or had not attempted to perpetrate on the public, Cook scarcely deserved such treatment, nor indeed the head-lines that appeared all over the United States, such as DR. COOK ADMITS FAKE! and DR. COOK MAKES PLEA OF INSANITY! (quoted in Cook 1911a: 555). Yet when Cook's book appeared in 1911 giving his version of the story, *The Times* gleefully taunted his "retraction" under the headline DR. COOK CONFESSES HE DIDN'T CONFESS (3 September 1911). Four more years passed before Lilian Kiel, a copyreader at *Hampton*'s admitted to a Congressional subcommittee that the magazine had purposely changed everything Cook had written. Ms Kiel stated:

> We cut through the galley proofs and inserted what has been known to the world as Dr. Cook's confession of mental unbalancement. The 'confession' was dictated to me by a sub-editor. Dr. Cook was on the ocean to Europe to get his wife and children. I then thoroughly believed the confession was authorized by Dr. Cook. I was horrified later to find that he knew absolutely nothing about it. (quoted in Wright 1970: 247)

In the meantime, according to McIntyre's biographer, "the whole world was led to believe that Dr. Cook had confessed that he had perpetrated a fraud and that he had never reached the Pole at all. Dr. Cook had done no such thing, but his name and reputation were ruined forever . . . it was the most dastardly deed in the history of journalism" (Driscoll 1938: 221–2).

That the press had (and since has) never done anything worse than change Cook's story is dubious, but the incident did destroy his last vestiges of hope to gain any type of public acceptance for his claim of having reached the North Pole. The publication of the altered feature led to an enormous jump in the magazine's circulation, at the same time that *Hampton*'s actions clearly showed the depths to which the print medium had plunged, becoming what perhaps has best been described by Charles Reich (writing of the modern corporate state) as "an immensely powerful machine, ordered, legalistic, rational, yet utterly out of human control, wholly and perfectly indifferent to any human values" (Reich 1970).

10

Conclusion

Historical postscript

So Cook had lost and Peary had won. Or had they? Certainly Cook never restored his reputation. And, in fact, his troubles continued. In 1910 two expeditions to Alaska apparently proved that he had faked his ascent of Mount McKinley. One, which included Belmore Browne and Herschel Parker, located the small peak on which Cook reputedly had taken the pictures he claimed showed the summit of McKinley (Browne 1913: 113–23). The other, which had been partly sponsored by *The New York Herald* and was sent to vindicate Cook's route to the summit, returned a failure. This party eventually reached a place where, it was stated, Cook's map "abruptly departs from reasonable accuracy into complete fantasy" (Moore 1967: 83). The leader of the expedition, C.E. Rusk, later commented:

> Dr. Cook had many admirers who would have rejoiced to see his claims vindicated, and I too would have been glad to add my mite in clearing his name. . . . But as we gazed upon the forbidding crags of the great mountain from far up the Ruth Glacier at the point of Cook's and Barrille's farthest advance [we] realized how utterly impossible and absurd was the story of this man. (quoted in Moore 1967: 85)

Cook's defenders later pointed to "proofs" that showed the findings of both of these expeditions to be inaccurate. In 1914 Ernest C. Rost indicated a close study revealed that Browne's peak differed from Cook's in at least eight respects. The geographer E.S. Balch later agreed with Rost's claim and also pointed out that Cook's descriptions of the northeast ridge of McKinley – about which nothing had previously been known – had been so closely corroborated by those who had since climbed the peak as to make it virtually certain that the explorer had indeed reached the top (Balch 1914).

Nevertheless, things went from bad to worse for Cook. In 1923 he was convicted of selling worthless stocks in Fort Worth, Texas, and was sentenced to almost 15 years in prison, despite the fact that the options he sold turned out later to be far more valuable than he had stated. He was released in 1930, and died a decade later, still claiming to have reached the North Pole.

Ultimately, Cook's reputation has taken little more of a beating than Peary's. The backlash against Peary's high-handed and evasive politicking for his recognition and pension began even before his death in 1920. In 1915 a resolution supporting Cook's claim was introduced in the House of Representatives (although it died in committee). The same year, a resolution was introduced for the correction of US Hydrographic Office maps containing certain fictional places of which Peary had claimed to be the discoverer, such as the Peary Channel in North Greenland and the island Crocker Land. In 1916 Henry Helgesen, a US Representative from North Dakota, read the most devastating portions of the already-scarce report of the House Naval Affairs Committee – those proving the lack of evidence required to affirm Peary's claim – into the *Congressional Record*, so that they would be preserved for posterity. Helgesen then introduced a bill before Congress to repeal the 1911 act that had recognized Peary's accomplishment and recommended his pension because Peary's "claims to discoveries in the Arctic regions have been proven to rest on fiction and not on geographical facts" and because "Robert E. Peary never reached, discovered, nor was approximately near to . . . the North Pole" (quoted in Rawlins 1973: 248). Had there been a hearing for Helgesen's bill, it is likely that Peary's proofs would have been closely examined by an official agency for the first time, but the matter was dropped when Helgesen died in April 1917.

But that was not the end of the question of Peary's attainment of the Pole. The year Helgesen died, Thomas F. Hall brought to light the dubious nature of Peary's speeds in his final days near the Pole; he indicated the lack of necessary observations Peary had taken; he pointed out the National Geographic Society's slipshod examination of Peary's proofs; and he suggested Peary had not attained a farthest north in 1906 (Hall 1917). Several years later, Clements R. Markham, formerly a friend and admirer of Peary, expressed his disbelief in Peary's success at reaching the Pole without the aid of regular observations (Markham 1921: 357). And eight years after that, the respected geographer J. Gordon Hayes pointed out the mistakes that Peary had made in his calculations in his earlier expeditions, made an even more in-depth – and even more devastating – appraisal of the explorer's claimed speeds, and reiterated arguments by both Greely and the distinguished Arctic scientist Albert I, the Prince of Monaco, against Peary's claims (Hayes 1929). In the mid-1930s, Henshaw Ward argued for a new appraisal of Peary by the public, stating: "Peary's claim of reaching the North Pole in 1909 is so highly improbable that our acceptance of it is absurd. Our unwillingness to listen to the evidence against his claim is a scandal" (Ward 1934: 41).

The evidence continued to mount against Peary. In 1973 Dennis

Rawlins, a professor of physics and astronomy at Johns Hopkins University, made the harshest condemnation yet of Peary, more closely examining the points already made by his predecessors, and also questioning Peary's movement of the fictional Jesup Land (supposedly discovered on his 1898–1902 expedition) to conform to Sverdrup's Axel Heiberg Island and his "discovery" of the non-existent Crocker Land in 1906 (1973: 49–52, 72–5). Rawlins concluded that Peary demonstrated a long-term pattern of lying in order to attain the glory he wished, a pattern undoubtedly continued on his final expedition.

Finally, in 1989 the noted Arctic traveler Wally Herbert became the first man allowed to study all of Peary's remaining personal papers, diaries, and observations (many had mysteriously disappeared through the years). Herbert, through scientific calculations, Peary's papers, the assessments (pro and con) of his predecessors, and, perhaps most important, his own years of Arctic travel, arrived at the conclusion that Peary most likely did not get closer than 100 miles to the North Pole (Herbert 1989).

Although Peary has been vigorously defended each time one of these works has appeared, the least that can be said is that his claim to have been the first man to reach the North Pole is now – and undoubtedly will continue to be – questionable.

And what of the other explorers who so thrilled the Anglo-American public? Gilder's travels eventually took him to the then-mysterious island of Borneo, and he later reported back from China when the French entered Cochin, now the southernmost region of Vietnam. He served for a brief while as editor of the *Sunday Standard* of Newark, New Jersey, and a short time before his death in 1900 he joined Hearst's *New York Journal and Advertiser*.

Stanley's reputation had been badly tarnished by his mismanagement of the Emin Pasha Relief Expedition, and he never was selected to lead another party into Africa. Although much of his heroic image remained intact with the public, he never was transformed into the same kind of mythic hero as Livingstone, nor was he ever popular with the English press. Yet he settled in England and retook British citizenship, in part so that he would be eligible for the knighthood he indeed received in 1899. Before he died in 1904, Stanley was able to see the role his efforts in the Congo basin played in the subsequent "Scramble for Africa," and the development of European imperialism in that continent.

Nansen's triumphs as a polar explorer were followed by equally successful careers in statesmanship, academics, and international affairs. When the union between Norway and Sweden was dissolved, Nansen was named his nation's first Minister to the Court of St James (1906–08). His reputation and popularity in London helped Norway achieve international recognition. In 1908 he was made professor of oceanography at the University of Christiania, where his work included the improvement and design of maritime instruments, an explanation of the wind-driven currents of the oceans, and an elucidation of the manner in which deep- and bottom-water is formed. In 1920 Nansen was appointed the head of the Norwegian delegation to the new League of Nations. In turn, the League appointed him high commissioner responsible for the repatriation from Russia of more than one-half million prisoners of war from the German and Austro-Hungarian armies. The government of the Soviet Union did not recognize the League of Nations, but Nansen had such stature that it negotiated directly with him. In 1921 the International Committee of the Red Cross and 48 national Red Cross organizations appointed him to direct an effort to bring relief to the famine-stricken Soviet Union. Although the League of Nations would not fund the relief efforts, Nansen obtained financial aid from private sources and brought great assistance to the Russian people. He was awarded the Nobel Prize for Peace in 1922 and died in 1930.

Amundsen achieved his greatest fame for his attainment of the South Pole in 1911. In 1918–23 he led the *Maud* expedition, which became only the second to complete the Northeast Passage. And in 1926 he led an expedition in the dirigible *Norge*, which flew across the Arctic basin and the North Pole. Since there are serious doubts about all previous claims to have reached the North Pole, Amundsen is not only definitely the first man to have attained both Poles, but most likely the first to have reached the northernmost place on earth. Two years later, in 1928, the most accomplished polar explorer of all time disappeared while attempting to rescue former associate Umberto Nobile's expedition, which had crashed and disappeared on the way back from the North Pole in the dirigible *Italia*.

And what happened to the newspapers and newspapermen who played such an important role in exploration? The biggest success story was certainly Peary's great supporter, *The New York Times*. With the help of the Cook-Peary controversy, its circulation rocketed (Berger 1951: 177), and then progressed even further during World War I. Until Ochs died in 1935, his paper continued to show an interest in exploration. Shortly after Peary's return, it purchased the American copyright to the South Pole stories of both Amundsen and Scott. In 1926 it sent a correspondent – Fredrick Ramm – on Amundsen's *Norge* expedition. And it received exclusive rights to the South Polar flight of Richard E. Byrd in 1929, when Russell Owen of *The Times* was also the official expedition historian. Byrd even named a glacier and several lakes after Ochs and his family. Today *The Times* cannot claim to be a specialist in exploration, but it is regarded by many as the "paper of record" in the United States.

The end was not so pleasant for the paper that had backed the loser in the North Pole débâcle. After its support of Cook, *The Herald* never entered exploration in a major way again. And after the man who had done so much to start the fascination with the unknown, James Gordon Bennett Jr, died in 1918, his paper was purchased by Frank Munsey, who in 1920 merged it with its old rival, *The Sun*. In 1924 Munsey sold *The Herald* to the family of Whitelaw Reid (who had died in 1912), which merged it with their paper, marking the beginning of the *New York Herald Tribune*. The New York edition of the *Herald Tribune* ceased publication in April 1966, although its Paris edition, today known as the *International Herald Tribune*, is successfully operated by *The New York Times* and *The Washington Post*.

Exploration also was rarely again a focus for *The World*, which lost much of its originality as well as its crusading spirit when Pulitzer died in 1911. Coincidentally, in 1931 the morning paper that had been the first to challenge the supremacy of *The Herald* disappeared in a merger with another former Bennett paper, *The Evening Telegram*, forming the *New York World-Telegram*. In the center of the United States, the *St. Louis Post-Dispatch* remains a successful paper today, still under the control of the Pulitzer family.

Stead played a new role in the growth of sensationalism in 1905, when, in an attempt to establish a permanent foreign desk, Hearst paid him £1,000 to act as London correspondent for the *New York American*. Stead's career – and life – came to a halt in a manner in which many of his contemporaries felt he would have approved. On 15 April 1912 he went out with the biggest story of the year – as a passenger on *Titanic*.

Newnes continued to develop new ventures that became fine magazines. He spent 20 of the last 25 years of his life as a Member of Parliament, first for Newmarket and then for Swansea. He died in 1910.

Both Hearst and Northcliffe maintained somewhat of an interest in exploration. Hearst's *New York American* was a major sponsor for several of Sir Hubert Wilkins' Antarctic expeditions as well as of his attempt to be the first man to take a submarine under the North Pole. Northcliffe contributed £5,000 to the first Antarctic expedition led by Robert Falcon Scott, although he eventually changed the focus of his attention to developments in aviation. Northcliffe died in 1922, but the remnants of his publishing empire, *The Times*, *Daily Mail*, and *Daily Mirror*, are among the most prominent and successful newspapers in Britain today.

Alternatively, although many parts of Hearst's empire still exist more than 40 years after his death in 1951, his centerpiece, the *New York Journal-American* (which was formed when he merged his morning and evening editions in 1937), outlived him by only 16 years. In 1966 it and two other papers in severe financial difficulty – the *New York Herald Tribune* and the *New York World-Telegram and Sun* – decided to merge to form one healthy paper. The three papers ceased individual publication in April 1966, but due to union difficulties the first edition of the new paper, the *World Journal Tribune*, did not appear until September of that year. When that paper died due to financial pressures in May 1967, it marked the end of the last traces in New York of the heritage of Day, Dana, Greeley, Reid, Pulitzer, Hearst, and the Bennetts.

Conversely, exploration, particularly in the Arctic, has never truly died out, although, after the Cook-Peary controversy had run its course in the newspapers, the far north began to recede in the public consciousness. First the Antarctic exploits of Amundsen, Scott, and Shackleton received the majority of polar coverage. Then, only five years after Cook and Peary arrived back from the north, the outbreak of World War I virtually eliminated the accounts of exploration in the newspapers. And during the next four years, the process of risking one's life in polar exploration lost some of its special meaning to a world numbed by the deaths of millions. As Hemingway commented in *A farewell to arms*: "abstract words such as

195

glory, honor, or courage were obscene besides the concrete names of villages . . . the numbers of regiments and the dates" (Hemingway 1929). During the Great War, exploration also lost its last great sponsor, a man who had followed in the footsteps of John Barrow and Roderick Murchison, who had been one of the key players in the establishment of the British Arctic Expedition in 1875, and who, as President of the RGS, had been greatly responsible for Britain's re-entry into the Antarctic. In 1916 Clements R. Markham died after setting light to his bedding while reading by candlelight.

Yet the last vestiges of the excitement of exploration did not die with Markham or the millions in World War I. Through the succeeding decades, science, exploration, and plain adventure continued. In 1930–31 Bertram Thomas made the first crossing of Rub' al Khali, the "Empty Quarter" of southern Arabia, one of the last genuinely unexplored regions of the world. In 1930–32 G.A. Ushakov mapped the little-known islands of Severnaya Zemlya. And throughout the 1920s and 1930s, the Americans, Australians, and Norwegians explored new sections of the Antarctic coast and interior. These little-known lands remained both working places and playgrounds, challenges to professionals and joy-seekers alike, into the 1990s.

In 1989, when Robert Swann's "Icewalk" to the North Pole – which was little closer to true exploration than would be a jaunt in the Devon countryside – received front-page coverage in *The Times*, it showed that the press' and the public's fascination with supposed exploration was still alive and healthy. And when a member of Swann's expedition commented that reports filed to *The Times* bore little resemblance to the sequence of events actually occurring in the far north, it helped to show that – despite the passing of Bennett, Gilder, Schwatka, and the others – the sensationalization of exploration still lives on.

Conclusion

Perhaps the most striking aspect of the linking of the press and explorers in the nineteenth century was that its origin lay in the realization by just one remarkably astute individual – James Gordon Bennett Jr – that the public could be intoxicated by exciting reports about heroic struggles to master nature, particularly in what were perceived as her most dangerous environments, Africa and the Arctic. Had Bennett been interested in staid, tediously factual articles, that emphasized the success of scientific endeavors or that stressed the similarities of Africa and the Arctic with the world familiar to the New York readership, *The Herald* could have published them. Instead, his paper concentrated on the exhilarating aspects of the exploration of blank spaces on the map, accentuated man's role as the conqueror of nature, presented stories that created national heroes by using sensational journalistic techniques, and, in so doing, established the role of the press in the creation of the modern image of the unknown, helping change it from the sublime and picturesque visions lingering from the eighteenth century, to the sensational perspectives that still exist today.

This indicates a need for a journalistic reappraisal of Bennett, who has long not only remained in the shadow of men such as his father and Pulitzer, but has been the victim of a negative historical bias because, during a life of personal luxury and professional extravagance, he spent more than $40 million, leaving *The Herald* in a difficult financial position that helped lead to its disappearance in the consolidation with the *Tribune*. Yet Bennett was uniquely skilled in the various technical arts involved in gathering and disseminating news. He was able to recognize stories that were appropriate for a mass-circulation journal, to embellish them so that their potential was not lost on the reader, and to entertain his readership with subjects of universal interest without crossing the line separating good taste from bad. Even more important, Bennett recognized that when the appropriate stories did not appear on their own, he could create them, thus becoming a founder of the modern concept that news is not simply whatever occurs, but is what the press wants to make news.

By observing the methods by which first *The Herald* and then other major newspapers presented exploration to the reading public, it has become obvious that, despite frequent assumptions to the contrary, sensationalism was present in the Anglo-American press throughout the 40-year period from 1870 to 1910, and certainly before Pulitzer came to New York. It has also become apparent that the newspapers involved in the coverage and sensationalization of exploration were not simply those that have long been accepted as sensational, but included those generally considered part of the quality press. This was particularly true of the coverage of the Cook-Peary controversy, which showed beyond question that the reputedly incorruptible *New York Times* was willing to engage in sensationalism, as well as aggressive and ethically questionable reporting, in order to better its position as one of the major newspapers in America.

The Cook-Peary controversy has traditionally been viewed by historians as a struggle between two explorers for the recognition of having attained priority in reaching the North Pole. However, it was equally a struggle between *The New York Herald* and *The New York Times*, and was dictated by their commercial interests. The controversy showed that the press had reached new heights (or depths) in the sensationalization of exploration. And although publishing reports of questionable accuracy or honesty and assailing competitors through vicious attacks on explorers sponsored by those competitors were practices previously "acceptable" within certain limits, the press, and particularly *The Times*, now went beyond even these boundaries. Ultimately the most important impact of the Cook-Peary controversy was that the dismissal of Cook as a fraud seriously injured the credibility of *The Herald*, while the recognition of Peary as the discoverer of the North Pole helped re-establish *The Times* as a journalistic power.

These events highlight the significant role of the press in Arctic exploration. Newspapers, their proprietors, and their reporters were much more influential in increasing knowledge about and interest in the far north than has traditionally been noted. Not only did newspapers sponsor numerous expeditions, the amount and style of the press coverage helped create an underlying interest among the public about exploration and explorers.

Several other conclusions about nineteenth-century exploration are also readily apparent. First, the role of science was highly variable. Although a number of explorers and sponsors were first and foremost devoted to the various branches of science, most individuals concerned with exploration, and certainly the majority of the press and the public, found it of secondary interest to the adventure. Although it validated the expeditions and was therefore deemed necessary, most people did not really want to know about scientific data or results. Second, nationalism played not only a major role in the expeditions themselves, but in their presentation to the public. Thus, the Anglo-American press did not give much coverage to explorers from other countries, and, with the exception of Nansen, rarely were such individuals promoted as heroic figures.

This second conclusion leads inextricably to another: that there was no relation between the success of an expedition and the amount of coverage it received or the level of sensationalism with which it was presented. Rather, the expeditions that tended to receive the most extensive and sensational coverage were those the results of which were the most disastrous, especially if they included great (and particularly gruesome) loss of life.

The accuracy of exploration accounts varied dramatically in the late nineteenth century. Early in the century, writers tended to exaggerate either the sublime or picturesque aspects of new lands, resorting to old clichés and demonstrating little factual accuracy in their comments. As these aesthetics were replaced by the sensational, the images of unknown areas were still often at a variance from the way these areas are now perceived to have been. As previously indicated, one reason for this was the desire of the press and explorers to make unknown lands as exciting, and therefore as saleable, as possible. Another was that individuals frequently went to areas knowing the reports of their predecessors and having therefore already drawn conclusions about them. They were thus sensitive to data that confirmed their preconceptions and insensitive to contradictory evidence. These errors of perception were perpetuated by journalists who had little experience with the remote areas about which they wrote, but who simply passed on the concept of the sensational first popularized by Bennett's correspondents.

Ironically, many of those first sensational accounts were written by reporters who were much more genuinely concerned with the accuracy of their articles than were their successors. Unlike many who followed them, J.A. MacGahan, William Henry Gilder, and Frederick Schwatka were simply talented enough to make life in the wild and the struggle with nature exciting to the common man. They were examples of traveler-writers who, while presenting sensational accounts of their experiences, nevertheless gave detailed and sensitive descriptions of the far north, which still enjoy the status of universally accredited truths.

Yet in the final assessment, it is perhaps a little sad that during the nineteenth century it was not the accuracy in the reporting of these men that was of the utmost importance to the press and public, nor was it the attainments of men such as Stanley or Amundsen, nor the scientific endeavors of Torell or Nordenskiöld, nor the fascination with the wilderness expressed by Hall or Thomson, nor even the heroic status achieved by Livingstone or Nansen. What counted was the controversy and the tragedy. Had Cook and Peary each accepted the other's claim, or had Greely (or Scott) been saved without loss of life, there would have been much less interest in them. Without the terrible winter at Cape Sabine, Greely would have remained a rather minor character on the Arctic stage. But by being enwrapped in a shroud of tragedy – the suffering, the deaths, and the rumors of cannibalism – he became an important figure, lifted to a higher plane, one that, as in the case of Franklin or Livingstone, could reach mythic status. And certainly for the vast majority of the newspapers in the United States and England, this kind of ennoblement (or, in the case of Cook, fall from grace) – and its consequent sensationalized story – was far more important than a scientific result or the conquest of some unknown land.

Appendix 1

Glossary of newspaper terminology

banner a main headline across the full width of the page.

box an item ruled off on all four sides, usually with heavy rule or border.

broadsheet a page the full size of a rotary press plate.

crosshead a centered sub-heading in the text.

deck a separate portion or section of a headline, usually applied to the subsidiary sections following the main headline, when there are three or more of these sections.

ear the advertising space beside the front-page title-line.

half-stick a small portrait measuring half a column.

halftone the process by which continuous tone is simulated by a pattern of dots of varying size; a photographic print in a newspaper made by this process.

intertype composing machine similar to the Linotype.

lead the main news story in the paper or the opening paragraph of any news story.

leader the British equivalent to the American editorial, in which the author, usually a member of the newspaper's staff or a well-known public figure, expresses his – or the paper's – viewpoint on a recent or impending event or political decision.

linotype the first keyboard-operated composing machine to employ the principle of the circulating matrix and to cast type in solid lines or slugs. Invented by the German-American engineer Ottmar Mergenthaler and first used in 1886.

make-up the sheet indicating the placing of the various items on a page; the process of actual assembly of the page.

perfector a press that prints both sides of the paper at a single pass. All letterpress rotaries and web-offset machines are perfectors.

point the standard unit of type size, 0.01383 inches or approximately 72 to the inch.

rotary a reel- or web-fed newspaper press perfecting from a cylindrical printing surface. Papers are delivered folded and counted, ready for dispatch.

run the period of printing an edition; the number of copies of an edition.

run-on where matter is not to be broken into paragraphs.

scarehead a headline intentionally worded in such way as to frighten or excite the readership.

sidehead a sub-heading in text set flush left.

smalls the run-on classified advertisements in a newspaper, usually set in 6-point or smaller.

streamer a multi-column headline leading a page, but not necessarily across its full width.

subhead a separate portion or section of a headline, usually applied to the subsidiary section or sections following the main headline, when there are only one or two of these sections.

tabloid a page half the size of a broadsheet.

titling a headline type available in capitals only.

turtle the segmental chase in which movable type was locked up in columns for printing on a type-revolver.

type-revolver the mid-nineteenth-century newspaper presses, devised by Hoe in New York and Applegarth in London, which were the first rotaries, that is, printing from a rotating drum on which the columns of type were locked. They were sheet-fed, however, and were not perfectors.

web-offset an offset press working from the web or reel of paper, delivering papers folded and complete, like the letterpress rotary.

woodcut an early form of newspaper illustration, using a wooden engraving made by hand.

Appendix 2

Primary newspaper sources

English morning dailies
The Times
> First issued 1 January 1785 as *The Daily Universal Register*; became *The Times or Daily Universal Register* 1 January 1788; became *The Times* 18 March 1788.

The Manchester Guardian
> First issued 5 May 1821 as *The Manchester Guardian*; merged with *British Volunteer* to become *The Manchester Guardian; and British Volunteer* 3 December 1825; became *The Manchester Guardian* 8 March 1828.

The Standard
> First issued 21 May 1827 as an evening paper; became a morning edition 29 June 1857.

The Daily News
> First issued 21 January 1846.

The Daily Telegraph
> First issued 29 June 1855 as *Daily Telegraph & Courier*; became *The Daily Telegraph* 20 August 1855.

Daily Mail
> First issued 4 May 1896.

English evening dailies
The Pall Mall Gazette
> First issued 7 February 1865 as *The Pall Mall Gazette/An Evening Newspaper and Review*; became *Pall Mall Gazette/An Evening Newspaper and Review* 1 January 1889; became *The Pall Mall Gazette* 18 February 1889.

The Echo
> First issued 8 December 1868; last issued 31 July 1905.

The Evening News
First issued 26 July 1881 as *The Evening News*; merged with *The Evening Post* to become *The Evening News & Post* 13 May 1889; became *The Evening News and Post* 12 August 1893; became *The Evening News* 17 September 1894; became *The Evening News and Evening Mail* 26 August 1901; became *The Evening News* 14 March 1905.

The Star
First issued 17 January 1888.

English weeklies
The Observer
First issued 4 December 1791.

The Sunday Times
First issued 18 February 1821 as *The New Observer*; became *The Independent Observer* 1 April 1821; became *The Sunday Times* 20 October 1822; became *Sunday Times* 10 July 1825; merged with *The Sunday Special* to become *Sunday Times and Sunday Special* 31 January 1904.

The Illustrated London News
First issued 14 May 1842.

Lloyd's Weekly Newspaper
First issued 27 November 1842 as *Lloyd's Illustrated London Newspaper*; became *Lloyd's Weekly London Newspaper* 15 January 1843; became *Lloyd's Weekly Newspaper* 14 January 1849; became *Lloyd's Weekly News* 30 November 1902.

The Weekly Times
First issued 24 January 1847 as *The Weekly Times*; merged with *The Weekly Echo* to become *The Weekly Times & Echo* 4 October 1885.

Reynolds's Newspaper
First issued 5 May 1850 as *Reynolds's Weekly Newspaper*; became *Reynolds's Newspaper* 16 February 1851.

American morning dailies
The Sun (New York)
First issued 3 September 1833 as *The Sun*; became *The New York Sun* 13 April 1840; became *The Sun* 29 September 1840.

The New York Herald
First issued 6 May 1835 as *The Morning Herald*; became *The Herald* 31 August 1835; became *The Morning Herald* 22 May 1837; became *The New York Herald* 21 September 1840.

New-York Tribune
First issued 10 April 1841 as *New-York Tribune*; became *New-York Daily Tribune* 22 April 1842; became *New-York Tribune* 10 April 1866.

The New-York Times
First issued 18 September 1851 as *New-York Daily Times*; became *The New-York Times* 12 September 1857; became *The New York Times* 1 December 1896.

The World (New York)
First issued 14 June 1860 as *The World*; became *The World and Morning Courier and New-York Enquirer* 1 July 1861; became *The World* 17 October 1863; became *The New-York World* 20 August 1881; became *The World* 11 May 1883.

New York Journal
First issued 19 November 1882 as *Morning Journal*; became *New York Morning Journal* 27 May 1888; became *The Journal* 7 November 1895; became *New York Journal* 19 July 1896; merged with *Morning Advertiser* to become *New York Journal and Advertiser* 2 April 1897; became *New York Journal and American* 11 November 1901; became *New York American and Journal* 10 March 1902; became *New York American* 2 March 1903.

The Chicago Daily Tribune
First issued 10 June 1847 as *Chicago Daily Tribune*; merged with *Chicago Daily Press* to become *Chicago Daily Press and Tribune* 1 July 1858; became *The Press and Tribune* 17 March 1859; became *Chicago Daily Tribune* 25 October 1860; became *Chicago Tribune* 21 August 1864; became *The Chicago Tribune* 15 September 1867; became *The Chicago Daily Tribune* 9 October 1872; became *The Chicago Tribune* 18 March 1886; became *The Chicago Daily Tribune* 19 July 1890.

The Examiner (San Francisco)
First issued 12 June 1865 as *The Evening Examiner*; became a morning edition as *The Examiner* 4 October 1880.

The Washington Post
First issued 6 December 1877.

American evening dailies

St. Louis Post-Dispatch
First issued as *St. Louis Union* 1862; became *The St. Louis Dispatch* 1864; first issue of *St. Louis Evening Post* 10 January 1878; merged into *St. Louis Post and Dispatch* 12 December 1878; became *St. Louis Post-Dispatch* 10 March 1879.

The Boston Daily Globe
First issued 4 March 1872.

The Chicago Daily News
First issued 23 December 1875.

American weeklies

Frank Leslie's Illustrated Newspaper
First issued 15 December 1855 as *Frank Leslie's Illustrated Newspaper*; became *Frank Leslie's Illustrated Weekly* 1891; became *Leslie's Illustrated Weekly* 1894; became *Leslie's Weekly* 1895; became *Leslie's Illustrated Weekly* 1907.

Harper's Weekly
First issued 3 January 1857 as *Harper's Weekly: A Journal of Civilization*.

References

Allen, W. 1840. *Picturesque views on the River Niger, sketched during Lander's last visit in 1832–33.* London: John Murray.

Alt, B.T., R.M. Koerner, D.A. Fisher, and J.C. Bourgeois. 1985. "Arctic climate during the Franklin era, as deduced from ice cores." In: Sutherland, P.D., ed. *The Franklin era in Canadian Arctic history 1845–1859.* Ottawa: National Museum of Man, Mercury Series, Archaeological Survey of Canada, 131: 69–91.

Altick, R.D. 1957. *The English common reader.* Chicago: University of Chicago Press.

Altick, R.D. 1987. *Evil encounters: two Victorian sensations.* London: John Murray.

Amdrup, G.C. 1913. "Report on the Danmark expedition to the north-east coast of Greenland 1906–1908." *Meddelelser om Grønland* 41 (1): 1–270.

American heritage dictionary of the English language. 1980. New college edition. Boston: Houghton Mifflin Company.

Amundsen, R. 1908. *The North West Passage.* 2 vols. London: Archibald Constable and Company.

Amundsen, R. 1912. *The South Pole.* 2 vols. London: John Murray.

Amundsen, R. 1927. *My life as an explorer.* London: William Heinemann.

Andrée, S.A., N. Strindberg, and K. Fraenkel. 1931. *The Andrée diaries: being the diaries and records of S.A. Andrée, Nils Strindberg, and Knut Fraenkel.* Edited by The Swedish Society of Anthropology and Geography. London: John Lane the Bodley Head.

Archer, M. 1980. *Early views of India: the picturesque journeys of Thomas and William Daniell 1786–1794.* London: Thames and Hudson.

Arnold, M. 1887. "Up to Easter." *The Nineteenth Century* 21 (123): 636–654.

Arnold, M. 1888. "Civilization in the United States." *The Nineteenth Century* 23 (134): 481–496.

Aspinall, A. 1949. *Politics and the press c. 1780–1850.* London: Home & Van Thal.

Bailey, P., ed. 1986. *Music hall: the business of pleasure.* Milton Keynes: Open University Press.

207

References

Baker, F.W.G. 1982. "The First International Polar Year." *Polar Record* 21 (132): 275–285.

Baker, S.W. 1855. *Eight years' wanderings in Ceylon*. London: Longman, Brown, Green, and Longmans.

Balch, E.S. 1914. *Mount McKinley and mountain climbers proofs*. Philadelphia: Campion and Company.

Baldwin, E.B. 1901. "How I hope to reach the North Pole." *McClure's Magazine* 17 (5): 415–422.

Barbeau, M. 1984. *Pantagruel in Canada*. Ottawa: National Museum of Man, Mercury Series, Canadian Centre for Folk Culture Studies, 48.

Barr, W. 1985. *The expeditions of the First International Polar Year, 1882–83*. Calgary: Arctic Institute of North America, technical paper 29.

Barr, W., ed. 1987. *Overland to Starvation Cove: with the Inuit in search of Franklin 1878–1880*. Toronto: University of Toronto Press.

Barr, W. 1988. "To the North Pole from York Factory." *The Beaver* 68 (2): 34–45.

Barrett, J.W. 1941. *Joseph Pulitzer and his World*. New York: Vanguard Press.

Barrow, J. 1846. *Voyages of discovery and research within the Arctic regions from the year 1818 to the present time*. London: John Murray.

Barrow, J. 1847. *An auto-biographical memoir of Sir John Barrow, Bart*. London: John Murray.

Barry, D.S. 1924. *Forty years in Washington*. Boston: Little, Brown, and Company.

Bartlett, R.A. 1931. *The log of Bob Bartlett: the true story of forty years of seafaring and exploration*. New York: Blue Ribbon Books.

Barttelot, W.G. 1890. *The life of Edmund Musgrave Barttelot*. London: R. Bentley & Son.

Baylen, J.O. 1972. "The 'New Journalism' in late Victorian Britain." *The Australian Journal of Politics and History* 18 (3): 367–385.

Baylen, J.O. 1988. "Politics and the New Journalism: Lord Esher's use of the *Pall Mall Gazette*." In: Wiener, J.H., ed. *Papers for the millions: the New Journalism in Britain, 1850s to 1914*. Westport, Connecticut: Greenwood Press: 107–141.

Beaglehole, J.C., ed. 1961. *The voyage of the Resolution and Adventure, 1772–1775*. Cambridge: Cambridge University Press for the Hakluyt Society.

Beaglehole, J.C. 1974. *The life of Captain James Cook*. London: Hakluyt Society.

Belich, J. 1986. *The New Zealand wars and the Victorian interpretation of racial conflict*. Auckland: Auckland University Press.

Bennett, N.R. 1970. *Stanley's despatches to the New York Herald*. Boston: Boston University Press.

Berger, M. 1951. *The story of the New York Times, 1851–1921*. New York: Simon & Schuster.

Berridge, V. 1976. Popular journalism and working class attitudes 1854–1886: a study of *Reynolds's Newspaper, Lloyd's Weekly Newspaper* and the *Weekly Times*. Unpublished PhD thesis. University of London.

Berridge, V. 1978. "Popular Sunday papers and mid-Victorian society.' In: Boyce, G., J. Curran, and P. Wingate, eds. *Newspaper history from the seventeenth century to the present day*. London: Constable and Company: 247–264.

Berry, W.T. 1958. "Printing and related trades." In: Singer, C., E.J. Holmyard, A.R. Hall, and T.I. Williams, eds. *A history of technology*. 5 vols. Oxford: Clarendon Press: V, 683–714.

Blackwood's Edinburgh Magazine. 1847. "The navigation of the Antipodes." *Blackwood's Edinburgh Magazine* 62 (385): 515–533.

Blackwood's Edinburgh Magazine. 1855. "Modern light literature – travellers' tales." *Blackwood's Edinburgh Magazine* 78 (481): 586–589.

Blake, E.V., ed. 1874. *Arctic experiences; containing Capt. George E. Tyson's wonderful drift on the ice-floe, a history of the Polaris expedition, the cruise of the Tigress, and the rescue of the Polaris survivors.* New York: Harper & Brothers.

Bleyer, W.G. 1927. *Main currents in the history of American journalism.* Boston: Houghton Mifflin Company.

Borchgrevink, C.E. 1901. *First on the Antarctic continent.* London: George Newnes.

Boston, R. 1976. "Fleet Street 100 years ago." *Journalism Studies Review* 1 (2): 16–20.

Boulding, K.E. 1956. *The image.* Ann Arbor, Michigan: University of Michigan Press.

Brannan, R.L., ed. 1966. *Under the management of Mr. Charles Dickens: his production of "the frozen deep".* Ithaca, New York: Cornell University Press.

Brantlinger, P. 1985. "Victorians and Africans: the genealogy of the myth of the Dark Continent." *Critical Inquiry* 12 (1): 166–203.

Brendon, P. 1982. *The life and death of the press barons.* London: Martin Secker & Warburg.

Bridges, R. 1982. "The historical role of British explorers in East Africa." *Terrae Incognitae* 14: 1–21.

Brown, E.H.P., and M.H. Browne. 1968. *A century of pay.* London: Macmillan and Company.

Brown, F. 1951. *Raymond of the Times.* New York: W.W. Norton & Company.

Browne, B. 1913. *The conquest of Mt. McKinley.* New York: G.P. Putnam's Sons.

Bullard, F.L. 1914. *Famous war correspondents.* Boston: Little, Brown and Company.

Bullard, F.L. 1933. "Januarius Aloysius MacGahan." *Dictionary of American biography* 12: 45–46.

Burke, E. 1758. *A philosophical enquiry into the origin of our ideas of the sublime and beautiful.* London: R. & J. Dodsley.

Burton, R.F. 1894. *First footsteps in east Africa, or, an exploration of Harar.* Memorial edition. 2 vols. London: Tylston and Edwards.

Cairns, H.A.C. 1965. *Prelude to imperialism: British reactions to Central African society, 1840–1960.* London: Routledge and Kegan Paul.

Cameron, I. 1980. *To the farthest ends of the earth: the history of the Royal Geographical Society.* London: Macdonald and Jane's.

Campbell, J. 1949. *The hero with a thousand faces.* Princeton: Princeton University Press.

Carey, J.W. 1983. "Technology and ideology: the case of the telegraph." *Prospects: the annual of American cultural studies* 8: 303–323.

Carlson, O. 1942. *The man who made the news.* New York: Duell, Sloan and Pearce.

Carpenter, K.J. 1986. *The history of scurvy and vitamin C.* Cambridge: Cambridge University Press.

Castberg, F. 1954. *The Norwegian way of life.* London: William Heinemann.

Century Illustrated Magazine. 1882. "Book review: *The voyage of the Vega round Asia and Europe.*" *The Century Illustrated Monthly Magazine* 24 (2): 303–305.

Clarke, T. 1950. *Northcliffe in history: an intimate study of press power.* London: Hutchinson & Company.

Cochrane, E. 1887. *Ten days in a mad-house; or Nellie Bly's experience on Blackwell's Island.* New York: N.L. Munro.

Coggeshall, W.T. 1856. *The newspaper record.* Philadelphia: Lay & Brother.

Cole, G.D.H. 1948. *A short history of the British working-class movement, 1789–*

References

1947. New edition. London: George Allen & Unwin.

Coleman, A.E. 1924–25. "A new and authentic history of the *Herald* of the Bennetts." *Editor and Publisher* 56–58 (29 March 1924–13 June 1925).

Collet, C.D. 1899. *History of the taxes on knowledge.* 2 vols. London: T. Fisher Unwin.

Conrad, J. 1926. "Geography and some explorers." In: Conrad, J. *Last essays.* London: J.M. Dent & Sons: 1–32.

Cook, F.A. 1911a. *My attainment of the Pole: being the record of the expedition that first reached the boreal center, 1907–1909.* New York: Polar Publishing Company.

Cook, F.A. 1911b. "Dr. Cook's own story." *Hampton's Magazine* 26 (1–4).

Cook, F.A. 1951. *Return from the Pole.* Edited by F.J. Pohl. New York: Pellegrini & Cudahy.

Corner, G.W. 1972. *Doctor Kane of the Arctic seas.* Philadelphia: Temple University Press.

Cray, E., J. Kotler, and M. Beller. 1990. *American datelines: one hundred and forty major news stories from colonial times to the present.* New York: Facts on File.

Crouthamel, J.L. 1964. "The newspaper revolution in New York." *New York History* 45 (2): 91–113.

Crouthamel, J.L. 1973. "James Gordon Bennett, the *New York Herald,* and the development of newspaper sensationalism." *New York History* 54 (3): 294–317.

Cruwys, E. 1990. "Henry Grinnell and the American Franklin searches." *Polar Record* 26 (158): 211–216.

Cruwys, E. 1991. "Profile: Henry Grinnell." *Polar Record* 27 (161): 115–119.

Curtin, P. 1965. *The image of Africa: British ideas and action, 1780–1850.* London: Macmillan & Co.

Cyriax, R.J. 1939. *Sir John Franklin's last Arctic expedition.* London: Methuen & Company.

Davis, E. 1921. *History of the New York Times: 1851–1921.* New York: Charles Scribner's Sons.

Dawson, L. 1946. *Lonsdale: the authorized life of Hugh Lowther, Fifth Earl of Lonsdale, K.G., G.C.V.O.* London: Odhams Press.

Dennis, C.H. 1935. *Victor Lawson: his life and his work.* Chicago: University of Chicago Press.

Dicken-Garcia, H. 1983. "Whitelaw Reid." *Dictionary of literary biography* 23: 292–305.

Dickens, C. 1854a. "The lost Arctic voyagers." *Household Words* 10 (245): 361–365.

Dickens, C. 1854b. "The lost Arctic voyagers." *Household Words* 10 (246): 385–393.

Dilliard, I. 1947. "How J.P. ran a newspaper – and his staff of editors." In: "Special Supplement Commemorating the 100th Anniversary of Joseph Pulitzer." *St. Louis Post-Dispatch* 6 April 1947.

Diubaldo, R.J. 1978. *Stefansson and the Canadian Arctic.* Montreal: McGill-Queen's University Press.

Dreiser, T. 1922. *A book about myself.* New York: Boni & Liveright.

Driscoll, C.B. 1938. *The life of O.O. McIntyre.* New York: Greystone Press.

Driver, F. 1991. "Henry Morton Stanley and his critics: geography, exploration and empire." *Past and Present* 133: 134–166.

Dwight, T. 1821–22. *Travels; in New-England and New-York.* 4 vols. New Haven, Connecticut: T. Dwight.

Eames, H. 1973. *Winner lose all: Dr. Cook and the theft of the North Pole.* Boston:

Little, Brown and Company.

Eberhard, W.B. 1970. "Mr. Bennett covers a murder trial." *Journalism Quarterly* 47 (34): 457–463.

Egan, M.F. 1910. "Dr. Cook in Copenhagen." *The Century Illustrated Monthly Magazine* 80 (5): 759–763.

Ellegard, A. 1958. *Darwin and the general reader: the reception of Darwin's theory of evolution in the British periodical press, 1859–1872. Göteborg Universitets Årsskrift* 64. Göteborg: Elanders Boktryckeri Aktiebolag.

Ellis, L.E. 1960. *Newsprint: producers, publishers, political pressures*. New Brunswick, New Jersey: Rutgers University Press.

Emery, M., and E. Emery. 1988. *The press and America: an interpretive history of the mass media*. Sixth edition. Englewood Cliffs, New Jersey: Prentice-Hall.

Fenton, A.H. 1941. *Dana of the Sun*. New York: Farrar & Rinehart.

Fermer, D. 1986. *James Gordon Bennett and the New York Herald*. New York: St. Martin's Press.

Fiala, A. 1907. *Fighting the polar ice*. London: Hodder & Stoughton.

Fine, B. 1933. *A giant of the press*. New York: Editor & Publisher Library.

Folkerts, J., and D.L. Teeter. 1989. *Voices of a nation: a history of media in the United States*. New York: Macmillan Publishing Company.

Foreign Quarterly Review. 1843. "The newspaper literature of America." *The Foreign Quarterly Review* 30 (59): 197–222.

Fox Bourne, H.R. 1887. *English newspapers*. 2 vols. London: Chatto & Windus.

Fox Bourne, H.R. 1891. *The other side of the Emin Pasha Relief Expedition*. London: Chatto & Windus.

Francke, W.T. 1974. Investigative exposure in the nineteenth century: the journalistic heritage of the muckrakers. Unpublished PhD dissertation. University of Minnesota.

Franklin, J. 1823. *Narrative of a journey to the shores of the Polar Sea, in the years 1819, 20, 21, and 22*. London: John Murray.

Franklin, J. 1828. *Narrative of a second expedition to the shores of the Polar Sea, in the years 1825, 1826, and 1827*. London: John Murray.

Freeman, A.A. 1961. *The case for Doctor Cook*. New York: Coward-McCann.

Freuchen, P. 1953. *Vagrant viking: my life and adventures*. London: Victor Gollancz.

Friederichs, H. 1911. *The life of Sir George Newnes, Bart*. London: Hodder and Stoughton.

Fyfe, H.H. 1934. *T.P. O'Connor*. London: George Allen & Unwin.

Fyfe, H.H. 1949. *Sixty years of Fleet Street*. London: W.H. Allen & Company.

Galton, F. 1878. "Letters of Henry Stanley from equatorial Africa to the 'Daily Telegraph'." *The Edinburgh Review or Critical Journal* 147 (301): 166–191.

Gardiner, A.G. 1926. *Portraits and portents*. New York: Harper & Brothers.

Geographical Journal. 1898. "Captain Sverdrup's expedition." *The Geographical Journal* 12 (1): 82.

Gerin, W. 1971. *Emily Brontë: a biography*. Oxford: Oxford University Press.

Gibbs, P. 1923. *Adventures in journalism*. London: William Heinemann.

Giddings, T.H. 1958. "Rushing the transatlantic news in the 1830s and 1840s." *New York Historical Society Quarterly* 42 (1): 47–59.

Gilder, W.H. 1881. *Schwatka's search: sledging in the Arctic in quest of the Franklin records*. London: Sampson Low, Marston, Searle, and Rivington.

Gilder, W.H. 1883. *Ice-pack and tundra*. New York: Charles Scribner's Sons.

Gilder, W.H. 1893. "An expedition to the North Magnetic Pole." *McClure's Magazine* 1 (2): 159–162.

References

Gilpin, W. 1792. *Three essays: on picturesque beauty; on picturesque travel; and on sketching landscape*. London: R. Blamire.

Gombrich, E.H. 1960. *Art and illusion: a study in the psychology of pictorial representation*. Princeton: Princeton University Press.

Goodbody, J. 1988. *"The Star*: its role in the rise of the New Journalism." In: Wiener, J.H., ed. *Papers for the millions: the New Journalism in Britain, 1850s to 1914*. Westport, Connecticut: Greenwood Press: 143–163.

Great Britain. 1854. *Arctic expeditions*. Great Britain. House of Commons. *Parliamentary Papers* 21. *Accounts and papers* 42 (129): 45242. Ordered, by the House of Commons, to be printed.

Greely, A.W. 1886. *Three years of Arctic service: an account of the Lady Franklin Bay expedition of 1881–84 and the attainment of the farthest north*. 2 vols. London: Richard Bentley and Son.

Greely, A.W. 1888. *Report on the proceedings of the United States expedition to Lady Franklin Bay, Grinnell Land*. 2 vols. Washington, DC: US Government Printing Office.

Greely, A.W. 1894. "Will they reach the Pole?" *McClure's Magazine* 3 (1): 39–44.

Green, F. 1926. Peary: *the man who refused to fail*. New York: G.P. Putnam's Sons.

Griest, G.L. 1970. *Mudie's circulating library and the Victorian novel*. London: David & Charles.

Grinnell, H. 1850–73. Letters and telegrams to Jane Franklin, 4 March 1850 to 22 November 1873. Unpublished documents. Cambridge: Scott Polar Research Institute, MS 248/414/2–112.

Guttridge, L.F. 1986. *Icebound: the Jeannette expedition's quest for the North Pole*. Annapolis, Maryland: Naval Institute Press.

Hall, C.F. 1865. *Life with the Esquimaux*. 2 vols. London: Sampson Low, Son, and Marston.

Hall, C.F. 1873. "Report of the reception, by the American Geographical Society, of Captain Hall and his officers, previous to their departure for the Arctic regions, held June 26th, 1871." *The Journal of the American Geographical Society of New York* 3: 401–415.

Hall, R. 1974. *Stanley: an adventurer explored*. London: William Collins Sons & Company.

Hall, T.F. 1917. *Has the North Pole been discovered?* Boston: Richard G. Badger.

Hayes, C.W. 1892. "An expedition through the Yukon district." *National Geographic Magazine* 4: 117–162.

Hayes, I.I. 1867. *The open polar sea*. London: Sampson Low, Son, and Marston.

Hayes, J.G. 1929. *Robert Edwin Peary: a record of his explorations 1886–1909*. London: Grant Richards & Humphrey Toulmin.

Hearne, S. 1795. *A journey from Prince of Wales's fort in Hudson's Bay, to the northern ocean undertaken by order of the Hudson's Bay Company, for the discovery of copper mines, a north west passage, etc. in the years 1769, 1770, 1771 & 1772*. London: A. Strahan and T. Cadell.

Hearst, W.R. 1948. *Selections from the writings and speeches of William Randolph Hearst*. San Francisco: privately printed.

Heilprin, A. 1893. "The Peary relief expedition." *Scribner's Magazine* 13 (1): 3–24.

Helly, D.O. 1987. *Livingstone's legacy: Horace Waller and Victorian mythmaking*. Athens, Ohio: Ohio University Press.

Hemingway, E. 1929. *A farewell to arms*. New York: Charles Scribner's Sons.

Henson, M.A. 1912. *A negro explorer at the North Pole*. New York: Frederick A. Stokes Company.

Herbert, W. 1989. *The noose of laurels*. London: Hodder & Stoughton.

Herd, H. 1952. *The march of journalism*. London: George Allen & Unwin.

Herschel, J.F.W. 1871. *A manual of scientific enquiry; prepared for the use of officers in Her Majesty's navy, and travellers in general*. 4th edn. London: John Murray.

Hesselman, H. 1933. "Aleksander Sibiriakoff." *Ymer* 53 (5): 446–448.

Himmelfarb, G. 1959. *Darwin and the Darwinian revolution*. Garden City, New York: Doubleday.

Hitchman, J.F. 1880. "The newspaper press." *The Quarterly Review* 150: 498–537.

Hobhouse, L.T. 1910. "The contending forces." *The English Review* 4 (2): 359–371.

Hodgson, M. 1985. "The literature of the Franklin search." In: Sutherland, P.D., ed. *The Franklin era in Canadian Arctic history 1845–1859*. Ottawa: National Museum of Man, Mercury Series, Archaeological Survey of Canada, 131: 1–11.

Hohenberg, J. 1964. *Foreign correspondence: the great reporters and their times*. New York: Columbia University Press.

Holland, C. In press. *An encyclopedia of Arctic expeditions, early times to 1920*. New York: Garland Press.

Howe, E. 1943. *Newspaper printing in the nineteenth century*. London: privately printed.

Hudson, F. 1873. *Journalism in the United States, 1690–1873*. New York: Harper & Row.

Hughes, H.M. 1981. *News and the human interest story*. 2nd edn. New Brunswick, New Jersey: Transaction Books.

Hunt, W.R. 1986. *Stef: a biography of Vilhjalmur Stefansson, Canadian Arctic explorer*. Vancouver: University of British Columbia Press.

Huntford, R. 1980. *Scott and Amundsen*. New York: G.P. Putnam's Sons.

Huntzicker, W.E. 1989. "Frank Leslie." *Dictionary of literary biography* 79: 209–222.

Hussey, C. 1927. *The picturesque: studies in a point of view*. London: Frank Cass & Company.

Hutt, A. 1973. *The changing newspaper: typographic trends in Britain and America 1622–1972*. London: The Gordon Fraser Gallery.

Ireland, A. 1938. *An adventure with a genius; recollections of Joseph Pulitzer*. London: Lovat Dickson.

Irwin, W. 1911a. "The fourth current." *Collier's* 46 (22): 14–19.

Irwin, W. 1911b. "The American newspaper." *Collier's* 46 (28): 18–21, 34.

Isaacs, G.A. 1931. *The story of the newspaper printing press*. London: Co-operative Printing Society.

Jackson, F.G. 1899. *A thousand days in the Arctic*. 2 vols. London: Harper & Brothers.

Jackson, F.G. 1935. *The lure of unknown lands*. London: G. Bell and Sons.

Jackson, M. 1885. *The pictorial press: its origins and progress*. London: Hurst and Blackett.

Jackson, P.H. 1962. *Meteor out of Africa: Henry Morton Stanley's journey to find Livingstone, 1871*. London: Cassell & Company.

Johnson, G.W. 1946. *An honourable titan: a biographical study of Adolph S. Ochs*. New York: Harper & Row.

Johnson, H. 1907. *The life and voyages of Joseph Wiggins, F.R.G.S*. London: John Murray.

Johnson, R.E., M.H. Johnson, H.S. Jeanes, and S.M. Deaver. 1984. *Schwatka: the life of Frederick Schwatka (1849–1892), M.D., Arctic explorer, cavalry officer*.

References

Montpelier, Vermont: Horn of the Moon Enterprises.

Jones, K. 1919. *Fleet Street and Downing Street.* London: Hutchinson and Company.

Juergens, G. 1966. *Joseph Pulitzer and the New York World.* Princeton: Princeton University Press.

Kane, E.K. 1854. *The U.S. Grinnell expedition in search of Sir John Franklin: a personal narrative.* London: Sampson Low, Son, and Company.

Kane, E.K. 1856. *Arctic explorations: the second Grinnell expedition in search of Sir John Franklin, 1853, '54, '55.* 2 vols. London: Trubner and Company.

Kennan, G. 1909a. "Commander Peary's return." *The Outlook* 93 (5): 252–255.

Kennan, G. 1909b. "Arctic work and Arctic food." *The Outlook* 93 (7): 338–342.

Kennan, G. 1909c. "Arctic work and Arctic food." *The Outlook* 93 (12): 625–630.

Kern, S. 1983. *The culture of time and space 1880–1918.* London: Weidenfeld and Nicolson.

Kinsley, P. 1943–46. *Chicago Tribune: its first hundred years.* 3 vols. New York: Alfred A. Knopf.

Kish, G. 1973. *North-east Passage: Adolf Erik Nordenskiöld, his life and times.* Amsterdam: Nico Israel.

Knight, R.P. 1805. *An analytical inquiry in the principles of taste.* London: T. Payne and J. White.

Krech, S. 1989. *A Victorian earl in the Arctic.* London: British Museum Publications.

Lamont, J. 1861. *Seasons with the sea-horses.* London: Hurst and Blackett.

Lee, A.J. 1974. "The radical press." In: Morris, A.J.A., ed. *Edwardian radicalism 1900–1914.* London: Routledge & Kegan Paul: 47–61.

Lee, A.J. 1976. *The origins of the popular press 1855–1914.* London: Croom Helm.

Lee, A.J. 1978. "The structure, ownership and control of the press 1855–1914." In: Boyce, G., J. Curran, and P. Wingate, eds. *Newspaper history from the seventeenth century to the present day.* London: Constable and Company: 117–129.

Lee, A.M. 1973. *The daily newspaper in America.* New York: Octagon Books.

Lefranc, A. 1905. *Les navigations de Pantagruel: Étude sur la géographie Rabelaisienne.* Paris: Librairie Henri Leclerc.

Leslie, A. 1879. *The Arctic voyages of Adolf Erik Nordenskiöld.* London: Macmillan and Company.

Livingstone, D. 1857. *Missionary travels and researches in south Africa.* London: John Murray.

Loomis, C.C. 1972. *Weird and tragic shores.* London: Macmillan.

Lundberg, F. 1936. *Imperial Hearst: a social biography.* New York: Equinox Cooperative Press.

MacGahan, J.A. 1876. *Under the northern lights.* London: Sampson Low, Marston, Searle, & Rivington.

Mack, E.L. 1941. *Public schools and British opinion since 1860.* London: Methuen & Company.

Mackenzie, A. 1801. *Voyages from Montreal, on the River St. Laurence, through the continent of North America, to the frozen and Pacific Oceans; in the years 1789 and 1793.* London: T. Cadell.

MacKenzie, J. 1984. *Propaganda and empire: the manipulation of British public opinion, 1880–1960.* Manchester: Manchester University Press.

MacKenzie, J. 1992. "Heroic myths of empire." In: MacKenzie, J., ed. *Popular imperialism and the military 1850–1950.* Manchester and New York: Manchester University Press.

Mackinnon, C.S. 1985. "The British man-hauled sledging tradition." In:

Sutherland, P.D., ed. *The Franklin era in Canadian Arctic history 1845–1859*. Ottawa: National Museum of Man, Mercury Series, Archaeological Survey of Canada, 131: 129–140.

MacLaren, I.S. 1984. "Retaining captaincy of the soul: responses to nature in the first Franklin expedition." *Essays on Canadian Writing* 28: 57–92.

MacLaren, I.S. 1985. "The aesthetic map of the north, 1845–1859." *Arctic* 38 (2): 89–103.

Maitland, A. 1971. *Speke*. London: Constable & Company.

Mårdh, I. 1980. *Headlinese: on the grammar of English front page headlines*. Lund Studies in English, 58. Malmö: GWK Gleerup.

Markham, C.R. 1873. *The threshold of the unknown region*. London: Sampson Low, Marston, Low, and Searle.

Markham, C.R. 1874. "Dr. Petermann's letters to the presidents of the Royal Geographical Society in 1865 and 1874." *Nature: a Weekly Illustrated Journal of Science* 11 (3 December): 85–87.

Markham, C.R. 1909. *Life of Admiral Sir Leopold McClintock, K.C.B., D.C.L., LL.D., F.R.S., V.P.R.G.S.* London: John Murray.

Markham, C.R. 1921. *The lands of silence*. Cambridge: Cambridge University Press.

Marsh, G.P. 1864. *Man and nature*. London: Sampson Low, Son and Marston.

Martin, C. 1988. "William Scoresby, Jr. (1789–1857) and the open polar sea – myth and reality." *Arctic* 41 (1): 39–47.

Massingham, H.W. 1892. *The London daily press*. London: The Religious Tract Society.

Maury, M.F. 1859. *The physical geography of the sea*. London: Sampson Low, Son, and Company.

Mawson, D. 1915. *The home of the blizzard*. London: William Heinemann.

Mayhew, H. 1861–62. *London labour and the London poor*. 4 vols. London: Griffin, Bohn, and Company.

McClintock, F.L. 1859. *The voyage of the 'Fox' in the Arctic Seas: a narrative of the discovery of the fate of Sir John Franklin and his companions*. London: John Murray.

McCormick, R., and C. Dickens. 1850. "Christmas in the frozen regions." *Household Words* 2 (39): 306–309.

McCullagh, F. 1929. "The Gordon Bennetts and American journalism." *Studies: an Irish Quarterly Review of Letters Philosophy & Science* 18 (71): 394–412.

McIlraith, J. 1868. *Life of Sir John Richardson*. London: Longmans, Green, and Company.

McLynn, F. 1989. *Stanley: the making of an African explorer*. London: Constable and Company.

McLynn, F. 1991. *Stanley: Sorcerer's apprentice*. London: Constable and Company.

McManis, D.R. 1975. "In search of a rational world: the encyclopedist's image of northern and western North America." *Historical Geography Newsletter* 5 (2): 18–29.

Melville, G.W. 1885. *In the Lena delta*. London: Longmans, Green, and Company.

Mikkelsen, E. 1955. *Mirage in the Arctic*. London: Rupert Hart-Davis.

Mills, J.S. 1921. *Sir Edward Cook K.B.E.: a biography*. London: Constable & Company.

Monk, S.H. 1960. *The sublime: a study of critical theories in xviii-century England*. Ann Arbor, Michigan: University of Michigan Press.

Montefiore, A. 1895. "The Jackson-Harmsworth North Polar expedition." *The*

References

Geographical Journal 16 (6): 499–520.

Moore, T. 1967. *Mt. McKinley: the pioneer climbs.* Anchorage, Alaska: University of Alaska Press.

Moorehead, A. 1960. *The White Nile.* London: Hamish Hamilton.

Morison, S. 1932. *The English newspaper: some account of the physical development of journals printed in London between 1622 and the present day.* Cambridge: Cambridge University Press.

Morison, S.E. 1971. *The European discovery of America: the northern voyages.* New York: Oxford University Press.

Morley, H. 1857a. "The lost English sailors." *Household Words* 15 (360): 145–147.

Morley, H. 1857b. "Official patriotism." *Household Words* 15 (370): 385–390.

Morris, T.N. 1958. "Management and preservation of food." In: Singer, C., E.J. Holmyard, A.R. Hall, and T.I. Williams, eds. *A history of technology.* 5 vols. Oxford: Clarendon Press: V, 26–52.

Mott, F.L. 1930–68. *A history of American magazines.* 5 vols. Cambridge, Massachusetts: Harvard University Press.

Mott, F.L. 1952. *The news in America.* Cambridge, Massachusetts: Harvard University Press.

Mott, F.L. 1962. *American journalism.* 2nd rev. edn. New York: Macmillan Company.

Murchison, R.I. 1852. "Address to the Royal Geographical Society of London." *The Journal of the Royal Geographical Society of London* 22: lxii–cxxvi.

Musson, A.E. 1958. "Newspaper printing in the Industrial Revolution." *The Economic History Review*, Second series 10 (3): 411–426.

Myers, G. 1901. *The history of Tammany Hall.* New York: privately printed.

Nansen, F. 1887. *The structure and combination of the histological elements of the central nervous system.* Bergen: John Grieg.

Nansen, F. 1890. *The first crossing of Greenland.* 2 vols. London: Longmans, Green, and Company.

Nansen, F. 1893a. "How can the North Polar region be crossed?" *The Geographical Journal* 1 (1): 1–32.

Nansen, F. 1893b. "Towards the North Pole." *The Strand Magazine* 6 (72): 614–624.

Nansen, F. 1894. *Eskimo life.* London: Longmans, Green, and Company.

Nansen, F. 1897. *Farthest north.* 2 vols. London: Archibald Constable and Company.

Nansen, F. 1911. *In northern mists.* 2 vols. London: William Heinemann.

Nares, G.S. 1878. *Narrative of a voyage to the polar sea during 1875–76 in H.M. ships 'Alert' and 'Discovery'.* 2nd edn. 2 vols. London: Sampson Low, Marston, Searle, & Rivington.

Nathorst, A.G. 1897. "Oscar Dickson." *Ymer* 17 (2): 159–165.

Nathorst, A.G. 1900. "Otto Torell: den vetenskapliga polarforskningens grundläggare." *Ymer* 20 (4): 454–459.

Nathorst, A.G., G. DeGeer, and J.G. Anderson. 1909. "Swedish exploration in Spitzbergen 1758–1908." *Ymer* 29 (1): 4–89.

Nature. 1874. "Notes." *Nature: a Weekly Illustrated Journal of Science* 11 (19 November): 55.

Navy, The. 1876. "The polar failure." *The Navy* 5 (128): 441.

Neatby, L.H. 1970. *The search for Franklin.* London: Arthur Barker.

Nevins, A., ed. 1936. *The diary of Philip Hone.* New York: Dodd, Mead & Company.

Nevius, B. 1976. *Cooper's landscapes: an essay on the picturesque vision.* Berkeley:

University of California Press.

Nicholson, M.H. 1959. *Mountain gloom and mountain glory: the development of the aesthetics of the infinite*. Ithaca, New York: Cornell University Press.

Nilsson, N.G. 1971. "The origin of the interview." *Journalism Quarterly* 48 (4): 707–713.

Nordenskiöld, A.E. 1881. *The voyage of the Vega round Asia and Europe*. 2 vols. London: Macmillan and Company.

Nordenskiöld, A.E. 1885. "Reply to criticisms upon 'The voyage of the Vega round Asia and Europe.'" *The Journal of the American Geographical Society* 17: 267–298.

Nourse, J.E., ed. 1879. *Narrative of the second Arctic expedition made by Charles Francis Hall*. Washington, DC: US Government Printing Office.

O'Brien, F. 1918. *The story of the Sun, New York, 1833–1918*. New York: D. Appleton and Company.

O'Connor, R. 1962. *The scandalous Mr. Bennett*. Garden City, New York: Doubleday.

O'Connor, T.P. 1929. *Memoirs of an old parliamentarian*. 2 vols. London: E. Benn.

Older, C.B. 1936. *William Randolph Hearst: American*. New York: D. Appleton-Century Company.

Osborn, S., ed. 1856. *The discovery of a North-West Passage by H.M.S. "Investigator," Capt. R. M'Clure, 1850, 1851, 1852, 1853, 1854*. London: Longman, Brown, Green, Longmans, and Roberts.

Osborn, S. 1865. "On the exploration of the North Polar region." *Proceedings of the Royal Geographical Society* 9 (2): 42–71.

Park, M. 1799. *Travels in the interior districts of Africa*. London: W. Bulmer and Co.

Parkman, F. 1872. *The Oregon trail; sketches of prairie and Rocky-mountain life*. 4th edn. Boston: Little, Brown.

Parkyns, M. 1853. *Life in Abyssinia: being notes collected during three years' residence and travels in that country*. 2 vols. London: John Murray.

Parry, W.E. 1821. *Journal of a voyage for the discovery of a North-West Passage from the Atlantic to the Pacific; performed in His Majesty's ships Hecla and Griper*. London: John Murray.

Parton, J. 1866. "The *New York Herald*." *The North American Review* 102: 375–419.

Payer, J. 1876. *New lands within the Arctic circle*. 2 vols. London: Macmillan and Company.

Payne, G.H. 1920. *History of journalism in the United States*. New York: D. Appleton and Company.

Peary, J.D. 1893. *My Arctic journal: a year among ice-fields and Eskimos*. London: Longmans, Green, and Company.

Peary, R.E. 1898. *Northward over the "great ice": a narrative of life and work along the shores and upon the interior of the ice-cap of northern Greenland in the years 1886 and 1891–97*. London: Methuen & Company.

Peary, R.E. 1899. "Moving on the North Pole – outlines of my Arctic campaign." *McClure's Magazine* 12 (5): 417–426.

Peary, R.E. 1907. *Nearest the Pole – a narrative of the polar expedition of the Peary Artic Club in the S.S. Roosevelt, 1905–1906*. London: Hutchinson & Company.

Peary, R.E. 1910a. *The North Pole: its discovery in 1909 under the auspices of the Peary Arctic Club*. New York: Frederick A. Stokes Company.

Peary, R.E. 1910b. "The discovery of the North Pole." *Hampton's Magazine* 24

References

(4–6); 25 (1–6).

Peary, R.E. 1910c. "The discovery of the North Pole." *Nash's Magazine* 2 (11): 321–342; (12): 429–450; (13): 531–551; (14): 633–653; (15): 761–780; (16): 874–891; (17): 1005–1040; (18): 1166–1184.

Peary, R.E. 1917. *The secrets of polar travel*. New York: The Century Company.

Peary, R.E., and H.L. Bridgman. 1901. "Peary's latest work in the Arctic." *McClure's Magazine* 14 (3): 235–240.

Petermann, A. 1852. *The search for Franklin*. London: Longman, Brown, Green, and Longmans.

Plant, M. 1939. *The English book trade: an economic history of the making and sale of books*. London: George Allen & Unwin.

Pound, R., and G. Harmsworth. 1959. *Northcliffe*. London: Cassell & Company.

Powell, J. 1961. *The long rescue: the story of the tragic Greely expedition*. London: W.H. Allen.

Powell, J.M. 1977. *Mirrors of the New World: images and image-makers in the settlement process*. Hamden, Connecticut: Archon Books.

Pray, I. 1855. *Memoirs of J.G. Bennett and his times by a journalist*. New York: Stringer and Townsend.

Rabelais, F. 1900. *Gargantua and Pantagruel*. 3 vols. London: David Nutt.

Rae, J. 1854a. "The lost Arctic voyagers." *Household Words* 10 (248): 433–437.

Rae, J. 1854b. "Dr. Rae's report." *Household Words* 10 (249): 457–459.

Rae, J. 1855. "Sir John Franklin and his crews." *Household Words* 11 (254): 12–20.

Rae, J. 1953. *John Rae's correspondence with the Hudson's Bay Company on Arctic exploration 1844–1855*. Edited by E.E. Rich. London: Publications of the Hudson's Bay Record Society, 16.

Rammelkamp, J.S. 1967. *Pulitzer's Post-Dispatch*. Princeton: Princeton University Press.

Rand, S.B. 1902. "Robert E. Peary and his campaign for the Pole." *McClure's Magazine* 18 (4): 354–363.

Random House dictionary of the English language. 1978. Unabridged edn. New York: Random House.

Rawlins, D. 1973. *Peary at the North Pole: fact or fiction?* Washington, DC: Robert B. Luce.

Rawlinson, H.C. 1872. "Address to the Royal Geographical Society." *Proceedings of the Royal Geographical Society* 16 (4): 291–377.

Redivivus, B. 1899. "Special newspaper trains." *The Railway Magazine* 5 (29): 410–412.

Reich, C.A. 1970. *The greening of America*. New York: Random House.

Richards, R.L. 1985. *Dr John Rae*. Whitby, England: Caedmon of Whitby Publishers.

Richardson, J. 1831. *Fauna boreali-Americana*. 2 vols. London: John Murray.

Riffenburgh, B. 1991. "James Gordon Bennett, the *New York Herald*, and the Arctic." *Polar Record* 27 (160): 9–16.

Rittenhouse, M. 1956. *The amazing Nellie Bly*. New York: Dutton and Company.

Robinson, B. 1947. *Dark Companion*. New York: Robert M. McBride & Company.

Rosebault, C.J. 1931. *When Dana was the Sun, a story of personal journalism*. New York: Robert M. McBride & Company.

Rosewater, V. 1930. *History of cooperative news-gathering in the United States*. New York: D. Appleton and Company.

Rotberg, R. 1970. *Africa and its explorers: motives, methods and impact*. Cambridge, Massachusetts: Harvard University Press.

Ruggles, R.I. 1971. "The west of Canada in 1763: imagination and reality." *Canadian Geographer* 15 (4): 235–261.

Ruggles, R.I. 1988. "Beyond the 'furious over fall': map images of Rupert's Land and the northwest." In: Davis, R.C., ed. *Rupert's Land: a cultural tapestry.* Waterloo, Ontario: Wilfrid Laurier University Press: 13–50.

Ruskin, J. 1866. *The crown of wild olive: three lectures on work, traffic, and war.* London: Smith, Elder & Company.

Sasser, E.L. 1967. An experimental study of the effects of headline size and writing style in newspapers. Unpublished PhD dissertation, University of Illinois.

Saturday Review. 1856. "Kane's Arctic explorations." *The Saturday Review of Politics, Literature, Science and Art* 2 (56): 660–662.

Saturday Review. 1872. "Mr. Stanley and Dr. Livingstone." *The Saturday Review of Politics, Literature, Science and Art* 34 (887): 526–528.

Saturday Review. 1878. "Mr. Stanley's explanations." *The Saturday Review of Politics, Literature, Science and Art* 45 (1,164): 207–208.

Schley, W.S., and J.R. Soley. 1885. *The rescue of Greely.* London: Sampson Low, Marston, Searle and Rivington.

Schults, R.L. 1972. *Crusader in Babylon: W.T. Stead and the Pall Mall Gazette.* Lincoln, Nebraska: University of Nebraska Press.

Schwatka, F. 1885a. *Along Alaska's great river.* New York: Cassell & Company.

Schwatka, F. 1885b. *Report of a military reconnaissance in Alaska made in 1883.* Washington, DC: US Government Printing Office.

Schwatka, F. 1885c. *Nimrod in the north; or hunting and fishing in the Arctic regions.* New York: Cassell & Company.

Schwatka, F. 1893. *In the land of cave and cliff dwellers.* Edited by A.B. Schwatka. New York: The Cassell Publishing Company.

Scott, D.M. 1980. "The popular lecture and the creation of a public in mid-nineteenth century America." *The Journal of American History* 66 (4): 791–809.

Scott, J.W.R. 1950. *The story of the Pall Mall Gazette, of its first editor Frederick Greenwood and of its founder George Murray Smith.* London: Oxford University Press.

Scott, J.W.R. 1952. *The life and death of a newspaper.* London: Methuen & Co.

Scott, R.F. 1913. *Scott's last expedition.* 2 vols. London: Smith, Elder & Co.

Scottish Geographical Magazine. 1892. "Notes." *Scottish Geographical Magazine* 8 (8): 445.

Seitz, D.C. 1924a. "Portrait of an editor." *The Atlantic Monthly* 134 (3): 290–300.

Seitz, D.C. 1924b. *Joseph Pulitzer; his life & letters.* New York: Simon and Schuster.

Seitz, D.C. 1928. *The James Gordon Bennetts: father and son, proprietors of the New York Herald.* Indianapolis: Bobbs-Merrill Company.

Shaw, F.H. 1958. *Seas of memory.* London: Oldbourne.

Shelley, M.W. 1818. *Frankenstein, or the modern Prometheus.* 3 vols. London: Lackington, Hughes, Harding, Mavor, & Jones.

Sherwood, M.B. 1965. *Exploration of Alaska 1865–1900.* New Haven, Connecticut: Yale University Press.

Smith, E.C. 1938. *A short history of naval and marine engineering.* Cambridge: Cambridge University Press.

Smith, I.R. 1972. *The Emin Pasha Relief Expedition 1886–1891.* Oxford: Clarendon Press.

Southworth, A.S. 1875. *Four thousand miles of African travel.* London: Sampson Low and Company.

Speke, J.H. 1864. *What led to the discovery of the source of the Nile.* Edinburgh and

London: William Blackwood and Sons.

Springhall, J. 1989. "'Healthy papers for manly boys': imperialism and race in the Harmsworths' halfpenny boys' papers of the 1890s and 1900s." In: Richards, J., ed. *Imperialism and juvenile literature*. Manchester: Manchester University Press: 107–125.

Stafford, R.A. 1989. *Scientist of empire: Sir Roderick Murchison, scientific exploration and Victorian imperialism*. Cambridge: Cambridge University Press.

Stamp, T., and C. Stamp. 1975. *William Scoresby: Arctic scientist*. Whitby, England: Caedmon of Whitby Press.

Stanhope, A. 1914. *On the track of the great: recollections of a 'special correspondent'*. London: Eveleigh Nash.

Stanley, D., ed. 1909. *The autobiography of Henry M. Stanley*. London: Sampson Low, Marston, and Company.

Stanley, H.M. 1872. *How I found Livingstone: travels, adventures, and discoveries in central Africa*. Second edition. London: Sampson Low, Marston, Low, and Searle.

Stanley, H.M. 1872–74. Personal and expedition journals. London: British Museum, Stanley MSS, RP 2435 (i).

Stanley, H.M. 1874. *Coomassie and Magdala: the story of two British campaigns in Africa*. London: Sampson Low, Marston, Low, and Searle.

Stanley, H.M. 1878. *Through the dark continent*. 2 vols. London: Sampson Low, Marston, Searle and Rivington.

Stanley, H.M. 1885. *The Congo, and the founding of its Free State*. 2 vols. London: Sampson Low, Marston, Searle and Rivington.

Stanley, H.M. 1890. *In darkest Africa, or the quest, rescue, and retreat of Emin, governor of Equatoria*. 2 vols. London: Sampson Low, Marston, Searle and Rivington.

Stanley, H.M. 1895. *My early travels and adventures in America and Asia*. 2 vols. London: Sampson Low, Marston and Company.

Startt, J.D. 1988. "Good journalism in the era of the New Journalism: the British press, 1902–1914." In: Wiener, J.H., ed. *Papers for the millions: the New Journalism in Britain, 1850s to 1914*. Westport, Connecticut: Greenwood Press: 275–298.

Stead, E.W. 1913. *My father: personal & spiritual reminiscences*. London: William Heinemann.

Stead, W.T. 1886. "Government by journalism." *The Contemporary Review* 49 (5): 653–674.

Stead, W.T. 1893. "Character sketch February: the 'Pall Mall Gazette'." *Review of Reviews* 7 (38): 139–156.

Stead, W.T. 1909. "Character sketch and interview: Dr. F.A. Cook." *Review of Reviews* 40 (238): 323–339.

Stefansson, V. 1943. *The friendly Arctic*. New edn. New York: Macmillan Company.

Stevens, T. 1887. *Around the world on a bicycle*. 2 vols. London: Sampson Low, Marston, Searle and Rivington.

Stevens, T. 1890. *Scouting for Stanley in east Africa*. London: Cassell & Company.

Stevens, T. 1891. *Through Russia on a mustang*. London: Cassell & Company.

Stone, I.R. 1987. "'The contents of the kettles': Charles Dickens, John Rae and cannibalism on the 1845 Franklin expedition." *The Dickensian* 83 (411): 7–16.

Stone, C. 1938. *Dana and the Sun*. New York: Dodd Mead.

Stone, M.E. 1922. *Fifty years a journalist*. London: William Heinemann.

Sutherland, D. 1965. *The yellow earl: the life of Hugh Lowther 5th Earl of*

Lonsdale, K.G., G.C.V.O., 1857–1944. London: Cassell & Company.

Sverdrup, O.N. 1904. *New land: four years in the Arctic regions.* 2 vols. London: Longmans, Green, and Company.

Swanberg, W.A. 1961. *Citizen Hearst: a biography of William Randolph Hearst.* New York: Charles Scribner's Sons.

Taft, R. 1938. *Photography and the American scene.* New York: The Macmillan Company.

Taylor, E.G.R., ed. 1935. *The original writings and correspondence of the two Richard Hakluyts.* London: Hakluyt Society, Second series: 77.

Tebbel, J. 1952. *The life and good times of William Randolph Hearst.* New York: Dutton.

Tebbel, J. 1976. *The media in America.* New York: New American Library. (Originally published 1974, New York: Thomas Y. Crowell.)

Thoreau, H.D. 1854. *Walden.* Boston: Ticknor and Fields.

Three Lookers-on in Venice. 1840. *The war of the giants against James Gordon Bennett, and other recent matters.* New York: privately printed.

Trevelyan, G.M. 1901. "The white peril." *The Nineteenth Century and After* 50 (298): 1043–1055.

Troup, J.R. 1890. *With Stanley's rearguard.* London: Chapman and Hall.

Tuckey, J.K. 1818. *Narrative of an expedition to explore the River Zaire, usually called the Congo, in south Africa, in 1816.* London: John Murray.

US Bureau of the Census. 1975. *Historical statistics of the United States: colonial times to 1970.* Bicentennial edition. 2 vols. Washington, DC: US Government Printing Office.

Van Deusen, G.G. 1953. *Horace Greeley: nineteenth century crusader.* Philadelphia: University of Pennsylvania Press.

Vizetelly, E.H. 1901. *From Cyprus to Zanzibar by the Egyptian delta.* London: C. Arthur Pearson.

Vrangel', F.P. 1844. *Narrative of an expedition to the polar sea, in the years 1820, 1821, 1822, and 1823.* 2nd edn. Edited by J. Sabine. London: James Madden and Company.

Wadsworth, A.P. 1955. "Newspaper circulation 1800–1954." *Transactions of the Manchester Statistical Society*, session 1954–55. Manchester: Norbury, Lockwood & Co.

Wallace, H.N. 1980. *The Navy, the Company, and Richard King.* Montreal: McGill-Queen's University Press.

Ward, H. 1934. "Peary did not reach the Pole." *The American Mercury* 33 (129): 41–48.

Watson, J.W. 1969. "The role of illusion in North American geography: a note on the geography of North American settlement." *Canadian Geographer* 13 (1): 10–27.

Webb, R.K. 1955. *The British working class reader, 1790–1848: literacy and social tension.* London: George Allen & Unwin.

Wechter, D. 1941. *The hero in America: a chronicle of hero worship.* New York: Charles Scribner's Sons.

Weems, J.E. 1967. *Peary: the explorer and the man.* London: Eyre & Spottiswoode.

Wendt, L. 1979. *Chicago Tribune: the rise of a great American newspaper.* New York: Rand-McNally Corporation.

Whitaker, I. 1982. "The problem of Pytheas' Thule." *The Classical Journal* 77 (2): 148–164.

Whyte, F. 1925. *The life of W.T. Stead.* 2 vols. London: Jonathan Cape.

References

Wickwar, W.H. 1928. *The struggle for the freedom of the press 1819–1832*. London: George Allen & Unwin.

Wiener, J.H. 1988. "How new was the New Journalism?" In: Wiener, J.H., ed. *Papers for the millions: the New Journalism in Britain, 1850s to 1914*. Westport, Connecticut: Greenwood Press: 47–71.

Wikoff, H. 1880. *Reminiscences of an idler*. 2 vols. London: Robson and Sons.

Williams, F. 1984. *Dangerous estate: the anatomy of newspapers*. Cambridge: Patrick Stephens.

Williams, G. 1962. *The British search for the Northwest Passage in the eighteenth century*. London: Longmans, Green and Company.

Williams, G. 1970. "The Hudson's Bay Company and its critics in the eighteenth century." *Transactions of the Royal Historical Society*, fifth series 20: 149–171.

Williams, R. 1961. *The long revolution*. London: Chatto and Windus.

Winkler, J.K. 1928. *William Randolph Hearst: an American phenomenon*. New York: Simon & Schuster.

Wright, J.K. 1953. "The open polar sea." *The Geographical Journal* 43 (3): 338–365.

Wright, T. 1970. *The big nail: the story of the Cook-Peary feud*. New York: The John Day Company.

Yule, H., and H.M. Hyndman. 1878. *Mr. Henry M. Stanley and the Royal Geographical Society: being a record of protest*. London: Bickers & Son.

Index

Newnes, George 102, 148–150, 152, 195
New York American 170, 172, 174, 179, 186, 188, 195
New York Herald, The 1, 4, 18–23, 26, 47, 51–53, 57–66, 68–70, 72–79, 81, 84–87, 89, 93–95, 101, 105, 107, 110–112, 116, 120–130, 133–136, 144–146, 149, 153, 166, 169–170, 172–175, 177–181, 183–184, 186–187, 189, 191, 194
New York Journal 124, 144–147, 172, 179
New-York Times, The 1,5, 21, 26, 48, 52, 57, 68, 74, 85, 89, 92–94, 105–112, 116–117, 119, 122–135, 145, 147–148, 153, 156, 159, 165, 168–172, 174, 177–181, 183–187, 189–190, 194, 197
New-York Tribune 21, 47, 52, 57, 64, 69, 87, 89, 92, 94, 105–107, 122-128, 131, 145–146, 157, 174–175, 178, 180, 182, 185, 194, 197
Niger River 14–16, 64
Nile River 9, 14, 34–35, 44, 50, 55–56, 64–65, 132
Nordenskiöld, Adolf Erik 37, 69–71, 73, 77, 87, 113–116, 142, 160, 164, 199
Northwest Passage 10–11, 13–16, 24, 26–27, 36, 41, 73, 161–164

Ochs, Adolph 147, 194
O'Connor, T.P. 101–102

Pall Mall Gazette, The 4, 61, 63–64, 66, 97–102, 115, 117–118, 128, 132–134, 136, 140, 149
Pandora 73–74, 77, 84, 121
Park, Mungo 14
Parry, William Edward 16, 30
Payer, Julius 83
Peary Arctic Club 34, 167, 169–170, 184–186
Peary, Jo 116
Peary, Robert E. 1, 2, 47, 112, 114, 116, 134–135, 137, 157, 160, 162, 165–172, 175–184, 186–189, 191–195, 197, 199
Petermann, August 76, 82–83
picturesque 11–13, 17, 24–25

popular press, birth of (Britain) 8, 18, 23, 45
popular press, birth of (US) 18–19, 23
Pulitzer, Joseph 4, 53, 87–97, 101, 112, 121–122, 130, 133–134, 136–137, 143–147, 179, 195, 197

Rae, John 18, 25, 28–30, 36, 41, 75, 161, 169
Rawlins, Dennis 192–193
Raymond, Henry J. 21–22, 52, 147
Rear column 124, 132–133
Reick, William 178
Reid, Whitelaw 52, 157, 174, 194–195
Rennell, James 15
Reynolds's Newspaper 23–24
Richardson, John 13, 17, 25, 30, 36
Roosevelt 168, 171, 178
Ross, James Clark 16, 25–26, 30, 36
Ross, John 16, 30, 39
Royal Geographical Society (RGS) 33–34, 38, 43, 49–50, 60, 62, 66, 668–69, 81, 117, 188, 196
Ruskin, John 5–6, 33, 97

St. James's Gazette 132, 136
St. Louis Post-Dispatch 87–0, 121–124, 195
Schley, W.S. 104–105, 108, 128, 166, 179, 188
Schwatka, Frederick 75, 109–111, 121, 131–132, 135, 169, 196, 198
Scott, Robert Falcon 7, 164, 175, 194–195, 199
sensationalism 3, 8, 20–21, 24, 26, 28–29, 46–48, 54, 63, 68, 70, 80, 84–88, 90–103, 105–109, 111, 119–129, 134, 143–148, 195–199
birth of in US 19–20
conventional view of 4–5, 47
definition of 4
growth of in Britain 23–24, 46, 54–55, 63–65, 68
in illustration 21, 92–94
in *The New York Herald* 20–23, 47, 53, 72–79, 81, 196–199
New Journalism 64, 89, 96–103, 151, 177
sensational vs quality press 4–5, 119, 122–129
yellow journalism 143–147